This boo... ...or before the ... te stamped ...low.

18. SEP. 1985

27. MAR. 1989

...1986

01. SEP 90

21. SEP

12. OCT 9...

26. OCT 8...

06. ...

20...

04. FEB 91

25. MAR 91

22. NO...

...D...

E

A Country Parson

James Woodforde's Diary 1759–1802

Illustrated

Weston Longeville Church

A Country Parson

James Woodforde's Diary 1759–1802

Illustrated

Foreword by JOHN JULIUS NORWICH
Introduction by RONALD BLYTHE
Drawings by ROSALIND CALDECOTT

CENTURY PUBLISHING LONDON

OXFORD UNIVERSITY PRESS
OXFORD   NEW YORK   TORONTO   MELBOURNE

This selection first published jointly in 1985 by
Century Publishing Co Ltd,
Portland House,
12–13 Greek Street
London W1V 5LE
and Oxford University Press,
Walton Street, Oxford OX2 6DP

British Library Cataloguing in Publication Data
Woodforde, James
The diary of a country parson. *Selections*
A Country parson: James Woodforde's diary 1758–1802.
1. England—Social life and customs—18th century.
I. Title II. Michie, James   III. A country parson:
942.07'3   DA485

ISBN 0-7126-0730-7 (UK & Eire)
ISBN 0-19-520488-3 (export only)

The Diary of a Country Parson was first
published in five volumes between 1924 and 1931
by the Oxford University Press. A one-volume
edition was subsequently published in 1935.

**Designed and produced by
Robert Adkinson Limited, London**

Editorial Director
Clare Howell

Art Director
Christine Simmonds

Phototypeset in 11/12pt Bembo by
Tradespools, Frome, Somerset

Colour and black-and-white illustration
origination by East Anglian Engraving Limited,
Norwich

Printed and bound in Belgium by
Brepols, Turnhout

❧ CONTENTS ❧

Foreword
by
John Julius Norwich

January 1, 1937: Hung about. So runs, in all its completeness, the first entry of the journal that I began at the age of seven and kept up, on much the same level of interest, for several weeks. Since then I have started – and stopped – more diaries than I care to remember, ending with that upon which I embarked exactly forty-seven years later and which, to my utter astonishment, is still going strong. I have therefore had plenty of opportunity to learn just what an art good diary-keeping is – and just how far I am, alas, from acquiring it. No matter: I have consoled myself by reading, over the years, as many diaries of other people as I have been able legitimately to lay my hands on, and like to think that I must now qualify as something of an expert in the genre.

Parson James Woodforde is, as a diarist, unlike any other I know. He has none of the driving ambition of Pepys, none of the self-conscious turgidity of Evelyn, none of the literary snobbery of William Allingham (one of my particular favourites, none the less), none of the suave sophistication of Harold Nicolson. Superficially, I suppose, he comes closest to the Rev. Francis Kilvert: they were both, after all, quiet country parsons. But whereas Kilvert in his piety, his sentimentality, his earnestness and his almost unbearable sexual repression radiates the High Victorian spirit from every pore, Woodforde is the eighteenth century through and through. He strives for no effects, he pretends to no elevated sentiments, he doesn't care a row of beans whether anybody reads him or not. He is no great intellectual, nor would he ever claim to be; but there is an earthy, no-nonsense quality about him that his parishioners must surely have appreciated. To them, as to us, he is superbly approachable. He was, I suspect, a first-rate parson.

I well remember my first introduction to him, when I found the little navy-blue Oxford edition on my bedside table in a friend's house. Opening it at random, I read:

> **April 15 [1778]. . . .** Brewed a vessell of strong Beer today. My two large Piggs, by drinking some Beer grounds taking out of one of my Barrels today, got so amazingly drunk by it, that they were not able to stand and appeared like dead things almost, and so remained all night from dinner time today. I never saw Piggs so drunk in my life...

> **April 16** . . . My 2 Piggs are still unable to walk yet, but they are better than they were yesterday. They tumble about the yard and can by no means stand at all steady yet. In the afternoon my 2 Piggs were tolerably sober.

These remain my favourite entries; but in Parson Woodforde's Diary the value, and indeed the ultimate interest, resides less in individual episodes like this one than in the ensemble. Woodforde builds up his picture very slowly and entirely without artifice – for the simple reason that he has no idea that he is building it up at all. A brilliant analysis of this extraordinary work is provided, however, by Mr Ronald Blythe in his admirable Introduction. All that remains for me to do is to commend his words and, in the pages that follow, wish the reader what Woodforde must so often have wished himself – finding, almost invariably, his wish fulfilled: Bon Appétit.

The Reverend James Woodforde, *Samuel Woodforde, R.A. (1763–1817)*

Introduction
by
Ronald Blythe

It was just after World War I that a Hertfordshire doctor persuaded his neighbour John Beresford to take a look at a diary kept by an ancestor who had been the rector of a village near Norwich during the years 1776–1802. The diary actually began on 21 July 1759 when its owner, James Woodforde, heard that he had been accepted as a scholar of New College, Oxford. Beresford was enthralled, as every reader of Parson Woodforde has been to this day, and in 1924 he published the first of his five-volume extract of the diary, complete with notes and a now somewhat bland assessment of its author. Its popularity is now only equalled by that other and quite different clerical masterpiece, *Kilvert's Diary*, which was published a decade or so later. As their authors were the very epitome of the country clergy of their day, the one late Georgian, the other late Victorian, no two journals could be less alike. For they are, amongst so much else, brilliant pictures of traditional English rural society viewed from its orthodox religious base.

Woodforde's is the spirtually comatose base of the Church of England still unawakened by Wesley and by the sacramentalists of the Oxford Movement. He himself is a country gentleman occupying a living and doing his duty, a sociable bachelor who is looked after by his niece Nancy and five servants. Strangely it may seem, for he is neither eccentric nor passionate, clever, saintly, nor scandalous, this very ordinary figure for his time is now among the most unforgettable characters of English literature. The reason for this is that in his diary he neither puffs nor censors himself but simply allows his ordinariness to fill its pages – in very beautiful handwriting, as it happens. He has a reverence for small events and the domestic odds and ends of existence. 'This I thought deserving of notice, even in so trifling a book as this is,' he writes on 27 November 1789, as he puts down a cure for the cramp. In his autobiographical *Finding the Gate* V.S. Naipaul remarks, '. . . as diarists and letter-writers repeatedly prove, any attempt at narration can give value to an experience which might otherwise evaporate away.' The world can only guess at James Woodforde's motive for not letting his very solid life vanish into thin air, although it certainly wasn't vanity.

James Woodforde was born in 1740 at Ansford, Somerset, the second son of the vicar. His father also held the living of nearby Castle Cary. The Woodfordes had been significant priests of the Church of England for three generations and the diarist's grandfather, through his friendship with Izaak Walton and Thomas Ken, had links with the sacred world of George Herbert and Nicholas Ferrar. But all that James inherited from his forebears were the conventions of the country parson's role, plus a modest but unfailing kindness and level-headedness.

He was ordained at twenty-three and spent the next decade as a curate in his father's parishes. It was on Guy Fawkes Day 1774, while working as a proctor at New College, Oxford, that he heard of a vacancy in one of the many livings which were in the gift of his college, '. . . in Norfolk, by name of Weston Longeville worth it is said £300 per annum.' Five weeks later, '. . . I was declared and presented with the Presentation of the Rectory.' The immortal days ten miles from Norwich had begun. But there is no rush. This is the Church of England of George III's reign and it takes the new parson a year and a half to take up residence. He does so with his handsome nephew Bill whose effect on the servants makes him 'uneasy'.

The first of a memorable line of male servants, which was to include the Shakespearianly-named Brettingham Scurl and Barnabas Woodcock, also appears. Woodforde always refers to his five servants as 'our folk'. They and he, and everybody in the village, observe rank and are at ease with each other in a way which would be incomprehensible a century later. Pregnancies among the maids are more of an economic than a moral disaster – his neighbour's footman has got two maids with child more or less at the same moment – and willing lads grow up to become 'saucy' young men. It is in his dealings with the staff that we catch rare snatches of emotion and revelation in Woodforde, and also of what it was like to live with six boisterous unmarried people, for his niece Miss Woodforde arrived as soon as the rectory was in order to do the honours, and was never to leave until her uncle died. The more one reads his diary, the more each member of the little household takes on the mystery and interest of a character in a great novel, which is curious, because Woodforde is above all one of those writers who never 'draws' a person. He is artless.

Among so much else, this remarkable diary is one of the most candid statements on the national Church in its doldrums. It is no wonder that another clergyman, the Reverend Charles Wesley, had forsaken snug rectories to re-teach the Gospel throughout Britain. Parson Woodforde disapproved of such 'enthusiasm', as it was called, just as he disapproved of singing in church, and anything which went beyond the formal Christian duties which regulated society. 'I read Prayers and Preached this Afternoon at Weston' sums up his weekly labours. He is very put out when anything occurs which enlarges these duties, such as being required to give a sermon in Norwich Cathedral. Many of his ceremonies are carried out in his best parlour and not in the church, and these include many christenings. Although he has some 360 parishioners, he thinks it quite good to have 'two rails' or thirty communicants at Easter and Christmas. His church is only full for thanksgivings for military victories and recoveries from sickness of members of the royal family. He does no teaching and long before he himself is too ill to take services he pays a curate £30 a year to officiate for him.

Yet, spiritually defunct though his religion is, and unthinking and, to us, deplorable though so many of his ways are, we take to him. He is dully good and yet far from admirable, and the reader intuitively understands his difficulties and his humanity. For one thing, in spite of so much company, he is clearly rather lonely. Not that he ever complains about it, or about his lot generally. Being far more an English gentleman than a complex priest, his code would not allow it. Parson Woodforde is a stoic.

No day passes without its charity being listed, if it is only a penny to a beggar. The rectory is first port of call in Weston for the destitute who drift through it, little boys, soldiers, pedlars, homeless women. There are many funerals and Woodforde is an authority on how we used to die. He watches executions, once of five young men together at Norwich. He buys smuggled goods. He is a freemason and a pillar of the Establishment. He is discreet and not a gossip. He is a giver of accurate, unadorned information and not a storyteller. But he needs to know what is going on and is always sending Scurl his servant to Norwich for news.

The unfolding in the diary of the English countryside as it was just before the Industrial Revolution and the nineteenth-century Enclosure Acts is magnificent. Woodforde actually says very little about agriculture and its economics, then the nation's chief business activity, but he often provides the nearest thing which we have to a total documentary of a winter or summer day in the 1780s. He and the gentry 'rotate', as they call it, entertaining each other to dinner, backgammon and cards in turn, and again the movement and conservation of some half dozen families, thrown together for the best part of the year due to bad roads and a network of rural dependencies, contain the inner drama of the classic country novel, although one low in dialogue. Woodforde is no Boswell and reports little conservation. He reports what is eaten and what is done, not what is said. His observations are masculine and they lack nuance, insight or even inquisitiveness, though never truthfulness. He ties in human behaviour to the season's food and weather, and, somewhat perfunctorily, to the Church calendar. The diary is one of the most English books ever written.

And here one must say something about what he said so much – meals. The emphasis placed on them is so disproportionate to that placed on anything else that Woodforde has acquired a reputation for gluttony, when he should only have been indicted for conviviality or, as it seems as one reads him into late middle age, for attempted conviviality. The old custom of loading the table with a great many dishes of roasts, fish and game all at once, instead of serving them as courses, now suggests gross appetites, but while Woodforde certainly put eating high on the list of his enjoyments, it would be unfair to say that this is what he lived for. He lived for agreeable company and the intimacy and pleasure it brought to his essentially lonely existence, his niece Nancy notwithstanding. When, last thing before sleeping, he confides the day's menus to his diary it often reminds us of a child's blissful recollections of a party.

Dinner, with dear ones, is the zenith of his day and he never stints himself in the recording of it. The first full appreciation is at Oxford when he is nineteen.

> '*DEC. 25.* I received the Sacrament being Xmas Day. The Warden dined in Hall with us. The Bursars give us Scholars 8 Bottles of Port Wine to drink at dinner time. They likewise give us a qutr of a Cheshirc Cheese. We have 2 large Grace Cups between courses. We have rabbits for supper, 1 Rabbit between three at the expense of the Domus. Sent a letter to my Father.'

Over forty years later come his very last diary words, written ten weeks before his death.

> 'Very weak this Morning, scarce able to put on my Cloaths and with great difficulty, get down Stairs with help. Mr Dade read Prayers & Preached this Morning at Weston Church – Nancy at Church. Mr. & Mrs. Custance & Lady Bacon at Church. Dinner to day, Rost Beef &c.'

There is no development in Woodforde from teenager to elderly country cleric either as a man or stylist. His diary is extraordinary for the way in which it reveals a person who never changed any of his ideas from beginning to end. He carries within himself the manners, conventions, pleasures, attitudes and hopes of the middle-class man of his age, never decorating, analysing or out-growing them, and there are few books which allow us to step so immediately into the rooms and fields of Georgian England. Woodforde even costs his world, for the diary is also a meticulously kept account book, with the price of wages, food, stagecoaches, household necessities, tips, gifts, clothes, theatres, candles, hairdresses, medicines, etc., all carefully entered.

His income was about £400 a year and he lived in some style within it, never grousing about money or trying to get more of it. His conscience and, to a degree, his indifference to wealth earned him a local reputation for generosity, although we, recognizing the tremendous comfort in which he lived, compared with the majority of his parishioners and the citizens of Norwich, might find this easily earned. But Weston Rectory was often very reminiscent of a little medieval hospital in the way it distributed comforts and funds to itinerates, and Woodforde never took fees, although entitled to do do, when he married, buried or in any other way legalized the lives of the poor. Once a year the local farmers bring him their tithes and spend the afternoon with him having a drunken 'tithe frolic', and scarce a week passes without seasonal offerings of fruit, game, fish and other delicacies from the big houses all around.

Not even below the surface, but in plain view of this bounty, is misery and hardship of such chronic proportion and familiarity that Woodforde and his circle are able to live with it without guilt. A similar pragmatism applies to his attitude towards hangings and bloodsports. What Woodforde and his civilization could countenance without a qualm, and this might even include their shocking diets, is the most intriguing revelation here. We read things like the following, realizing that we are indeed in a cool era.

> 'We dined at 3 o'clock and after we had smoked a Pipe etc., we took a ride to the House of Industry about 2 miles West of Dereham, and a very large building at present tho' there wants another Wing. About 380 Poor in it now, but they don't look either healthy or cheerful, a great Number die there, 27 have died since Christmas last [in three months]. We returned from thence to the King's Arms and then we supped and spent the evening together. To Mr Hall's Clerk of Garvaston who came to give him notice of a Burial on Friday, being very poor, gave, O.I.O.'

The other sombre aspect of the diary and part of those dark realities which balance up its enchanting canvas of Gainsborough-like rural society in amiable movement round the respectable figure of a sporting parson, is of illness. Due to Woodforde's honesty and lack of euphemism when it comes to the failings of the flesh – in both senses – we have a record of his health in all its phases. In many ways he was wise about treatment, keen on vaccination and full of practical measures when any of his little household was sick. But we also see how people had to live with all kinds of non-diagnosable complaints, deal with pain and ignorance, especially of what their heavy eating and drinking could do to their bodies. Nor was Woodforde the type of man who thought of a village as a retreat and all through his diary we are ceaselessly aware that we are in one of history's epoch-changing revolutionary periods,

But the overall power of this rich diary stems from its perfect chronicling of the heart of an eighteenth-century clergyman.

THE ENGLAND OF
PARSON WOODFORDE

England is governed by the Aristocracy and the King. The Rotten Boroughs return members at their bidding. Only the County Members are rather more free, and even their return is largely dependent on the support of the great lords; moreover, in any case, the county franchise is limited to forty shillings a year freeholders. The Prime Minister is the actual nominee of the King, not of the Party. Only members of the Anglican Church are legally eligible for national or municipal office, or for admittance to the universities; a certain number of Dissenters, however, manage to scrape in through the loophole of occasional conformity or the Indemnity Acts. The criminal law is immensely rigorous, and thefts of the value of 40*s.* or over are punished by death. There are 160 capital offences. Small-pox carries off the thirteenth or fourteenth part of each generation. The Slave Trade is regarded as a legitimate commercial enterprise, and slavery itself as a respectable institution. The Society for the Propagation of the Gospel owns slaves in Barbadoes, and Whitefield has slaves in Georgia. Men are 'impressed' when necessary for the navy, and, by a variety of means, not seldom forced into the army. France is regarded as the age-long enemy of England. Though the Jacobites cease, after the suppression of the dangerous outbreak of 1745–6, to be a serious political menace, the Catholics are hated or feared by the people, and subject to outbursts of mob violence, as in the Gordon Riots in 1780. The theory of Free Trade is but just born, and high Protection— with the consequent smuggling—is practised universally. There is no system of public health or public education. In the civil service promotion depends on patronage, and in the army on purchase. There are, of course, no railroads, and the roads, such as they are, are controlled by a net-work of turnpikes. Travelling is by horseback, coach, or post-chaise. The existence of highwaymen adds a certain excitement to long journeys.

(From John Beresford's introduction to
The Diary of a Country Parson, Oxford, 1924)

PRINCIPAL DATES IN
PARSON WOODFORDE'S LIFE

JUNE 27 (June 16 O.S.) 1740 born at Ansford, Somerset, baptized three days later, 'being very ill', by his father who was Rector of Ansford and Vicar of Castle Cary.

1752 elected scholar of Winchester College.

JULY 21, 1759 elected scholar of New College, Oxford.

JULY 21, 1761 elected fellow of New College.

MAY 29, 1763 ordained deacon at Oxford.

JUNE 1, 1763 B.A. degree.

SEPTEMBER 12, 1763 leaves Oxford for Somerset.

OCTOBER 8, 1763 Curate of Thurloxton, Somerset.

JANUARY 12, 1764 Curate of Babcary, Somerset.

SEPTEMBER 29, 1764 ordained Priest at Wells.

MAY 26, 1765 Curate of Castle Cary (gives up Babcary in October).

OCTOBER 1765 takes up residence in the Lower House, Ansford.

MAY 23, 1767 M.A. degree.

JUNE 4, 1771 takes up residence in Ansford Parsonage, on his father's death, and continues as Curate of Castle Cary and Ansford till 1773.

DECEMBER 1773 leaves Ansford to take up residence at New College, Oxford, of which he becomes Sub-Warden.

APRIL 13, 1774 Pro-Proctor.

DECEMBER 15, 1774 presented to the living (Rectory) of Weston Longeville, Norfolk, but continues to reside at New College till February 15, 1776, when he goes home to Ansford.

NOVEMBER 24, 1775 Bachelor of Divinity degree.

MAY 9, 1776 leaves Ansford with his nephew Bill for Weston Longeville, which they reach on May 24.

MAY 24, 1776 to January 1, 1803 lives at Weston Longeville Parsonage, where he died on the latter date. In December 1778 his nephew Bill leaves Weston, and in October 1779 Nancy, his niece, arrives and lives with him for the rest of his life. Parson Woodforde never married. He proposed to a Miss Betsy White, of Shepton Mallet, on May 28, 1774, but she jilted him later for a rich Mr. Webster, of Devonshire, whom she married on September 6, 1775.

Babcary Church, where James Woodforde was curate in 1764–65

THE DIARY

PART I

OXFORD AND THE SOMERSET CURACIES, 1759–76

1759

The detailed Diary begins on July 21, 1759, with the laconic entry: 'Made a Scholar of New College'. In August and September of this year he is at home at Ansford.

DEC. 3. I first began on the Spinnet, Mr. Philip Hays, my Tutor.

DEC. 8. ... Had a Half-Crown Bowl of Punch from Kennerslys. I laid in Mr. Nicolls rooms with Mr. Hearst, who turned me out of Bed, and locked me out of the room naked.

1760

JAN. 30. Mr. Pye the Subwarden set me Part of the 1st Lesson for this morning service to translate into Sapphic Metre, for not being at Prayers this morning.

1761

JAN. 7. Peckham, Loggin and Webber went with me to Halse's the Sadler, where I threshed his apprentice Crozier for making verses on me.

FEB. 2. ... Went and saw Dumas alias Darking, a famous Highwayman, in the Castle. Gave a girl there, in for stealing a Shift 0. 0. 2*d*.

MAR. 6. Went up into the Hall this afternoon after the Judge was in, and I could not get a tolerable Place some time, but at last I jumped from two men's shoulders and leaped upon the Heads of several men and then scrambled into the Prisoners

Place where the Judge said I must not stay, so one of the Counsellors [i.e. Barristers] desired me not to make a noise, and he would let me have his Place, which was immediately under the Prisoners and opposite the Judge, where I sat and heard three or four tryalls, and likewise condemnation passed on Dumas, alias Darking, alias Hamilton, alias Harris. Was up there from 5 till 9, and then the Judge had finished everything. 1 condemned to die, 4 transported for seven years, 1 burnt in the hand and acquitted.

A view of the City of Oxford

MAR. 23. Mr. Darking alias Dumas etc., was hanged this morning about a quarter before eight, and after he was cut down he was carried by the Bargemen to St. Thomas Church to be buried. All the College gates was shut from ten o'clock last night till nine this morning by an Order of the Vice-Chancellor and Procters.

JUNE 14. . . . Hearst, Bell and myself, being in Beer, went under Whitmore's window, and abused him very much, as being Dean, he came down, and sent us to our Proper Rooms, and then we Huzza'd him again and again. We are to wait on him to-morrow.

JUNE 15. We waited on Whitmore this morning and he read to us a Statute or two and says he shall not mention again provided the Senr. People do not. I am to read the three first Books of Hutchinson's Moral Philosophy, and I am to give a summary account of them when I am examined for my Degree. . . .

On July 21st, 1761, he is made a Fellow of New College, and treats the Bachelors' Common Room 'all the evening with Wine and Punch'.

NOV. 4. . . . Dyer laid Williams 2*s*. 6*d*. that he drank 3 Pints of Wine in 3 Hours, and that he wrote 5 verses out of the Bible right, but he lost. He did it in the B.C.R. [Bachelors' Common Room], he drank all the Wine, but could not write right for his Life. He was immensely drunk about 5 Minutes afterwards.

1762

NOV. 26. . . . I began this very day to take upon me the Stewardship of the College, viz: to see the Meat of the College weighed every day in Kitchen for one week and for which I receive of the Manciple at the end of the week 0. 6*s*. 6*d*. All Fellows of this College above three years standing, and that here in College are, take the Stewardship by turns every week from Year's end to Year's end, and so on ad infinitum. Had a dunning Letter from Robinson & Hartley for the payment of £8. 15. 0 for half a Hogshead of old Port, that I had from Southampton last year.

1763

JAN. 24. We skated down to Abington where we dined and for our dinners there etc. each of us pd. 2*s*. 6*d*. We were going down about an hour and half; N.B. We walked above 2 miles out of it. It is about 10 miles by water.

An early nineteenth-century view of Abingdon Bridge and Church

FEB. 17. I dined at the Chaplain's table with Pickering and Waring, upon a roasted Tongue and Udder, and we went on each of us for it 0. 1. 9. N.B. I shall not dine on a roasted Tongue and Udder again very soon.

An early nineteenth-century etching of Christ Church Cathedral, Oxford

MAY 23. . . . I went this afternoon at five o'clock to C.C.C. to Mr. Hewish the Bishop of Oxford's Chaplain, before whom I was examined for deacon's Orders, and I came of very well. I was set over in the middle of the fifth Chapter of St. Paul to the Romans and construed that Chapter quite to the end. I was quite half an hour examining. He asked a good many hard and deep questions. I had not one question that Yes, or No, would answer. . . . Mr. Hewish is a very fair Examiner, and will see whether a Man be read or not soon. . . .

MAY 29. At nine o'clock, this morning went to Christ Church with Hooke, and Pitters, to be ordained Deacon; and was ordained Deacon there by Hume Bishop of Oxford. There were 25 Ordained Deacons and 13 Priests. We all received the Sacrament. . . . We were in C. Church Cathedral from nine o'clock this morning till after twelve. For wine this afternoon in the B.C.R. pd. 0. 0. 6.

JUNE 1. I took my B.A. Degree this morning. . . . Reynels, myself, Lucas, Peckham and Webber treated (as is usual) the B.C.R. after dinner with Wine, and after Supper with Wine and Punch all the evening. We had 27 People in the B.C.R. this evening. . . . I sat up in the B.C.R. this evening till after twelve o'clock, and then went to bed, and at three in the morning, had my outward doors broken open, my glass door broke, and pulled out of bed, and brought into the B.C.R. where I was obliged to drink and smoak, but not without a good many words. Peckham broke my doors, being very drunk, although they were open, which I do not relish of Peckham much.

JUNE 6. Had a Letter from Fitch, with a Promise from his Father of my taking the Curacy of his at Thurloxton near Taunton.

JUNE 29. ... For a Pocket Pistol alias a dram bottle to carry in one's pocket, it being necessary on a Journey or so, at Nicholl's pd 0. 1. 0.

JULY 3. Went this morning to Ardington by Wantage in Berks for Mr. Sheffield, who desired me to change Churches with him for this Sunday, it is about twelve miles of Oxford: I preached and read Prayers there in the morning and Churched a woman; and read Prayers there in the afternoon. Coming out of Church in the morning a woman that I had Churched gave me in the middle of the Church 0. 0. 6. which I received and pocketed. ...

AUG. 17. Dined in Hall at the High Table upon a neck of Venison and a Breast made into Pasty, a Ham and Fowls and two Pies. It is a Venison Feast which we have once a year about this time ... 2 Bucks one year, and 1 Buck another year is always sent from Whaddon Chase and divided between the Wardens, the Senr Fellows, and us. For an ounce of Indian Bark to put into my Pipe when smoking pd. 0. 0. 6*d*. It gives the tobacco a pretty smell and taste.

SEPTEM. 7. ... Had three bottles of Wine out of my room in ye B.C.R. this afternoon and Waring had another, out of his room. Waring was very drunk and Bedford was but little better. N.B. I was very sober, as I had made a resolution never to get drunk again, when at Geree's rooms in April last, when I fell down dead, and cut my Occiput very bad indeed.

On September 12th he leaves Oxford, having completed his course. On October 7th he sets out for Thurloxton, near Taunton, to take up his curacy.

NOV. 16. ... I lent Doctor Clarke a pamphlet called a sure Guide to Hell this evening, and a very good moral book it is, taken properly.

On November 29th he arranges with the old Rector of Babcary for the curacy of that place—it being only six miles from his home at Ansford—at £5 a quarter, the surplice fees, Easter offerings, and free use of Parsonage, gardens and stables, &c. On December 30th he rides over from Ansford to Babcary to see his new cure. He sees Farmer Bower, apparently the principal parishioner, who is much vexed to hear there is only to be one service on Sunday. Woodforde agrees to have two if his salary is increased to £30 per annum.

1764

JAN. 12. ... After breakfast I rode upon Cream to my Curacy at Babcary about six miles from hence, where I dined upon a Sheep's heart that I carried there in my pocket, at the Parsonage house, where I am to be when I go to Babcary on any occasion.

MAR. 26. I churched a poor woman at Babcary yesterday and she gave me sixpence, which I sent to her again. Mr. Gapper has been so good to serve my Church for me during my absence, and I sent him yesterday a genteel note to thank him. . . .

A view of Babcary Church

AUG. 18. . . . I have made a promise to-day concerning a certain thing (in eating); which every time I break that promise I pay—1—0.

AUG. 19. . . . After the Afternoon Service [Babcary] . . . I returned to Ansford—and the first news I heard was, that poor Miss Milly Chiche (a niece of Mrs. Chiche's) was dead; and she died about 11 o'clock this morning. I hope to God that she (poor dear creature) is happy. I believe verily that she was good to everyone, but herself, and I am afraid that drinking was her death. . . .

1765

JAN. 9. . . . Mr. Bridges Priest Vicar of the Cathedral at Wells called upon me this afternoon, and laid at our house all night. I took him with me up to Mr. Clarke's where we supped and spent the evening. . . . Mr. Bridges made himself very disagreeable to all the Company, and exposed himself much. We had great part of Cato★ performed this evening, and done tolerably well.

JAN. 10. . . . Mr. Bridges breakfasted with me, and afterward he went home to Wells. I am not sorry for it.

FEB. 11.

. . . For things that my old Woman at Babcary has bought me this last week— paid her	0.	0.	7½
Viz. for half a pound of Butter	0.	0.	4
For one pound of beef Stakes	0.	0.	3
For some Cream	0.	0.	0½
Gave Mary for her trouble	0.	0.	4½

★ Addison's tragedy.

For laying a wager with Betty Crich my old Woman's daughter concerning frosty weather last Thursday, and losing with her paid.......................... 0. 0. 6

MARCH 4. . . . I called upon Mr. Andrew Russ at Clanville, and spent the afternoon with him, Mr. Dod a Baker and a Roman Catholick, Mr. Thomas and Seth Burge. Mr. Dod and myself touched a little upon Religion, which I own was not right at all. . . .

MAY 24. . . . We got home to Ansford to dinner, where I dined, supped and laid at my Father's house. Blessed be Almighty God for sending me safe home to my dear Parents again. . . .

On May 26th he begins his curacy at C. Cary, and gets £20. 0. 0 a year from his father for it: this means he can only take one service at Babcary on Sunday.

JULY 8. . . . Brother John breakfasted, dined, supped and laid here again. Brother John is very indifferent by his being too busy with Girls. . . .

On July 11th he gives a dinner party at Babcary to fourteen C. Cary gentlemen, 'one of whom', he observes, 'was not invited'.

Babcary Church

We all spent the greatest part of the afternoon in the Churchyard at Babcary, where we were diverted by some of the Gentlemen playing at Ball,★ at which I won a betting 0. 2. 9. The Gentlemen seemed well pleased at the Entertainment, which gave me infinite satisfaction. A terrible accident happened whilst we were

★ 'Fives', probably, against the church wall.

at dinner, which many of us went to see the Body; viz. a Poor Boy was dragged and killed by a Horse about half a mile from us on the Ilchester Road. The boy was about fourteen years old. I hope to God the Poor Boy is happy. There was no bone broken, neither was his skull fractured, but he is dead. We all came home singing, and I thank God well. My Brother John was indisposed, therefore he could not go. . . .

JULY 30. . . . Jack [John] made Papa this evening very angry and uneasy by his defending suicide and talking so saucy to him. Jack is much altered indeed within these two years. I am afraid he will be ever miserable, but God forbid!

John Woodforde

SEP. 28. . . . Dr. Clarke's cook maid, Mary, was this morning found out in concealing a dead child in her box of which she had delivered herself yesterday morning, whether she murdered it or not is not yet known, but will be tried by the Coroner and Jury next Monday. . . .

SEP. 30. The Coroner, Mr. Norton with the Jury took inquest this afternoon upon the deceased child (a boy) of Dr. Clarke's maid, Mary, and brought her in not guilty.

DEC. 1. . . . I read Prayers and preached this afternoon at C. Cary Church. Mrs. White, Mrs. Sam White, Mr. Andrew Russ, Mr. James and Richard Clarke and Brother Heighes, supped and spent the evening with us at the Parsonage. My father did not come downstairs all the evening on account of the Company and Mama being ill. It vexed my Father and Mother greatly to have company brought to the house by Jack on a Sunday, and especially as my Mother is so bad.

~ 1766 ~

FEB. 4. . . . Our dear Mama is much worse and daily taking her leave of all of us.

FEB. 7. . . . Poor Mama sent for me and Jack this afternoon up into her room and very solemnly took her leave of us; therefore I do not believe she can exist very long in this world. . . .

FEB. 8. It pleased Almighty God of his great goodness to take unto himself my dear good Mother this morning, about 9 o'clock, out of this sinful world, and to deliver her out of her miseries. She went out of this world as easy as it was possible for anyone. I hope she is now eternally happy in everlasting glory. . . .

   O Lord God Almighty send help from Thy Holy Place to my dear Father, and to all my dear Mother's relations, to withstand so great a shock, and to live and dye so easy as she did. . . .

FEB. 14. . . . Papa gave me this afternoon my money box that Poor Mama kept for me from a Boy in which was half a guinea, two half crown pieces, a sixpence, two small silver coins and $\frac{1}{2}$d.

SEP. 14. . . . I was taken extremely bad this evening just after I was in bed in a fainting fit, but, I thank God (through Jack's assistance etc.), I soon got better. If my brother had not laid in the same room, I do believe I must have expired this evening.

SEPT. 29. N.B. We had a Pine Apple after dinner, the first I ever saw or tasted.

OCT. 18. . . . I entirely forgot that this was St. Luke's Day, and therefore did not read Prayers at C. Cary which I should have done otherwise. As it was not done willfully, I hope God will forgive it.

~ 1767 ~

FEB. 3. . . . I spent the evening and supped at Ansford Inn, there being a Masquerade Ball there this evening, and very elegant it was, much beyond my expectation in all respects. . . . Parson Penny, Gapper, Baily, Witwick and Overton and myself were the Clergymen that were there. . . . Brother John [was in the character of] a Counsellor, Brother Heighes, King Richard the Third; John Burge, Othello; Sister Jane, Shepherdess; Sally Clarke, Diana Trapes★ . . . cum multis aliis, all in very rich dresses but in no particular characters. . . . I did not dance the whole evening. We had good musick viz., four Violins, a Bass Viol, a Taber and Pipe, a Hautboy and French horn played by Mr. Ford.

★ A character in Gay's *Beggar's Opera.*

MARCH 7. ... I have taken for these last three mornings one hour before breakfast, the second rind of Alder stick steeped in water, and I do really think that I have gained great benefit from it, half a pint each morning; it must be near the colour of Claret wine. N.B. Very good to take every Spring and Fall.

MARCH 24. I was bleeded this morning by Mr. James Clarke, and had two ounces of blood taken from me, for which I gave him 2. 6.
   N.B. My blood was very rich and, therefore, proper to be bled.

APRIL 10. ... Jack did not please at Parsonage this evening being very much disguised in Beer, but it is but seldom and I hope will be more seldom, the more so the better.

APRIL 14. I read prayers this morning again at C. Cary Church. I prayed for poor James Burge this morning, out of my own head, hearing he was just gone off almost in a consumption. It occasioned a great tremulation in my voice at the time. I went after prayers and saw him, and he was but just alive. He was a very good sort of a young man and much respected. It was the evil which was stopped and then fell upon his lungs. Grant O Almighty God that he may be eternally happy hereafter. ...

Castle Cary Church

OCT. 10. ... My Father let Jack have this morning 60. 0. 0 to equip himself for the [Somerset] Militia, he being an Ensign in it.

NOV. 24. ... Colonel Cox's brother and Mr. Wm. Melliar waited on me this morning at the Lower House, and desired my vote for Sir Charles Tynte and his brother, Colonel Cox [as nominees to represent the County in Parliament], which I promised him. ...

DEC. 3. My man Luke Barnard, acquainted me this morning that he did not like his wages, and unless I would raise them, he must leave me, which he is to do at Lady Day next, and his year being up yesterday, I am to give him at the rate of five pounds a year till Lady Day without any new cloathes etc. I am not very sorry. He is a willing fellow but indolent and too fond of Cyder. He is going to farm, that is the reason of his leaving me. ... Mrs. Melliar was *fashionably* frightened into a fit by a cat after supper at the Doctor's, but soon well. ...

DEC. 11. I dined, supped and spent the evening at Justice Creeds, with him, his father, Mrs. Betty Baker, her three nieces of Bridgwater, that is, Miss Baker rather ordinary, Miss Betsy very pretty, and Miss Sukey very middling, rather pretty than otherwise, all very sensible and agreable, and quite fine ladies, both in Behaviour and Dress and Fortunes. ...

1768

JAN. 4. ... Jack did not come home till near four in the morning. He was much in liquor and quite unhappy. The Devil has had great power over him to-day. O Lord, grant him strength from Thy Holy Place, to withstand him better pro futuro.

FEB. 3. ... One Sarah Gore, came to me this morning and brought me an instrument from the Court of Wells, to perform publick Pennance next Sunday at C. Cary Church for having a child, which I am to administer to her publickly next Sunday after Divine Service.

MARCH 1. ... Great dinners etc., given to-day at the George Inn and the Angel by Sir Charles Tynte's and Mr. Cox's friends, viz. by Lord Ilchester, Lord Berkeley of Bruton and Mr. Mildmay, but neither were there. There were a great multitude of all sorts, gentle and simple. Mr. Cox himself was there. Bells ringing etc., and a great procession through Town with Musick playing and guns firing. They all came up in the afternoon as far as Justice Creeds, and Mr. Cox himself being there, we [the Diarist was dining with Justice Creed] both went out and spoke to him, and we both went back with him, with the Procession down to the George Inn, where we drank success to him, and was there for an hour in the large room with the multitude till Mr. Cox made a very handsome, sensible and genteel speech, and then he withdrew as did we immediately. Brother John dined and spent the evening with the multitude.

MARCH 4. ... I lent Brother John this afternoon at Lower House, to pay his expenses at Ansford Inn last Wednesday night, 1. 1. 0.
    N.B. It was the last guinea I had, but it was proper so to do, that he might by no means appear shabby. ...

MARCH 17. ... Great rejoicings this day at C. Cary, on account of Mr. Trevylyan's declining standing the Poll for this County of Somersett after so much hurry and disturbance. So that Sir Charles Tynte and Mr. Cox are to be our members. May they make great and worthy Representatives. ...

MARCH 29. ... My Father would not play cards, it being Passion Week and the Justice [Creed, who was visiting there] was not very pleased.

N.B. No cards this week at Parsonage which I think is not amiss, though there might be no harm.

APRIL 14. ... I went over to C. Cary this night after eleven o'clock and privately baptised a child born this day and very dangerously ill in convulsions, by name George, of Perry's a Mason and a poor man in South Cary.

Mem: Never did I any ecclesiastical duty with more pleasure as it gave such great satisfaction to its Parents, and that they were so good and charitably disposed to have it done. The poor innocent Babe was taken with a violent fit, immediately after I had named it, and I really thought was dead, but it pleased God to restore it again, which was undoubtedly a blessing from Heaven for their goodness. ...

APRIL 15. ... The poor little Infant which I privately baptized last night departed this world this afternoon. ...

APRIL 17. ... After Cary Service I buried that little Infant which I privately named two days ago,—2 days old, a very happy turn for the dear Innocent.

MAY 9. ... I never saw a Peacock spread his tail before this day at Justice Creeds and most Noble it is.—How wonderful are Thy Works O God in every Being.

MAY 23. I rec^d a note from my Father this morning by Sister Jane and wherein he insists on Jack's not coming to this house again for some time, as he disturbed him so much last night that he could not sleep.

SEP. 14. ... Mr. Hindley and Justice Creed called at Parsonage this evening in their Chair to ask me to dinner to-morrow to talk about going to Wells with them Friday, concerning the Gallery work, to wait on the Bishop, but I shall not go (I believe) nor interfere at all concerning it, but to live peaceably with all men. He is a little unreasonable to desire it, as I must then fly in the face of allmost all my Parishioners. Great and many are the divisions in C. Cary, and some almost irreconcilable. Send us Peace O Lord! With Thee O Lord all things are possible.

Squire Creed's man, for some reason, had been kept out of the gallery by the singers and the Squire wanted to have the gallery taken down.

OCT. 26. I had a poor little cat, that had one of her ribs broke and that laid across her belly, and we could not tell what it was, and she was in great pain. I therefore with a small pen knife this morning, opened one side of her and took it out, and performed the operation very well, and afterwards sewed it up and put Friars Balsam to it, and she was much better after, the incision was half an inch. ...

NOV. 5. ... The effigy of Justice Creed was had through the streets of C. Cary this evening upon the [Fire] Engine, and then had into the Park and burnt in a bonfire immediately before the Justice's House, for his putting the Church Wardens of Cary into Wells Court, for not presenting James Clarke for making a

Riot in the Gallery at Cary Church some few Sundays back. The whole Parish are against the Justice, and they intend to assist the Church Wardens in carrying on the cause at Wells. . . .

NOV. 22. I married Tom Burge of Ansford to Charity Andrews of C. Cary by License this morning. The Parish of Cary made him marry her, and he came handbolted to Church for fear of running away, and the Parish of Cary was at all the expense of bringing of them to, I rec^d of Mr. Andrew Russ the overseer of the Poor of Cary for it 0. 10. 6. . . .

DEC. 26. I was very bad in my throat all night, but towards the morning was rather better, only extremely hoarse. . . . I could not go to read Prayers this morning at Cary though it was St. Stephen, which I hope will be forgiven. . . . Sister Jane visited me this morning, and she being deaf and I not able to speak, was good company. . . .

1769

JAN. 1. . . . My ring which I had lost, was unaccountably found in little Sam: Clarke's breeches, he knowing nothing of it. I gave him 0. 1. 0.

On February 9th a meeting at the George Inn of some of the leading Cary parishioners including the Diarist composes the approaching Law Suit between Justice Creed and the Church Wardens, the agreement (this proposal had been rejected two days before) being 'that as the Gallery at Cary Church was large enough to contain between 3 & 4 score people, and the Singers being not above 30 in number that there should be a partition made in the gallery for the Singers, and the other part open to any body and also for Mr. Creed to pay his own costs and the Parish the other'.

The George Inn, Castle Cary

FEB. 26. ... The 36 Psalm was sung this afternoon in Cary Church by the Singers. Done out of Pique to old Willm. Burge. Old Mr. Burge concerns himself too much with the Singers.

On February 19th Burge had annoyed the singers by sending some persons into the singing part of the gallery contrary to the recent agreement.

MARCH 10. One Farmer Wittys of Butly whom I never saw but once before called upon me this morning, and desired me to lend him thirty Pound, but it was not convenient—Very odd indeed. ...

MARCH 12. ...
   Mem: As I was going to shave myself this morning as usual on Sundays, my razor broke in my hand as I was setting it on the strop without any violence. May it be always a warning to me not to shave on the Lord's Day or do any other work to profane it pro futuro. ...

JUNE 17. ... Jack made a terrible noise at Lower House with all the folks there. I got up out of my bed and came down at twelve at night and found the house in an uproar, Jack abusing of them all in a terrible manner. Very bad work indeed of a Saturday night in a Parson's House, it disturbed me all night.
   N.B. We must part.

JUNE 21. ... I played with Mr. James Clarke at Battledor and Shuttlecock, and we kept the cock up once upwards of 500 times.

SEP. 22. ... Great rejoicings at Cary to-day being the Coronation Day. Bells ringing all day, Cudgell playing at Crokers, a very large bonfire on the top of the hill and very grand fireworks in the evening with firing of many guns. All at Mr. Creed's, Mr. Hindley and Mr. Potts and Duck's expense. I was at all. At the Cudgell Playing I gave 0. 4. 5. The fireworks were sent from London and were Sky-Rocketts, Mines, Trees, Crackers, Wheels and divers Indian Fireworks. Old Mrs. Burge and daughter etc., etc., etc., drank tea and coffee, supped and spent the evening at Justice Creed's. We did not break up till near two in the morning. Everything extremely handsome and polite indeed. ...

OCT. 1. ... I read Prayers, churched a woman [and] read the Act of Parliament against profane swearing as directed by Law. ...

NOV. 12. ... I was disturbed this morning at Cary Church by the Singers. I sent my Clerk some time back to the Cary Singers, to desire that they would not sing the Responses in the Communion Service, which they complied with for several Sundays, but this morning after the first Commandment they had the Impudence to sing the Response, and therefore I spoke to them out of my desk, to say and not sing the Responses which they did after, and at other places they sang as usual. The Singers in the Gallery were, John Coleman, the Baker, Jonathan Croker, Willm Pew Junr., Thos Penny, Willm Ashford, Hooper the Singing Master, James Lucas, Peter, Mr. Francis's man, Mr. Melliar's man James, Farmer Hix's son, Robert Sweete and the two young Durnfords. ...

NOV. 26. I read Prayers and Preached this morning at C. Cary Church. N.B. No singing this morning, the Singers not being at Church, they being highly affronted with me at what I lately had done. . . .

DEC. 5. . . . A strange man was found this evening in my father's little house.★ N.B. A Farmer's daughter near Bristol who was to sleep at my Father's to-night had occasion to go to the Necessary House and there was a man there, but he got clear of. He was upon no good there.

DEC. 17. . . . The Singers at Cary did not please me this afternoon by singing the 12 Psalm, New Version, reflecting upon some People. . . . Some people have been about my Father's house again this evening, about 8 o'clock. Jenny and the maid being at the Little House, some person or another came to the door of it and rapped against it three times with a stick. What it means I know not. Brother Heighes, Jack and myself all armed, took a walk at twelve this evening round the Parish to see if we could meet any idle Folks but we did not, and therefore came home about two. We waited at my Father's some considerable time, till Brother Heighes was very uneasy, being cold in his feet.

DEC. 24. To Cary Singers this evening being Xmas Eve at Parsonage after giving them a Lecture concerning their late behaviour in Church, on promise of amendment gave 0. 2. 0.

1770

JAN. 26. At two o'clock this afternoon I went up to Justice Creed's and heard my Wood Stealers examined before the Justice. Robert Biggin was found guilty and

Justice Creed's house, Castle Cary

★ Lavatory.

his brother Nath was acquitted, therefore Robert was ordered to pay me six shillings by the 9 of February, if he does not he is to be whipped from Cary Cross to Ansford Inn. . . .

Lower House, Ansford

FEB. 12. . . . I went to Mr. Willm Melliar's and Mr. Creed's and Mr. Clarke's to desire all three of them to drink a dish of coffee with me this afternoon at Lower House and if possible to reconcile all animosities in Cary and to stop and put an end to all Law Suits now subsisting. It was agreeable to all Parties for Mr. Creed and Mr. Melliar to settle all matters and to make Peace. Mr. Creed and Mr. Melliar agreed to meet each other this afternoon at my house. I dined and spent part of the afternoon at Mr. Creed's with him and his Father, and after the Justice took a walk with me to my house and drank a dish of coffee with me. Mr. Willm Melliar and Dr. Clarke also drank a dish of coffee with me and after coffee we talked over the Parish Affairs. After much altercation it was settled for Peace. The terms were these as underwritten. . . .

That all Prosecutions between the contending parties in the Parish of Castle Cary, and all animosities between the Houses of Creed and Melliar, should from that time cease, and be buried in the Gulf of Oblivion. . . . After the above [numerous technical details of settlement of Prosecution costs etc., etc.] was agreed to by all four and Mr. Melliar had made a Memorandum of it in writing, Mr. Creed and Mr. Melliar hobbed and nobbed in a glass of Wine and drank success to Peace. . . .

APRIL 18. . . . I dined at old Mr. Willm Burge's being the day of Mr. Wilkes's enlargement, and spent the afternoon and former part of this evening there with old Mr. Willm Burge etc., etc. . . . Cary bells ring all day upon the occasion. Two British Flaggs also displayed, one at Cary Cross and another on Cary Tower. A hogshead of Cyder given to the Populace at the Cross. Many loyal toasts and worthy men drank upon the occasion, and Mr. Burge's house handsomely illuminated in the evening. The Flagg on the Tower had on it Liberty and Property, the small one had on it Mr. Wilkes's Head and Liberty. Everything was conducted with great decorum and broke up in good time. We had for dinner [apparently for 15 people] a boiled Rump Beef 45 pd. weight, a Ham and half a dozen Fowls, a roasted Saddle of Mutton, two very rich puddings, and a good Sallet with a fine cucumber. . . .

JULY 15. I read Prayers and preached at Cary Church and whilst I was preaching one Thos Speed of Gall-hampton came into the Church quite drunk and crazy and made a noise in the Church, called the Singers a Pack of Whoresbirds and gave me a nod or two in the pulpit. The Constable Roger Coles Senr took him into custody after and will have him before a Magistrate to-morrow. . . .

1771

JAN. 10. . . . Brother John was greatly astonished by a light this evening as he came thro' Orchards, a field by Ansford Church, which light seemed to follow him close behind all the way through that field, and which he could not account for. I hope it is no Omen of death in the Family. N.B. The Reflection of the snow I apprehend occasioned the light that my Brother saw.

JAN. 20. . . . My Poor Father rather worse than better. He wastes very fast. . . .

FEB. 19. . . . My Father was brave and in good spirits this morning, but in the evening was as bad as ever and talked very moving to Sister Jane and me about his Funeral and that he wanted to alter his Will, and mentioned the underwritten to me and my Sister Jane, 'that he desired that his maid should have that house where Grace Stephens lives at present during her life, and after her life to go to my sister Jane, as well as all the other Poor Houses and Mrs. Parr's House and the Field called Four Acres to her my Sister Jane. That Sister White has one Hundred Pounds to make her equal to her Sister Clarke in Fortune. That I have all his Books and Book-case in his Study. And that he would have no people invited to his funeral to make a show, but that he is carried to Ansford Church by six of his poor neighbours, Robin Francis and his Brother Thomas were mentioned and that they have half a crown a-piece.—To be laid in the vault where my Mother is, by her side. And that a little monument be erected in the side wall near the vault in memory of him and his wife.' My poor Father is I think much in the same way as my poor Mother was. . . . Grant him O Lord an easy and happy exit. Better Parents no children ever had than we have been blessed with—blessed be God for it—and make us more worthy than we are, for all thy goodness to us. . . .

I played at Back Gammon with my Father in the evening, it takes him in some degree off from thinking of his Pain. I won—0: 6. . . .

MAY 16. . . . My Poor Father worse than ever a great deal, and altered greatly after 12 at night, and in great agonies all the morning; and it pleased the Almighty Creator to deliver him out of all his Pain and Trouble in this world about $\frac{1}{2}$ an hour after one o'clock at noon, by taking him to himself—blessed therefore be the name of the Lord.—It is the Lord, let him do what seemeth him good. The Lord gave and the Lord hath taken away, blessed be the name of the Lord. Have mercy upon us O Lord, miserable sinners—and send us comfort from above.

The Diarist was left sole executor of all his Father's real and personal property left between him, Brother John, and Sister Jane.

MAY 17. . . . My Brother John, myself and Sister Jane, examined this morning, my poor Father's Bureau etc. at Parsonage and we found in Cash in all the places

the sum of 518 : 9 : 6; Mortgages, Bonds and Notes of Hand 533 : 16 : 0. . . . I sent poor old Alice Stacy by her daughter this morning to cheer up her spirits a little, 0–1–0. The poor creature begged most heartily to sit up with my Poor Father, all night, which she did with Christian Speed.

JUNE 5. . . . This morning between James Woodforde, Jane Woodforde, and John Woodforde, Housekeeping was settled as follows: that I should keep house at Parsonage, Jack at Lower House and that Sister Jane should board with me for sixteen pounds per annum, Tea, Sugar and Wine excepted. . . .

On June 25th he rides over to see his cousin Mr. Dolton, Parson of Cucklington, who is to hold the living of Ansford for Frank Woodforde, and on July 9th he duly inducts him to Ansford Rectory where the Diarist and his sister Jane are to live; Mr. Dolton promising not to turn them out.

On September 25th he goes over to dine with Mr. Wickham at Shepton Mallett, and brings back with him in the chaise Miss Betsy White of Shepton, to whom he refers as follows: 'She is a sweet tempered girl indeed, and I like her much, and I think would make a good wife, I do not know but I shall make a bold stroke that way.' He sees a good deal of her.

Ansford Church

1772

FEB. 29. This morning after Breakfast I went down to Henbridge, when I saw and spent the morning with Mrs. Grant and her two daughters, Miss Jenny Wason and Miss Nancy Wason. They all seemed to be very uneasy, particularly Mrs. Grant, who said, that my Brother seemed too gay to be able to make a good Husband to her daughter, kept too much Company for his circumstances etc. etc. I told her that he had some failings as other young men, but I thought his good ones overbalanced them as I never saw anything tending to any very bad. I staid at Henbridge till after one and then returned and dined, supped, and slept again at Parsonage. Brother John went home well pleased at my going down. . . .

APRIL 21. . . . Whilst we were at dinner they [Parson and Mrs. Wickham] came to us to the Parsonage and caught my Sister Jane at table with her hair up in papers, as she is going this evening to Shepton Assembly, but they excused it very kindly.

MAY 1. . . . Brother John supped and spent the evening at Parsonage, was very much in liquor and behaved like a madman. N.B. He has received a letter from Nancy Wason, which I saw and I think she has used Jack very ill, she declares of [off] entirely, and will answer no more letters of his. It is I believe her Mother's and Sister's doing all this. . . .

JUNE 7. . . . Mr. Creed called upon me in the evening and we took a walk—after I had buried a child of Giles Francis's by name J. Francis—aged 5 years. The child died at Bath owing to a kick in the groin by another lad. Giles works at Bath, and he and his son brought the child in a coffin upon their heads from Bath, they set out from Bath last night at 12. . . .

1773

FEB. 10. . . . I went in the evening to the Play with the Justice [Creed]. The Play was Hamlet and the entertainment—Hob in the Well.

MARCH 1. . . . Brother John spent the evening at Parsonage but was noisy, being merry, and his seeing Nancy Wason ride by our house this aft. and is reported to be married to And^w Russ this morning. Parson Rawkins and another Person with her. . . .

MARCH 28. . . . Mr. John Pouncett of Cole spent the afternoon, supped and spent the evening at Parsonage. He has an inclination for my Sister Jane. I think it would do well. . . .

MAY 21. . . . A grey owl was found in my back-kitchen this morning. He came down the chimney. I gave him his Liberty again. . . .

JULY 8. . . . We all went from Sister Clarke's up into South Cary to the Royal Oak to see Mr. Nevil's grand machinery, being the whole of the woolen manufactory, from one end of it to the other, and all in motion at once. It is very curious indeed—three thousand movements at once going—composed by Mr. Nevil himself, and which took him ny thirty years in completing it. . . .

JULY 19. . . . Mr. Frank Woodforde was this morning inducted into the Living of Ansford, and he immediately sent me a Line that he intends serving Ansford next Sunday himself, which notice of my leaving the Curacy is I think not only unkind but very ungentlemanlike. I must be content. Far be it from me to expect any favour at all from that House. All their actions towards me are bad. . . . I intend to quit the Parsonage House when my year is up, which will be Lady Day next, and to take up my residence once more at New College. . . .

AUG. 24. . . . I called at Mrs. White's and stayed with her and her daughter Betsy till 8 o'clock this evening. . . . Betsy White came from London only last Saturday. She is greatly improved and handsomer than ever. . . .

On September 6th he hands Mr. Wickham notice of his giving up Cary curacy at Michaelmas, and visits 'my dear Betsy White', and on September 13th he enters that Andrew Russ and Nancy Wason are married that day. On December 14th he leaves Ansford to take up residence at Oxford.

DEC. 24. (Mem:) I dreamt very much of poor old Alice Stacy of Ansford and my man Willm Corpe last night—the former that she had a vast discharge of matter from her Breast—the latter that he was very drunk and almost killed by a fall from a Horse—both which I thought I saw very plainly.

DEC. 25. . . . I dined in the Hall and 14 Senr Fellows with me. I invited the Warden to dine with us as is usual on this day, but his Sister being here, could not. We had a very handsome dinner of my ordering, as I order dinner every day being Sub-Warden.

We had for dinner, two fine Codds boiled with fryed Souls round them and oyster sauce, a fine sirloin of Beef roasted, some peas soup and an orange Pudding for the first course, for the second, we had a lease of Wild Ducks rosted, a fore Qu: of Lamb and sallad and mince Pies. We had a grace cup before the second course brought by the Butler to the Steward of the Hall who was Mr. Adams a Senior Fellow, who got out of his place and came to my chair and there drank to me out of it, wishing me a merry Xmas. I then took it of him and drank wishing him the same, and then it went round, three standing up all the time. From the high Table the grace Cup goes to the Batchelors and Scholars. After the second course there was a fine plumb cake brought to the sen^r Table as is usual on this day, which also goes to the Batchelors after. . . .

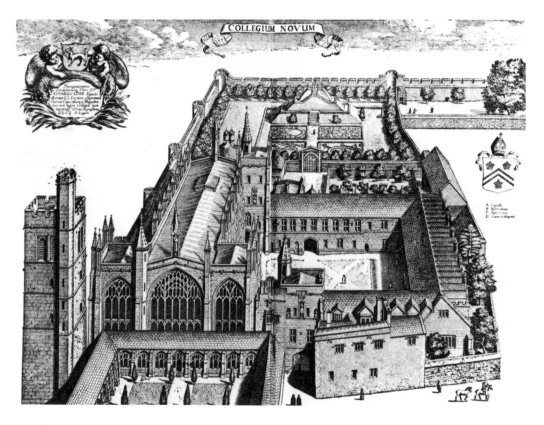

A late seventeenth-century engraving of the buildings and gardens of New College, Oxford

1774

FEB. 1st. . . . I got to Ansford, I thank God safe and well this evening about 6 o'clock. It snowed all the way from Old Downe to Ansford and the wind blowed very rough and it was very cold indeed. Gave the old Downe driver a dram at Gannard's Grave and another at home, and gave him also 0. 1. 6. I found Mr. Pouncett and my sister Jane at home by themselves, and I supped and slept at Parsonage. Brother John supped and spent the evening with us. . . .

MARCH 13. . . . Mr. Pouncett slept at Parsonage. I talked with him pretty home about matters being so long doing—[i.e. the marriage arranged between Mr. Pouncett and Sister Jane being delayed].

MARCH 16. . . . I took a ride this morning to Shepton Mallett . . . When I came to Shepton I got of at Mr. White's and there I spent most of my time with Mrs. White and my dear Betsy White. They wondered not to see me before. . . .

MARCH 23. I breakfasted at Parsonage this morning as did Mr. Pouncett, who after breakfast went home and returned about 12 to take his leave of me. I got up very early this morning, packed up my things, settled all accounts with my People, dined at 12 and at one set of in Ansford Inn Chaise with a very heavy Heart for Oxford thro' Bath. I left with Mr. Pouncett two guineas to be given to the Poor of Ansford, as directed by me in writing. I left with him also one guinea to be given to the Poor of Cary as also directed by me in writing. . . .

I left all my House in Tears and I could not refrain myself from the same. Pray God bless them all. This day left of all House-keeping to Mr. Pouncett. We had some Trout for dinner to-day, but my Heart was so full that I could eat but little. . . .

APRIL 20. . . . I went to Chapel this morning at 11 o'clock it being Term Time and Wednesday. There should have been Declamations to-day but there was none: Cooth and Trotman should have declaimed, therefore I shall punish them. . . .

AP. 21. . . . I went with Holmes to-day to the Free-Masons Lodge held this day at the New Inn, was there admitted a Member of the same and dined and spent the afternoon with them. The Form and Ceremony on the occasion I must beg leave to omit putting down. Paid on admission for fees etc. £3. 5. 0. It is a very honourable as well as charitable Institution and much more than I could conceive it was. Am very glad on being a Member of it. . . .

MAY 12. . . . Whilst I was at supper I was sent for to quell a riot in Hollinwell. I left my supper and went with Holmes and Oakely into Hollinwell, but it was pretty quiet. However I met with two gentlemen going into a House and I accosted them, and I believe they were the same that made the disturbance. I asked them to go to their Colleges directly and wait on me tomorrow morning at New College. Their names were Taylor of Worcester Coll: and Duprie of Exeter College. I received a letter this evening from my Sister Jane, who acquainted me that my poor old servant man William Corpe dropped down in an Apoplectic Fit

Nancy Woodforde

May 2, and expired directly. He was that morning married to his old Sweet-heart, and this happened in the evening in the street. I am exceedingly sorry for him indeed and her also. I hope he is everlastingly happy in a better state: Pray God make us all wise to consider our latter end, for Death comes upon us we see at an hour when we little think upon it, and sometimes very sudden. . . .

MAY 20. . . . I got home to Ansford this evening about 8 o'clock and I thank God safe and well, to the Old House. . . .

MAY 22. . . . Have been very naughty to-day, did not go to either Ansford or Cary Church. . . . Have mercy on me O Lord a miserable, vile sinner, and pardon my failings.

MAY 24. . . . After breakfast I went down to Ansford Church and married my Sister Jane and Mr. Pouncett by license. Pray God send Thy Blessing upon them both, and may they be long happy in each other. I would not have anything for marrying them but Mr. Pouncett gave Mr. Frank Woodford 1. 1. 0. . . .

MAY 28. I supped and spent the evening at Brother John's with him, Nancy, Sister White and Betsy White, Sister Jane and Mrs. Pouncett. . . . Mrs. Pouncett, Sister White and Betsy dined at Jack's. I went home with Betsy White and had some talk with her concerning my making her mine when an opportunity offered and she was not averse to it at all.

MAY 30. I breakfasted at Parsonage and about 9 set forth on my bay Mare for the University of Oxford. . . . Mr. Pouncett went with me as far as Alfred's Tower. I left my Sister Jane very low on my going away. . . .

JULY 5th. . . . A little after 4 this aft: went to the Theatre and heard the oratorio of Hercules, for a ticket pd 0. 5. 0. There was a good deal of Company present. The Music was very fine—A Miss Davies from the Opera House sung most delightfully, Miss Molly Linley sung very well. A Mr. Gosdall gave us a fine Solo on the Violincello as did Mr. Fisher on the Hautboy. Miss Davies is to have they say sixty guineas. . . . Mr. Woodhouse a gent: Com: of University College was very drunk at the Theatre and cascaded in the middle of the theatre. Mr. Highway one of the nominal Proctors for this week desired him to withdraw very civilly but he was desired by one Mr. Peddle a gent: com: of St. Mary Hall not to mind him, my seeing Highway in that distress I went to them myself and insisted upon Woodhouse going away immediately from the Theatre, and then Peddle behaved very impertinently to me, at which I insisted upon his coming to me to-morrow morning. Mr. Woodhouse after some little time retired, but Peddle remained and behaved very impertinently, I therefore intend putting him in the black Book. . . .

An eighteenth-century engraving of the Sheldonian Theatre, Oxford

JULY 27. . . . Mr. Hindley, Dr. Thurlowe, Dr. West, Dr. Burrows and Mr. Bowerbank, supped and stayed with me till after one. Mr. Hindley, Dr. Burrows, Mr. Bowerbank and myself got to Cards after coffee. At whist I won 1. 0. 6 out of which, Mr. Hindley owes me 0. 5. 0. I gave my company only for supper cold mutton. After supper I gave them to drink some Arrac Punch with Jellies in it and some Port wine. I made all my Company but Dr. West quite merry. We drank 8 bottles of Port one Bottle of Madeira besides Arrac Punch, Beer and Cyder. I carried of my drinking exceedingly well indeed.

OCT. 15. . . . I caught a remarkable large Spider in my Wash Place this morning and put him in a small glass decanter and fed him with some bread and intend keeping him. . . .

DEC. 15. . . . We had a meeting of the whole House in the Hall at 12 o'clock, to present a Person to the Living of Weston Longeville and to seal the remaining Leases. The former came on first. Hooke and myself were the two candidates proposed. Many learned and warm arguments started and disputed, and after 2 hours debate the House divided and it was put to the Vote, when there appeared for me 21 votes, and for Mr. Hooke 15 only, on which I was declared and presented with the Presentation of the Rectory. The chief speakers for me were the Warden, Mr. Holmes, Mr. Webber, Mr. Gauntlett, and Dr. Wall. The chief speakers for Mr. Hooke were Mr. Caldecott, Mr. Coker Senr, Mr. Adams, Mr. Thorpe and Mr. Milton, the latter talked nothing but nonsense. [The Diarist very sensibly voted for himself.]

. . . A little after 11 o'clock this evening I went down into the Junr Common Room attended with Master Senr, Cooke, Adams, Townshend and Holmes to thank them for the favour conferred on me. We stayed there till after 12 and returned then to the Senr Common Room and stayed till near 4 o'clock. We were exceeding merry in the Junr Common Room and had many good songs sung by Swanton, Williams Junr and Wight. And also a very droll one by Busby, which occasioned great laughter. . . .

1775

FEB. 17. . . . Mr. Peddle gent: Com: St. Mary Hall whose name is in the black Book put in by me in July last, waited on me this morning to desire me to take his name out of the same, which I promised to do upon his bringing me a Declamation on—Nemo omnibus horis sapit, and asking pardon of Highway of Baliol. . . .

FEB. 20. . . . Mr. Peddle brought me his Declamation this morning. I went to Highway of Baliol about him, and he is satisfied, therefore this aft: I sent to the Senr Proctor for the black Book and erased his name, and put satisfecit.

FEB. 28. . . . It being Shrove Tuesday we had Lambs Wool to drink, a composition of Ale, sugar etc., Lobsters, Pancakes etc., to eat at Supper, and the Butler there gives a Plumb Cake with a copy of Verses of his own making upon it. . . .

On April 9th he enters that he is very busy packing up for 'my Norfolk Expedition'—an expedition to take possession of his living at Weston. This is a temporary visit, as he does not go into residence till over a year later.

APRIL 10. I breakfasted in my room this morning at 7 o'clock upon some chocolate as did Cooke with me. After breakfast about 8 o'clock I set of in Jones's Post Coach for the City of London. Cooke went with me in the same, and I promised to frank him all the way to Norfolk as he goes to oblige me. . . .

An eighteenth-century print of the Oxford Coach leaving Hyde Park Corner

APRIL 16. We breakfasted, supped and slept at Weston Parsonage. A man and his wife, by name Dunnell live at the Parsonage House and are good kind of people. We went to Church this morning at Weston, and Cooke read Prayers and preached for Mr. Howes [his curate]. I also administered the H: Sacrament this morning at Weston Church being Easter Day—I had near 40 Communicants. N.B. No money collected at the Sacrament, it not being usual at Weston. My clerk is a shocking Hand. The worst singing I ever heard in a Church, only the Clerk and one man, and both intolerably bad. Mrs. Howes and her niece Mrs. Davy were at Church and they would make us get into their Chaise after Church and go with them to Hockering to Mr. Howes, where we dined and spent the afternoon and came back to Weston in the evening in Mr. Howes's Chaise about 8 o'clock—Gave his driver 1. 0. Mr. Howes' is about 2 miles West of Weston. Cooke likes my House and Living very much. For my part I think it a very good one indeed. I sleep in the Garrett at Weston as I would not let Cooke sleep there, but immediately under in the New Building which is very good. Cooke is mightily pleased with his Scheme [i.e. the whole expedition].

The Diarist and his friend Cooke remain together at Weston till April 26th. The time is taken up in viewing the glebe, making expeditions, interchanging visits with the Howes's, transacting on the Diarist's part a variety of ecclesiastical business, such as being inducted by Mr. Howes, taking the Oath of Abjuration★ before the Justices at Norwich, reading the 39 Articles in Weston Church before a crowded congregation, and 'declaring my assent and consent to the Liturgy'.

On May 16th he and Cooke stay two nights in London at the Turk's Head. On the 18th whilst walking in St. James's Park, 'the King and Queen with their guards went by us in Sedan Chairs from the Queen's Palace to St. James's Palace, there being a Levee at St. James's to-day at 1 o'clock. The King did not look pleasant but the Queen did.' They went to Covent Garden Theatre and saw the Merchant of Venice. *'We separated coming out of the Play House and Cooke went home by himself and I by myself. I met many fine women (Common Prostitutes) in my return home, and very impudent indeed. . . .*

Next day they return to Oxford.

New College, Oxford

JUNE 13. . . . A Chinese man about 25 years of age attended by a multitude of People came to see our College and Gardens this morning, I was in the garden with him. He talks English very well. He had on his head a Cap like a Bell covered with a red Feather and tyed under his Chin, a kind of a Close Coat on his back of pink Silk quilted, over that a loose Gown of pink silk quilted also, which came down to his heels, and over that a black Gauze or Crape in imitation of a long Cloak, a pr of Breeches or drawers of pink silk also and quilted, and a kind of

★ The oath abjuring the descendants of James II was by the Act of 1702 made a
necessary qualification for every employment in Church or State.

silk Boots of the same colour and quilted also, and a pr of red Morocco Slippers.
His hands were also covered with some thin silk of pink. He had a Fan tyed to a
Sash before him. He was of a moderate stature, a tawny complexion, black hair
tyed in a kind of tail, small eyes, short nose, no beard, in short as to his whole
Face, it was uncommonly ugly, not unlike one of the runabout gipsies. . . . After
prayers I went with Acton one of our Gent: Com: to have my Profile taken of by
a Lady who is come to town and who takes of great likenesses. I was not above a
minute sitting for the same. . . .

Mid-eighteenth-century engravings of Chinese mandarins

Parson Woodforde

A period of nearly three months at Ansford begins in mid-July.

AUGUST 10. . . . Jenny Clarke returned from Devonshire last night. Betsy White of Shepton is to be married in a fortnight to a Gentleman of Devonshire by name Webster, a man reported to have 500 P^d per annum, 10,000 P^d in the Stocks, beside expectations from his Father. He has settled 300 P^d per annum on Betsy.

SEP: 13. . . . Jenny Clarke told me that she was at Shepton Mallett yesterday, and that Miss White was Married to Mr. Webster this day sennight the 6 Instant.

SEP: 16. . . . Mr. and Mrs. Webster (late Betsy White) came to Sister White's on Horseback this morning, and they dined, spent the afternoon there, and returned to Shepton in the Even^g. I did not go to Mrs. White's today tho much pressed in the aft:. Brother Heighes and myself took a walk in the evening down to Allhampton Field, and in our return back we met Mr. and Mrs. Webster in the Turnpike Road. Mrs. Webster spoke as usual to me, but I said little to her, being shy, as she has proved herself to me a mere Jilt. Lawyer White at Mrs. White's— quite drunk this evening. . . .

SEP: 27. . . . Gave a poor old man at Rachel Pounsett's by name Curtis, who is now in his 95 year, and walks strong, sees tolerable, and hears quick, and who has thatched some Hayricks this year tho' so old . . . 0. 1. 0. . . .

On October 3rd he sets out for Oxford.

OCT: 30. . . . Very busy again in the Audit House [doing the College Accounts] from 10 till 2 o'clock. Betting with Cooke and Boys this morning in the Audit House about casting up a sum won 0. 10. 6. which they owe me at present. . . .

NOV. 28. . . . The warden sent down a note to the Junr C. Room to acquaint the young gentlemen that if any of them should make any future noise in the College, they would suffer the greatest rigour of the Statutes. We have of many nights past had very great Hallowing★ etc. in the Courts, what is facetiously called the upright . . . Lee, Warton, Alcock, Bingham, Awbery and Busby the principal gentlemen, but Lee is far the worst. They are called in the University the black Guards of New College for their noises in the street. I have been disturbed two or three nights lately by their great disturbance in the Court. The Junr Com: Room Chimney Piece was pulled down Saturday night by the above Rioters.

1776

JAN. 18. . . . Williams Senr and Jeffries played at all fours this evening in M.C.R. They had very high words at last and Williams threw the cards in Jeffries's face, the whole pack, being in a very violent passion. They were both to blame, but Williams much more so. Jeffries went to his room soon after and their [there] stayed. . . .

On February 15th he sets out for Ansford.

The next three months at Ansford passed in the usual quiet country way, except for an incident on March 5th. The Diarist was congratulating himself on feeling 'brave' again after a disorder which had 'proceeded from eating great quantities of water-cresses', when 'at one o'clock . . . as a leg of mutton was rosting by the Kitchen fire, a very dreadful fire happened in the chimney'. Pails of water were thrown down the chimney as well as wet rugs and blankets, and in two hours the fire was extinguished. 'My Uncle sent down some Cyder in Pails to the people and we gave them more. I offered a guinea to the people upon the house but they would not take it, Mr. Burge would not suffer it.' The fire was all due to the chimney's not having been swept 'for above twelve months. . . . It is amazing that Mr. Pounsett should neglect it so long, very wrong indeed of him only to save sixpence.'

MAY 9. . . . This morning at 9 o'clock took my final leave of the old Parsonage House at Ansford and went up to Mr. White's and there I breakfasted with him, Sister White, Mr. Pounsett and Jenny, Brother Heighes, his son Willm and Sam and James Clarke. . . . After breakfasting at Mr. White's about 10 o'clock I took my leave of my Friends at Ansford and set forth on my mare for Norfolk, and Bill Woodforde and my boy Will. Coleman went with me. I left my friends very low on the occasion.

The Diarist, his nephew Bill, and William Coleman proceeded to Norfolk via Oxford and Cambridge.

MAY 20. We breakfasted at College and about 10 took my final leave of my Rooms at College . . . When we got to Tame was very uneasy on account of my

★ Hallooing, riotous noise.

leaving at Oxford this Book and my Baldwins Journal. I sent a man immediately from Tame with a letter to Master Sen[r] to send back the same, and in about three hours he returned and brought me back both very safe. I was then quite happy—p[d] him for going 0. 2. 6. . . .

MAY 22. We breakfasted at Cambridge and then set forward. Bill and myself went after Breakfast and saw Kings Chapel, the finest I ever saw, all fine carved Stone, the Roof of the same—most capital piece of Architecture indeed, gave a man that shewed it to us 0. 1. 0. The gentlemen Commoners were [wear] black Gowns and gold trimmings made slight upon the sleeves of the same and very small gold Tossills to their square Caps of cloth. The members of Trinity Coll: undergraduates all wear Purple Gowns—gentlemen Commoners were purple Gowns trimmed with silver instead of gold and silver tossills. The Buildings are grand at Cambridge but few of them. . . .'

King's College Chapel, Cambridge

Renshaw & Tichman Bridge Row.

Weston Longeville Church

PART II

WESTON LONGEVILLE, NORFOLK

May 24th, 1776, to January 1st, 1803

Weston Longeville owed its second name to the priory of Longeville in Normandy, to which its tithes were transferred at the end of the eleventh or the beginning of the twelfth century—a common mediaeval practice—by its then Norman Lord of the Manor. The population in 1776 probably did not exceed 360—its population in 1801 was 365. The church, exceptionally spacious and beautiful, is of the perpendicular period, and dedicated to All Saints. The living is still in the gift of New College, Oxford. The rectory is not, alas, as known by the Diarist, but on the same site, about half a mile from the church.

JUNE 4. . . . My tooth pained me all night, got up a little after 5 this morning, & sent for one Reeves a man who draws teeth in this parish, and about 7 he came and drew my tooth, but shockingly bad indeed, he broke away a great piece of my gum and broke one of the fangs of the tooth, it gave me exquisite pain all the day after, and my Face was swelled prodigiously in the evening and much pain. Very bad and in much pain the whole day long. Gave the old man that drew it however 0. 2. 6. He is too old, I think, to draw teeth, can't see very well.

JUNE 5. Very much disturbed in the night by our dog which was kept within doors tonight, was obliged to get out of bed naked twice or thrice to make him quiet, had him into my room, and there he emptied himself all over the room. Was obliged then to order him to be turned out which Bill did. My face much swelled but rather easier than yesterday tho' now very tender and painful, kept in today mostly.

JULY 19th. Bill and myself took a ride in the afternoon to Mr. Howes at Hockering where we spent the remaining part of the afternoon with Mr. Howes and his Wife. Mr. Howes went to bury a corpse for Mr. du Quesne, and when he was gone Mrs. Howes told us that she lived very unhappy with her Husband, as he wants her to make her Will and give everything to his Family. I advised her to the contrary, and to give to her own.

SEP. 17th. I breakfasted at Weston and afterwards set of to Yarmouth [with Bill]. . . . We got to Yarmouth about 4 o'clock, and there we dined, supped and slept at the Wrestlers in Church Square kept by one Orton. A very good house. After we dined we took a walk on the Quay and viewed the Dutch vessells, about 70 sail which came in last night, to go a-fishing soon for Herrings. The Dutch are very droll fellows to look at, strange, heavy, bad dressed People with monstrous large Trousers, and many with large wooden shoes.

Dutch Fair, *George Vincent (1796–1831)*

SEP. 19th. . . . After breakfast we each took a Yarmouth coach and drove down
upon the coast, and called again at the Fort. . . . It was very pleasant and delightful
indeed. Nothing can beat what we saw to-day—immense sea Room, Shipps and
Boats passing and repassing—the Wind being rather high, the Waves like
Mountains coming into the Shore. We rode close to the Ocean, the Waves
sometimes coming into our Carriages. We returned about 3 o'clock. We had
some fine smelts, shoulder of Mutton rosted and Tarts. In the evening we took a
walk on the Quay, as fine a one as ever was seen. A great deal of company
walking backward and forward. We got on board an English vessel, and were
treated with Wine, Gin, etc. The sailors behaved very civil indeed to us, had a
difficult Matter to make them take anything, but at last I did, and all the silver I
had, being only 0. 1. 0. She was a Collier and going soon back to Sunderland.

OCT. 4th. . . . A Mr. Roop a young Man and is a Brother of Mrs. Davy's called
on me this morning, he drank a glass of Wine and decamped. I never saw him
before in my Life—he is a Prig.

NOV. 3rd. . . . Pray God my People and all others in the Small Pox may do well,
several Houses have got the Small Pox at present in Weston. O Lord send thy
Blessing of Health on them all.

DEC. 3rd. . . . My Frolic for my People to pay Tithe to me was this day. I gave
them a good dinner, surloin of Beef rosted, a Leg of Mutton boiled and plumb

Puddings in plenty. Recd. to-day only for Tithe and Glebe of them 236. 2. 0. Mr. Browne called on me this morning and he and myself agreed and he paid me for Tithe only 55. 0. 0 included in the above, he could not stay to dinner. They all broke up about 10 at night. Dinner at 2. Every Person well pleased, and were very happy indeed. They had to drink Wine, Punch, and Ale as much as they pleased; they drank of wine 6 Bottles, of Rum 1 gallon and half, and I know not what ale. . . . We had many droll songs from some of them. I made use of about 13 lemons and about 2 Pds of sugar. Bill and myself both well tired when we went to bed.

DEC. 10th. . . . Mr. Chambers the Schoolmaster who is lately come here called on me this morning to let me know that he would teach my Servants Ben and Will to write and read at 4/6d. a quarter each—which I agreed for.

DEC. 25th. . . . The undermentioned poor old People dined at my House to-day being Christmas Day and went to Church with me in the afternoon, to each of them gave 0. 1. 0.

Old Richard Bates	0.	1.	0
Old Richard Buck	0.	1.	0
Old Thos. Cushion	0.	1.	0
Old Harry Andrews	0.	1.	0
Old Thos. Carr	0.	1.	0
Old Robin Buck Mrs. Dunnell's man	0.	1.	0
James Smith the clerk	0.	1.	0

Storm on Yarmouth Beach, *John Sell Cotman (1782–1842)*

By God's Blessing I intend doing the same next Christmas Day. Gave old Richard Bates an old black coat and waistcoat. I had a fine surloin of Beef rosted and Plumb Puddings. It was very dark at Church this aft. I could scarce see. . . .

1777

FEB. 14th. . . . To 36 children being Valentine's day and what is customary for them to go about in these parts this day gave 0. 3. 0 being one penny apiece to each of them.

MARCH 18. . . . My Servants Will and Suky went to a Puppett Show this evening at Morton and kept me up till after 1 o'clock.

MARCH 23. . . . I gave notice this morning at Church that there would be Prayers on Friday night being Good Friday—there used to be none that day, which I think was very wrong.

MARCH 25. . . . My great Pond full of large toads, I never saw such a quantity in my life and so large, was most of the morning in killing of them, I daresay I killed one hundred, which made no shew of being missed, in the evening more again than there were, I suppose there are thousands of them there, and no froggs. . . .

MARCH 29. . . . Andrews the Smuggler brought me this night about 11 o'clock a bagg of Hyson Tea 6 Pd weight. He frightened us a little by whistling under the Parlour Window just as we were going to bed. I gave him some Geneva and paid him for the tea at 10/6 per Pd.

MAY 15. . . . Mr. Custance [the Squire's brother] called on me this morning to go a fishing. We rode down to the river. Mr. Custance's mistress a Miss Sherman and one Sandall an oldish man a broken gentleman and who keeps a Mistress also tho he has a Wife living, went with us on horseback. I returned home to dinner tho' very much pressed to dine with Mr. Custance. We had but middling sport—a lease of trout, 1 pike and some flat fish. Mr. Custance behaved exceedingly civil to me. He sent me the finest trout and the pike this evening by his man Phillips. . . .

JUNE 4. . . . The toads in my great Pond made an extraordinary loud noise for this last week past. This being his Majesty's Birth Day had my Blunderbuss fired of by Bill above 2 hands high three times in honour of the day, and with powder only. . . .

JUNE 17. . . . Bill made me very uneasy and very angry with him at breakfast by contradicting me in a very saucy manner. I therefore told him that I was determined that he should not return with me to Weston but that I would leave him in the West. This being my Rotation Day, the following Company dined and spent the afternoon with me. Mr. and Mrs. Howes and with them Mrs. Priest and daughter from Norwich, Mr. Bottom, Mr. Donne and Sister with one Miss Church a Lady rather deformed but dressed exceedingly well with a prodigious high Head indeed, but very sensible and the Rev. Mr. Du Quesne, Chancellor of St. David's. I gave for dinner a bad Leg of Mutton boiled scarce fit to be eat by being kept too long, and capers, some green Pease and a Pigg's face, a Neck of Pork rosted with gooseberries, a plumb Pudding, with Carrots, Turnips, etc. for Roots. . . .

On June 23rd he and his nephew, and the servant, Will Coleman, journeyed on horseback to Somerset to visit 'Sister Jane', Mrs. Pounsett.

JULY 3. I breakfasted, dined, supped and slept again at Mr. Pounsetts. Brother John being at the Christening last night being merry disturbed the whole Company so much that they were obliged to break up about 11 o'clock. Js. Clarke and Jack were going to fight. He made terrible work there I heard this morning. He is the worst Company I ever was in in my Life when he is got merry. Nothing pleases him then but making the whole Company uneasy. . . .

JULY 5th. . . . Brother Heighes and his son Sam dined etc. with us. Sam brought his violin with him and played several tunes to us—he is amazingly improved both in Painting and in Musick —he is a very clever youth. Gave Sam this afternoon 0. 2. 6. . . .★

JULY 22. . . . I breakfasted and slept again at Ansford. . . . Robert Biggen for stealing Potatoes was this afternoon whipp'd thro' the streets of Cary by the

The Angel, Ansford

★ Samuel Woodforde, the Diarist's nephew (1763–1817), was a considerable artist in his day, and was elected an associate of the Royal Academy in 1800, and an academician in 1807.

Hangman at the end of a Cart. He was whipped from the George Inn to the Angel, from thence back thro' the street to the Royal Oak in South Cary and so back to the George Inn. He being an old offender there was a Collection of 0. 17. 6 given to the Hangman to do him justice. But it was not much for all that—the Hangman was an old Man and a most villainous looking Fellow indeed. For my Part I would not contribute one Farthing to it.

The Diarist's stay at Ansford lasted for another month. They reached Weston again on August 29th, and found 'things in decent order'.

SEPT. 16. . . . Very busy with the engine [for pumping out the pond] this morning. Mr. du Quesne, Mr. Donne and Sister, Mr. Bodham, Mr. and Mrs. Howes and Mrs. Davy came to my House about 12 upon account of seeing some fishing before dinner as my great Pond was near empty. We were obliged to sink the engine lower, and in doing of the same in raising the engine one of the triangular Poles broke and very near killed my man Will Coleman, he was knocked down by the Pole falling on his Head, but it only stunned him for some time. I then gave him a dram and he was soon pretty well. It frightened us all very much. . . . I gave them for dinner half a dozen of my own fine Tench (taken out of my Pond in the yard) stewed, a Rump of Beef boiled, and a Goose rosted, and a Pudding. Mrs. Howes found great fault with many things especially about stewing the Fish—she could not eat a bit of them with such sauce etc. Mrs. Davy fell downstairs but did not hurt herself. Miss Donne swallowed a Barley corn with its stalk. Many accidents happened but none very bad. . . . They all admired my plated candlesticks and snuffers. . . .

SEPT. 21. . . . In the afternoon my dog Pompey came home shot terribly, so bad that I had her hanged directly out of her Misery. My greyhound Minx who was with her did not come and we suppose she has met with the same fate. It is supposed that Mr. Townshend's gamekeeper who goes by the name of black Jack, shot Pompey. . . .

SEPT. 27. . . . I took a walk about 5 o'clock this evening by myself to Mr. Townshend's at Honingham according to a promise from me to Mr. du Quesne,

Honingham Parsonage

At Honingham, *John Crome (1768–1821)*

and was very politely received, and drank Tea there with him, his Lady and Mr. du Quesne. The Hon: Charles Townshend handsomely apologised for my dogs being shot by his gamekeeper, and told me moreover that whenever I had an Inclination for a Hare I was very welcome to take a Course with Mr. du Quesne upon his Lands. . . .

OCT. 1. Harry Dunnell behaved very impertinent this morning to me because I would not privately name his child for him, he having one Child before named privately by me and never had it brought to Church afterwards. He had the Impudence to tell me that he would send it to some Meeting House to be named etc.—very saucy indeed. . . .

1778

JAN. 6. . . . Sukey's sister breakfasted here and then went home. I did not speak one word to her, as she came unasked. . . .

MAR: 2. . . . Poor Neighbour Gooch died this morning about 7 o'clock. I was quite surprised to hear of it indeed, as he did not appear to me yesterday near his latter end. I hope that as his Intention was to receive the Sacrament this morning, that his Will will be, to the Supreme Being, taken as if the Deed had been done. . . .

Honingham Church

APRIL 15. . . . Brewed a vessell of strong Beer today. My two large Piggs, by drinking some Beer grounds taking out of one of my Barrels today, got so amazingly drunk by it, that they were not able to stand and appeared like dead things almost, and so remained all night from dinner time today. I never saw Piggs so drunk in my life. I slit their ears for them without feeling.

APRIL 16. . . . My 2 Piggs are still unable to walk yet, but they are better than they were yesterday. They tumble about the yard and can by no means stand at all steady yet. In the afternoon my 2 Piggs were tolerably sober.

APRIL 24. . . . Who should come to my House about 2 o'clock this day but my cousin Js. Lewis from Nottinghamshire and on foot and only a dog (by name Careless) with him. He was most miserably clothed indeed in every respect. He dined and supped and slept at my House. . . .

APRIL 25. . . . Cousin Lewis breakfasted, dined, supped and slept again at Weston. I gave Lewis a Tobacco Box this morning, a Pr of Shoes, a Pr of Stockings, a Pr of Breeches and Shirt and Stock, and an old Coat and Waistcoat. . . .

MAY 21. . . . I walked up to the White Hart with Mr. Lewis and Bill to see a famous Woman in Men's Cloaths, by name Hannah Snell, who was 21 years as a common soldier in the Army, and not discovered by any as a woman. Cousin Lewis has mounted guard with her abroad. She went in the Army by the name of John Gray. She has a Pension from the Crown now of 18. 5. 0 per annum and the liberty of wearing Men's Cloaths and also a Cockade in her Hat, which she still wears. She has laid in a room with 70 Soldiers and not discovered by any of them. The forefinger of her right hand was cut by a Sword at the taking of Pondicherry. She is now about 60 yrs of age and talks very sensible and well, and travels the country with a Basket at her back, selling Buttons, Garters, laces etc. I took 4 Pr of 4d Buttons and gave her 0. 2. 6. . . .

JUNE 5. . . . Mr. Custance Senr of Ringland called on me this morn' caught me in a very great disabelle, and long beard. He stayed with me about half an Hour. Talked exceedingly civil and obliging and behaved very polite. . . .

JULY 6. . . . In the afternoon about 5 o'clock Mr. Pounsett and Sister took leave of Weston [where they had been staying since mid-May] and set of in Lenswade Chaise for Norwich, in which I went with them to Norwich and had my Mare led there by Will. . . . My poor dear Sister shook like an aspin leave going away, she never went in a stage Coach before in her Life.

AUG. 26. . . . Mr. Baldwin called on us this morning, and talked with us concerning a Midshipman's Place for Bill and desired us to drink a Dish of Tea

William Woodforde, *Samuel Woodforde (1763–1817).*
Parson Woodforde's nephew is shown as Lt.-Colonel in command of the Western Battalion of the
East Somerset Rifle Volunteer Infantry in 1805.

with him in the afternoon which we promised him. . . . In the afternoon took a walk with Bill to Mr. Baldwin's at Ling and there drank a dish of Tea with him, Miss Vertue Baldwin, Mr. Hammerton, Dr. Neale. Had a good deal of Chat with Mr. Hammerton about Bill. Bill is to go to London when Mr. Hammerton goes which will be very soon, to show himself to a Captain of a ship and that Mr. Hammerton will use all his Interest for him. I have been most uneasy and most unhappy all day about one thing or another. When Bill goes away I shall have no one to converse with—quite without a Friend.

AUG. 28. . . . Very low and ill withal especially going to bed. Sukey went before Justice Buxton today with her [Information?] to swear to the Father of the Child she is big with. I had a note from Mr. Buxton which Sukey brought to desire the Parish Officer the Overseer to come with her, and then he would take her Information.

AUG. 29. . . . My Maid Sukey went with Mr. Palmer to Mr. Justice Buxton and he granted a Warrant to take up Humphrey [the child's father].

SEPT. 3. I told Sukey this morning my Opinion of her respecting the late affair that has happened to her.

Weston Old Hall, seat of the Custance family before their move to Weston House

SEPT. 9. . . . I took a ride to Ringland about 2 o'clock and there dined, spent the afternoon and supped and spent the evening at Mr. Custance's with him, his Wife and an old maiden Lady by name Miss Rush. I spent a most agreeable day there and was very merry. Mrs. Custance and self played at Back Gammon together. Mr. and Mrs. Custance are very agreeable people indeed, and both behaved exceedingly polite and civil to me. I there saw an Instrument which Mrs. Custance played on that I never saw or heard of before. It is called Sticcardo pastorale. It is very soft Music indeed. It is several long pieces of glass laid in order in a case, resting on each end of every piece of glass, and is played in the middle parts of the glasses by two little sticks with Nobbs at the end of them stricking the glass. It is a very small Instrument and looks when covered like a working Box for Ladies. . . .

OCT. 14. . . . Paid my Servant Maid Sukey Boxly this morning a yrs wages due Oct. 10. The sum of 4. 0. 0. Gave to her besides her Wages, as going away 0. 4. 0. I sent Cary's Cart with one of my Horses by Ben to Little Melton about 4 Miles beyond Easton after my new Maid this afternoon, and she returned about 6 o'clock. Her name is Eliz: Claxton about 40 yrs of age, but how she will do I know not as yet but her Wages are 5. 15. 6 per annum, but out of that she is to find herself in Tea and Sugar. She is not the most engaging I must confess by her

first appearance that she makes. My other Maid came to me also this evening. Her name is Anne Lillistone of Lenswade Bridge about 18 years of age but very plain, however I like her better than the other at the first sight, I am to give her 2. 0. 0. per annum and to make her an allowance to find herself in Tea and Sugar. Sukey this evening left us, but in Tears, most sad.

Lenwade Mill, *John Thirtle (1777–1839)*

NOV. 21. . . . I told my Maid Betty this morning that the other maid Nanny looked so big about the Waist that I was afraid she was with Child, but Betty told me she thought not, but would soon inform me if it is so.

1779

JAN. 26. [Rotation Day at Mr. Howes.] . . . Just as the Company was gone Mrs. Howes attacked Mr. Howes about putting down the chaise and she talked very roughly to him and strutted about the Room. It was rather too much in her. I did not stay long to hear it, but soon decamped and was at home before 10.

MAR. 23. I breakfasted, and slept again at home. Memorandum. In shaving my face this morning I happened to cut one of my moles which bled much, and happening also to kill a small moth that was flying about, I applied it to my mole and it instantaneously stopped the bleeding.

MAY 18. . . . Mr. Howes and Wife and Mrs. Davy, Mr. Bodham and his Brother, and Mr. du Quesne all dined and spent the afternoon and part of the evening with us to-day. I gave them for dinner a dish of Maccarel, 3 young Chicken boiled and some Bacon, a neck of Pork rosted and a Gooseberry Pye hot. We laughed immoderately after dinner on Mrs. Howes's being sent to Coventry by us for an Hour. What with laughing and eating hot Gooseberry Pye brought on me the Hickupps with a violent pain in my stomach which lasted till I went to bed. At Cards Quadrille this evening—lost 0. 2. 6.

MAY 22. . . . My Boy Jack had another touch of the Ague about noon. I gave him a dram of gin at the beginning of the fit and pushed him headlong into one of my Ponds and ordered him to bed immediately and he was better after it and had nothing of the cold fit after, but was very hot. . . .

SEP. 18: . . . Soon after breakfast my Friend Mr. Hall called on me and dined and spent the afternoon with me. Poor Mr. Hall was very uneasy concerning an affair that happened at Walton about 3 weeks ago, where he was insulted in public Company by one Nelthorpe and endeavouring to come at him to lick him had greatly hurt his leg between a door and its lintel. Mr. Hall could not get at him or else would have licked him handsomely, I wish that he had done it. . . .

OCT. 12. . . . About 8 this evening my Sister Clarke, Nancy Woodforde and my Nephew Saml. Clarke arrived at Norwich [where the Diarist was meeting them] in the London Machine from the West greatly fatigued by being up all last night. . . .

Scene at Costessey, *John Thirtle (1777–1839).*

OCT. 23. . . . Had a letter this evening from Bill Woodforde from on board the Fortune Sloop of War, and now at Spithead performing Quarantine, being lately arrived from the Barbary Coast, had been out about 2 months. He informs me that he had suffered many hardships, and he seems to be tired of the Sea already. He now sincerely repents of his late behaviour at my House at Weston, and of his not taking my advice to him. He also tells me that he has bought some curious things for me and desires me to accept of them. . . .

DECEM. 4. . . . This evening by Mr. Cary came Bill's present to me, viz: a large Moorish sword and a curious Moor's purse made of Morocco leather with some coins in it. He also sent me two curious shells and a quill that came from Falklands Island. It is some gratitude in him I must confess—but he expects something in return as he complains in his letter to me of being very low in pocket. . . .

1780

JAN. 28. . . . Sister Clarke, Nancy and Sam breakfasted etc. here again. I went to Church this morning a little before 12 and publickly presented Mr. Custance's child in the Church. Sir Edmund Bacon and Lady, and Mr. Press Custance assisted as Sponsors. Mr. Custance was also at Church with the others. After the ceremony Mr. Custance came up to me and presented me with a Norwich Bank Note of five Guineas, wrapped up in some writing Paper. He asked me to dine with the Company at Ringland at 2 o'clock, therefore I walked by myself there and dined and spent the afternoon and stayed till after 7 in the evening and then walked back home. The Company present were Sir Edmund Bacon and Lady, Mr. and Mrs. Custance and Mr. Press Custance. Coming away gave George the servant 0. 2. 6. We had for dinner a Calf's Head, boiled Fowl and Tongue, a Saddle of Mutton rosted on the Side Table, and a fine Swan rosted with Currant Jelly Sauce for the first Course. The Second Course a couple of Wild Fowl called Dun Fowls, Larks, Blamange, Tarts etc. etc. and a good Desert of Fruit after amongst which was a Damson Cheese. I never eat a bit of a Swan before, and I think it good eating with sweet sauce. The Swan was killed 3 weeks before it was eat and yet not the lest bad taste in it.

JAN. 31st. . . . A very comical dull day with us all. Sister Clarke very low. In the evening Sam spoke in favour of the Methodists rather too much I think. We did not play Cards this evening as usual.

APRIL 17. . . . About 5 o'clock my Sister and Sam went of in Lenewade Chaise for Norwich, to take Coach for London this night. . . . We were all very low at parting with each other, poor Nancy very low indeed. I gave to Nancy this evening 0. 5. 0. . . . My Head Maid slept with Nancy and is so to do.

APRIL 26. . . . Busy in painting some boarding in my Wall Garden which was put up to prevent people in the Kitchen seeing those who had occasion to go to Jericho.★

MAY 3. I breakfasted, dined, supped and slept again at home. About ½ past 9 o'clock this morning my Squire called on me, and I took my Mare and went with him to the Hart just by the Church where most of the Parish were assembled to go the Bounds of the Parish, and at 10 we all set of for the same about 30 in number. Went towards Ringland first; then to the breaks near Mr. Townshend's Clumps, from thence to Attertons on France Green, where the People had some Liquor, and which I paid, being usual for the Rector—0. 4. 6. Mr. Press Custance was with us also. From France Green we went away to Mr. Dades, from thence towards Risings, from thence down to Mr. Gallands, then to the old Hall of my Squire's, thence to the old Bridge at Lenewade, then close to the River till we came near Morton, then by Mr. Le Grisse's Clumps, then by Bakers and so back till we came to the place where we first set of. Mr. Custance Senr then called the six following old men (that is) Richd. Bates, Thos. Cary, Thos Dicker, Richd Buck, Thos Cushion and Thos Carr, and gave each of them half a guinea—To

Ringland

★ The outside lavatory.

George Wharton, who carried a Hook and marked the Trees, my Squire gave also five shillings. To Robin Hubbard also who carried a Spade he gave 5 shillings, and sent all the rest of the People to the Hart to eat and drink as much as they would at his expense. The Squire behaved most generously on the occasion. He asked me to go home and dine with him but I begged to be excused being tired, as I walked most of the way. Our Bounds are supposed to be about 12 miles round. We were going of them full five hours. We set of at 10 in the morning and got back a little after 3 in the afternoon. Nancy was got to dinner when I returned. Ben, Will and Jack all went the Bounds. Ben's Father Wm. Legate in crossing the River on horseback was thrown of and was over head and ears in the River. My Squire's man John was likely to have had a very bad accident in leading the Squire's horse over a boggy place, both horses were stuck fast up to their Bellies, and by plunging threw him of in the mire and was very near being hurt by the horses plunging to get out, but by great and providential means escaped free from any mischief. The horses also were not injured at all. The man had his new suit of Livery on and new hat, which were made very dirty. Where there were no Trees to mark, Holes were made and Stones cast in.

JUNE 5. . . . Mr. Mann's Boy who was taking care of some Horses in a Field, where there was a large Clay Pitt full of water, by accident fell in and was drowned and found about Noon Time quite dead. He was a Child of one Spincks by the Church—a sad misfortune indeed, but hope the poor Lad is much happier than if he had stayed longer here. Mr. Mann very uneasy.

JUNE 19. . . . My Squire called on me this morn' and talked to me a good deal about his Brother's Mistress sitting in my Seat yesterday and whether she had leave, and also that she strutted by them in a very impudent manner coming out of Church—and stared at Mrs. Custance.

SEP. 22. . . . My Squire called on me this morning to desire me to come over in the afternoon and privately name his new born son. I married one John Wont and Rose Branton this morning by License at Weston Church—a compelled marriage. N.B. am owed by Mr. Mann the Church Warden for marrying them, as I could not change a Guinea—0. 10. 6. . . . Recd. a printed Letter from the Bishop to send him an account of the Roman Catholicks in my Parish—but I don't know of one in it.

OCT. 13. . . . Mr. Cary's daughter (the Widow Pratt) is we hear with child by her Servant that lived with her last year, but she pretends to say that she was ravished one night coming from her Father's by a man whom she does not know.

OCT. 15. . . . Will came home drunk this evening after Supper from Barnard Dunnell's at Morton and he and my head Maid had words and got to fighting. Will behaved very saucy and impudent and very bold in his talk to me. Shall give it to him to-morrow for the same. . . .

OCT. 16. . . . I gave Will a Lecture this morning concerning last night's work.

DEC. 15. . . . Mrs. Davie called here this aft. in Mr. Howes's Chaise with her daughter Betsy, who is just returned from School and is to spend a few days with

Nancy, therefore Mrs. Davie left her with us. . . . Betsy slept with my Niece Nancy Woodforde.

Nancy Woodforde

DEC. 31. . . . This being the last day of the year we sat up till after 12 o'clock, then drank a Happy New Year to all our Friends and went to bed. We were very merry indeed after Supper till 12. Nancy and Betsie Davie locked me into the great Parlour, and both fell on me and pulled my Wigg almost to Pieces.—I paid them for it however.

1781

FEB. 3. . . . Had but an indifferent night of Sleep, Mrs. Davie and Nancy made me up an Apple Pye Bed last night. . . .

FEB. 12. . . . We did not go to bed till after 12 this night, the Wind being still very high. We were as merry as we could be, I took of Mrs. Davie's Garter tonight and kept it. I gave her my Pair of Garters and I am to have her other tomorrow. . . .

Next day Mrs. Davie, who had been staying at the Rectory on and off since January 30th, went to Parson Howes's of Hockering, taking Betsy with her, who had been at the hospitable Diarist's since December 15th.

Hockering Rectory

MAR. 20. . . . About 12 o'clock I took a ride to Dereham . . . Soon after I got to Dereham I walked to Mr. Hall's Rooms, he lodges at a Barbers by name Field, and there I dined and spent the afternoon with him by appointment. We had for dinner a fine Lobster hot and some Mutton Stakes, had from the King's Arms. Before dinner Mr. Hall and myself took a Walk about Dereham, went and saw a whimsical Building called Quebec. We dined at 3 o'clock and after we had smoked a Pipe etc., we took a ride to the House of Industry about 2 miles West of Dereham, and a very large building at present tho' there wants another Wing. About 380 Poor in it now, but they don't look either healthy or cheerful, a great Number die there, 27 have died since Christmas last. . . .

MAY 16. . . . Between 7 and 8 o'clock this morning went down to the River a fishing with my Nets. Ben, Will, Jack, Harry Dunnell and Willm Legate (Ben's Brother) were my Fishermen. We begun at Lenewade Mill and fished down to Morton. And we had the best day of Fishing we ever had. We caught at one draught only ten full Pails of Fish, Pike, Trout and flat fish. The largest Fish we caught was a Pike, which was a Yard long and weighed upwards of thirteen pound after he was brought home. We caught about 20 brace of Pike, but threw back all the small ones—also we caught abt 15 brace of Trout, the largest not more than a Pound and half—all the smallest we threw back—3 brace also of Perch—one tolerable Tench and I dare say near if not quite five hundred Brace of Roach and Dace. Prodigious sport indeed we had today tho' cold and wet. As we were fishing by Coplin's, he came out and ordered my men of from his land, and behaved quite contrary to the opinion I had of him. After talking with him some little time he said I might fish, but then I would not, at which he seemed rather uneasy. We eat some cold meat which we carried about one o'clock and returned home to dinner at 4. For Beer at Barnard Dunnells of Morton, pd. 0. 1. 0. Gave Beeston, Cantrell, Palmer of Morton and Barnard Dunnell some Pike, and most of the flat Fish to the Poor at Lenewade and Morton and of my own Parish. Harry Dunnell and Will Legate dined etc. with our Folks. Paid them also for their labour today 0. 3. 0. I was rather fatigued this evening by Fishing.

JUNE 30. ... Nancy by being with Mrs. Davy had learnt some of her extravagant Notions, and talked very high all day. I talked with her against such foolish Notions which made her almost angry with me, but when we went to bed we were very good Friends and she was convinced.

JULY 24. ... I read a good deal of the History of England today to Nancy whilst she was netting her Apron. Very dry again. I feed my Geese with Cabbage now.

JULY 30. ... Nancy and myself get up every morning before 7 o'clock under the penalty of forfeiting sixpence each day—Sundays only excepted.

SEP. 19. ... Weston Bells rung yesterday and again to-day, on Mrs. Custance being brought to bed and in the New House.

Lenwade Mill

Evening River Scene with Bridge, Cows, Fisherman and Dog, *John Thirtle (1777–1839)*

OCTOB. 26. . . . Beckham the Net-Maker called here at dinner and he dined with our Folks. He fights cunning. He came to mend my dragg Net but I would not have him mend it at my House as I know him to be an expensive Boarder. If he has it to his House to mend it will cost me 1. 2. 9 which is very dear indeed. I told him that I would send it to his House, if it was to be mended by him. . . .

NOV. 15. . . . Will informed me to-night of his being ill in the venereal way.

DEC 1. . . . It is very true that L. Cornwallis and his whole army and 40 Ships 160 Cannon etc. are all taken by the Americans and French in Virginia. . . .

DEC. 7. . . . Immediately after breakfast I rode to Honingham and married a very odd Couple, a fine young Man about 22 years of age, by name Robert Martin and an old, infirm, weak Widow about 50 years of age, by name Jane Price, by License, and for du Quesne, as he was not returned home yet. . . .

1782

JAN. 21. . . . By one and another, hurried all the day long—almost.

FEB. 4. . . . To a poor old Man that plays on the Dulcimer gave 0. 0. 6.

FEB. 8. ... This Day being appointed to be observed as a Fast on the present Troubles and Wars abroad, ★ I went to Weston Church this morning at 11 o'clock and there read Prayers proper on the occasion—but there was no Sermon after. I had a large Congregation—Mr. Custance was at Church—Mrs. Custance not ...

FEB. 12. ... At 10 o'clock this morning took a walk to Hockering to attend poor Mrs. Howes's Funeral there today. ... I found all the Clergy in gowns and some in Cassocks also—I did not carry my gown, as I did not know whether or not the Clergy appeared in them—I borrowed one however, of Mr. Howes and likewise a Band. Before we went to Church there was Chocolate and Toast and Cake with red Wine and white. ..

Hockering Church

★ We were fighting at this time against the rebel Americans, the French, the Spaniards, and the Dutch, to say nothing of Hyder Ali in India.

FEB. 28. . . . Was rather uneasy to-day on Account of being afraid that I have got the Piles coming or something else—unless it is owing to my eating a good deal of Peas Pudding two or three days ago with a Leg of Pork.

MAR. 21. . . . The poor Woman whom I sent some Veal to Sunday died yesterday morning—She eat nothing afterwards till she died, But she eat hearty of the Veal I sent her.

APL. 1. . . . Mr. Custance sent after Nancy this morning to spend the Day with Mrs. Custance and to have her Hair dressed by one Brown, the best Ladies-Frisseur in Norwich. . . . Nancy returned home about ½ past 9 o'clock this Even', with her head finely dressed of but very becoming her. Mrs. Custance would not let Nancy pay the Barber, but she paid for her and it cost no less than half a guinea. Mrs. Custance gave the Barber for dressing her Hair and Nancys the enormous sum of one guinea—He came on purpose from Norwich to dress them. Mrs. Custance (God bless her) is the best Lady I ever knew.

MAY 29. . . . Very busy all the Morning, packing up our things for to go into the Country, as we set out in the Evening [for London]. Mr. Du Quesne, who goes to London with us dined and spent the Afternoon with us . . .

MAY 31. We breakfasted, dined and spent the Afternoon at our Inn. Before we breakfasted, I hired a Coach and we went in it to St. James Park. Will also went with us. From the Horse Guards we all walked up the Park to St. James's Palace and saw the Guards relieved at 9 o'clock—a very pretty sight. We also saw most

An early nineteenth-century view of the Horse Guards

of the State Rooms in the Palace. Gave to People at St. James's Palace 0. 3. 6. From thence we walked up the Park to the Queens Palace but did not go into that—the Royal Family being there. After that we walked down the Park back to the Horse-Guards and there took a Hackney Coach and returned to our Inn to breakfast. Mr. Du Quesne came to us at breakfast—and after breakfast, Nancy, myself and Will took a Coach and went to the Tower and saw the Horse Armory, the small Armory, the Artillery, the Regalia, and the wild Beasts. ★ . . . I went by myself and gave a Peep into St. Pauls Church this aft: To a Barber this Afternoon for shaving &c. gave 0. 1. 0. For 2 inside Places in the Salisbury Coach p^d 2. 2. 0. For 1 outside Place Do. p^d 0. 10. 6. Paid and gave at the Bell Savage for all of us abt. 1. 15. 0. They were very civil People at the Bell Savage Inn by name Barton and a very good House it is. About 10 o'clock at Night we set of in the Salisbury Coach from the same Inn for Salisbury, and the Coach guarded. I was bit terribly by the Buggs last Night, but did not wake me.

Cole Manor

JUNE 1. . . . We got to Cole about 10 o'clock and I thank God safe and well and found my good Friends there all well—blessed be God for all things—and accept my most sincere and unfeigned thanks for thy great goodness to us in preserving us from all the Dangers of so long a Journey that we have taken. My good Friends were very happy to see us and waiting impatiently for our arrival. Sister White and her Daughter were at Cole expecting us and they supped and slept at Cole. Nancy, myself and Will all supped and slept at Cole. I was terribly swelled in the face and hands by the Buggs. Mr. Pounsett with my Sister and little Maid very glad to see us.

★ Zoological gardens were as yet non-existent, and one went to the Tower to
see the wild beasts, specially the lions.

JUNE 18. . . . We heard at Ansford that there were 3 Men struck down in Pilton Church by the Lightning this morning. One of them killed instantly—but the others like to recover. The Man that was Struck dead was tolling a Bell for a Person lately dead, the other two were near him. Pray God have mercy on the poor Man.

JULY 20. . . . Mr. Thomas spent the Morning with us Yesterday, he came to ask me to preach for him on Sunday but I could not, as I brought no Sermon with me—The last Time I was in the Country I had some Sermons with me and was never asked to preach therefore I thought it of no Use to bring any now. . . .

The entries for nearly two months are now missing, from August 6th to October 2nd, 1782. Sometime in the interval he returned to Weston, where we rejoin him.

OCT. 19. . . . Busy in readg Evelina a Novel, lent Nancy by Mrs. Custance— there are 3. Volumes of it—wrote by a Miss Burney—they are very cleaver and sensible.

OCT. 24. . . . Mr. Hall, just returned from Andover in Hants, came here about Noon and he dined, supped and sat up all Night at my House, having no bed but mine which I offered to him, but he would not accept of it, therefore obliged me to sit up with him all Night. . . .

OCT. 25. . . . Hall went away about 10 o'clock. I was quite ill all day by setting up last night and will not do it again for any Hall in the Kingdom—He might have as well went to Lenewade and slept as he used to do—but he minds nothing but self and his Money. . . .

NOV. 16. . . . Cobb of Mattishall a Rat-Catcher and whom I formerly employed came to my House this morning by Order, and I engaged with him for to kill all my Rats at one Guinea Per Annum and likewise to kill all my Mice. And the first Guinea is to be paid the first of Decem^br 1783—I gave him for Entrance Mony 11. 0. He is to come as often as there is Occasion for him—And is to be kept in Victuals and drink.

NOV. 20. . . . Mr. Howes with Mrs. Davy and Nancy came here and they stayed and dined and spent the afternoon with me—and Mr. Howes with Mrs. Davy prevailed on me after many Entreaties and at last with great reluctance on my Part, to let Nancy return with them to Hockering as they are going to Norwich to-Morrow, which I did, tho' much against me. Poor Mr. Howes and Mrs. Davy had set their hearts so much on it, that they were made very uneasy at my refusing them at first, and they almost cried and said that they would never be friendly with me if I did not admit of it. Mr. Howes said he would never enter my Doors more. The chief and principal Reason I gave, was, I did not approve or ever could that my Niece should make so free at Mr. Priest's—Mrs. Davy having sent a note this morning before they came here, that she with Nancy intended dining with them to Morrow at Norwich. It made me rather uneasy after they were gone back as I cannot by any means approve of it on any Account neither should I at last, unless to make old Mr. Howes easy. . . .

DEC. 3. . . . This being the Day for my Tithe Auditt, the following Farmers paid me their Tithes, Girling, Peachman, Howlett, Rising, Forster, Herring, Dade, Mann, J^n_o Pegg, Page, Andrews, Wm. Bidewell, Case, Ringgar, J^n_o Pegg, Norton, Buck, Rush, Silvie, Cary, Burroughs, Baker, Thos. Leggatt, Wm. Leggatt, Rose Bean for the Widow Pratt, rec^d in all to day 265. 3. 0. They all dined here, but J^n_o Pegg and Mr. Mann and stayed till near 11 at night. Forster behaved so insolent towards me that I dont intend to have him ever again at my Frolick. Poor J^n_o Buck broke one of my Decanters. . . . J^s Smith, my Clerk, dined with our Folks in Kitchen. I dined with the Farmers in the great Parlour, Nancy dined by herself in the Study. Wine drank 6 Bottles. Rum drank 5 Bottles besides Quantities of strong Beer and Ale.

DEC. 25. . . . This being Christmas Day I went to Church this Morn' and then read Prayers and administred the Holy Sacrament. Mr. and Mrs. Custance both at Church and both received the Sacrament from my Hands. The following poor old Men dined at my House to day, as usual, Js. Smith, Clerk, Richd Bates, Richd Buck; Thos. Cary; Thos. Dicker; Thos. Cushing; Thos. Carr—to each besides gave 1/0—in all 0. 7. 0. I gave them for Dinner a Surloin of Beef rosted and plenty of plumb-Pudding. We had mince Pies for the first Time to-day.

1783

JAN. 13. . . . This Evening paid all my Servants their Years Wages—due January 6, 1783.

To my Head Maid, Betty Claxton p^d	5. 15.	6
,, ,, Lower ,, Lizzy Greaves p^d	2. 0.	6
,, ,, Man Will: Coleman p^d	4. 4.	0
To Ditto for Grains p^d	17.	0
To Ditto for dressing my Wiggs p^d	10.	0
To Ditto what he owed me I gave	1. 1.	0
To my Farming Man Ben Leggatt p^d	10. 0.	0
To my Boy, Jack Warton	10.	6
Gave to him besides as a free gift	2.	6

JAN. 25. . . . This Evening the Ipswich News brought us the joyful News of Peace being signed at Versailles the 20 of this month and recd. at London the 25. . . . The above Peace is with America, France and Spain, but not with the Dutch— Tho' daily expected by them.

MARCH 5. . . . Much colder than yesterday—Wind much higher and Frost more severe—The coldest Day for some years. I was very low and indifferent all day long. The Barometer very low, and the Wind being very rough when I went up to my Chamber to go to bed, being not the lest sleepy, I lighted my Fire, and sat down and read the Life of Lewis 14 of France till after 2 o'clock in the morning and then went to bed, the Wind still high. I heard some Noise between one and two but it did [not] last.

MARCH 6. . . . The first thing I was informed of when I came down stairs, was, that my Stable had been broken up, in the Night and that there was stolen out of it, a Hatchet, a Hook, a Bridle, and a pair of hedging Gloves of Bens. There was seen Yesterday a Couple of idle Fellows passing and re-passing my House, I saw them once go by, one of them was in a long blue Coat, the other in a brown one. They came in at the back Window of the Stable, which they cut away, to wrench it open with a large stick wch was found just by, they left behind them a P^r of Sheep Sheers broke directly in the middle—They also took Bens Cart Whip, which they left on the Muck-heap. I think myself well of, in having so few things stolen as there were so many in the Stable and in the Corn Room. . . .

MAR: 8. . . . A change of the Ministry will soon take place as mentioned on the Papers—Ld North and Charles Fox have shook hands—O North, how low art thou fallen.

MAR: 24. . . . About 6 o'clock this Morning we all got up to go to Norwich and after breakfast we set forth at 8 o'clock, Mrs Davy and Nancy in the Chaise, myself on Horseback, Will, Ben and Lizzy on horseback, Jack went behind the Chaise as I was willing that all sh^d go that could. Betty, my Upper Maid stayed at home being Washing Week. We all got to Norwich about 10 o'clock—The Road we went was filled with People on Horseback and foot, going to see the fine Sight—Ben carried Lizzy behind him on Phyllis and the first Time she ever carried any one, double, and she carried her very well and safe, to Norwich and back again. . . . The Order of the Procession was as follows.

Four Trumpeters
Marshal-Man
Peace
Orator
Banner of Brittania
Plenty
Drums and Fifes
20 Argonauts
Hercules

Lynceus Zetes	{ The Golden Fleece borne on a grand Palanquin by four Men }	Tiphy[s] Calais
Castor	{ Jason drawn in a Phaeton by four Horses }	Pollux

Standard of the Argonauts
20 Argonauts
Militia Band
Standard of the City
Two Vergers
Orator
{ Bishop's Chaplain
in a Phaeton and Pair }
{ Bishop Blaize
in a Phaeton drawn by 6 Horses
Standard of the City }

The book-keepers, Shepherds and Shepherdesses belonging to the different

The Market Place, Norwich

Societies of Combers 12 Companies—Seven Companies on foot—Five Companies on Horseback. . . .

We were all highly delighted indeed with this Days Sight—it far exceeded every Idea I c^d have of it. Hercules, Jason, and Bishop Blaize, were exceedingly well kept up and very superbly dressed. All the Combers were in white ruffled Shirts with Cross-Belts of Wool of divers Colours—with Mitred Caps on their heads—The Shepherds and Shepherdesses were little Boys and Girls on horseback, very handsomely and [with] great Propricty dressed. Orations spoke in most of the principal Streets. I never saw a Procession so grand and well conducted. ★

APRIL 10. . . . Mr Howes was this Day married to his 4th Wife, a Mrs Brown.

APRIL 30. . . . At Quadrille this Evening won 0. 4. 0. I played the finest Sans Prendre Vole to Night, that I ever had—Not a loosing Card in hand—It was Mattadores, 9 black Trumps in Spades and the King of Hearts—I was the last Player; after the first Card was played, I declared the Vole. I did not get home to

★ This procession was a combined celebration of the conclusion of peace, and of the patron saint of the Norwich woollen trade—Bishop Blaise, Bishop of Sebaste in Armenia, who perished sometime between A.D. 289 and 316 in one of the persecutions of the Christians.

Old Sheds, Thorpe Road, Norwich, *Henry Bright (1810–73)*

Weston till 10 at Night.

MAY 1. . . . The 2 Fellows who were suspected breaking open my Stable and many others, were tried this Day at the Sessions at Norwich and convicted of the Robbery of stealing a Sack from Mr Howlett and are to remain in Prison for three years—which I hope will do good.

MAY 15. . . . At half past 6 this morning took a black Dose of Physic in bed, then laid down till half past 7 then got up and came down to breakfast. I had a very disagreeable Night of rest, sweated a vast deal and started much in my Sleep, being in the Horrors. . . . I was brave (thank God) this Evening—my Physic having operated very well—Altho' hurried so much to day. I began taking going to bed some Camphire and Nitre Powders.

JUNE 5. [He had gone to Norwich the day before.] . . . About 1 o'clock I mounted my Mare and set of for Weston and did not get home till near 4 o'clock on Account of my poor Mare, she having filled herself so much on dry Meat last Night—I was afraid that she would have dropped on the road as she puffed and blowed so terribly—I walked her most part of the way—and I got of and walked many Times—It vexed and fretted me much on Account of having Company to Dinner.—It was also very hot and was obliged to wear my great Coat, the Pockets of which also were loaded with 2 Pounds of Pins &c., however I did get home at last as did my Mare—And I found Mr Smith and Mr Baldwin with my Ladies at home. I was pretty much fatigued with the Heat and fretting. . . .

JUNE 16. ... I saw Forster and Herring of Ringland—Mr. Forster was very sorry for what he had said and if I would forgive him, he w^d beg my Pardon—which I did and he promised never to affront me more—so that all matters are made up.★

Weston Longeville Church from the road to Ringland

JUNE 25. ... Very uncommon Lazy and hot Weather. The Sun very red at setting. To a poor old crazy Woman this morn' gave 0. 0. 6. Nancy and myself dined and spent part of the afternoon at Weston House with Mr. and Mrs. Custance—Mr. Rawlins dined also with us—whilst we were at Dinner Mrs. Custance was obliged to go from Table about 4 o'clock labour Pains coming on fast upon her. We went home soon after dinner on the Occasion—as we came in the Coach. We had for Dinner some Beans and Bacon, a Chine of Mutton rosted, Giblett Pye, Hashed Goose, a Rabbit rosted and some young Peas,—Tarts, Pudding and Jellies. We got home between 5 and 6 o'clock. After Supper we sent up to Mr. Custances to enquire after Mrs. Custance who was brought to bed of a fine girl about 7 o'clock and as well as could be expected.

JUNE 27. ... After breakfast Nancy and self dressed ourselves and walked to Hungate Lodge to make the first visit to Mr. and Mrs. Micklewaite who were both at home and appear to be tolerable agreeable People—He is very young. She is much older and appears rather high. We stayed about half an Hour with them and then returned.

JUNE 30. ... I privately named a Child this morning of Dinah Bushell's by name Keziah One of Job's Daughters Names. ...

★ It will be remembered that Forster had been insolent to the Diarist at the latter's frolic on 3 December 1782.

JULY 29. . . . About 1 o'clock I took a ride to Mattishall to Mr. Bodhams and there dined and spent the Afternoon with him, Mrs. Bodham, Mr. and Mrs. Ball of Catfield, Sister to Mrs. Bodham, Mrs. Davy, Mr. Smith, Mr. and Mrs. Howes, Mr. Ashull and Nancy.—We had for Dinner a Piece of boiled Beef, some Beans and Bacon, a couple of Ducks rosted, a Veal Pye and some Apricot Dumplins. At Quadrille this Evening won 0. 2. 0. As we were coming away Mrs. Howes came to me and asked me to their House it being their Rotation next, but I entirely refused to go, as they had not only kept away from mine very lately, but would not let Miss Howes come who was very desirous of coming to Weston. I gave it to her, and most of the Company seemed pleased with my behaviour. We did not get home till after 9 in the Evening. Nancy was obliged to change Horses, the flies teazing Phyllis very much which made her kick a little.

AUG. 28. ... About 2 o'clock Mr. and Mrs. Custance called here by appointment and took Nancy and self with them in their Coach to Mr. Townshends at Honingham where we dined and spent the Afternoon with Mr. and Mrs. Townshend, Mrs. Cornwallis, Widow of the late Arch-Bishop of Canterbury's and who is also Sister to Mr. Townshend, Mr. and Mrs. Custance, and Mr. Du Quesne—The latter of whom we were glad to see, as it was so long since we saw him. Mr. and Mrs. Townshend behaved very genteel to us. The drawing Room in which we drank Tea &c. was hung with Silk. The Chairs of the same kind of Silk and all the woodwork of them gilded, as were the Settee's. The looking glass which was the finest and largest I ever saw, cost at secondhand 150. 0. 0. The Height of the Plate was seven feet and half, and the breadth of it was five feet and half, one single Plate of glass only. The frame and Ornaments to

Mattishall Rectory

it, was carved and gilded and very handsome. There was two Courses at Dinner besides the Desert. Each course nine Dishes, but most of the things spoiled by being so frenchified in dressing. . . .

The Townshends' Dining Room at Honingham

SEP. 2. . . . Will: very bad all the time he was out to day. Ben also complained this Evening—Jack also bad to-day. Almost all the House ill in the present Disorder and which is called the Whirligigousticon by the faculty. It is almost in every House in every Village. . . .

SEP. 4. . . . To Largesses to day gave 0. 2. 0. About 1. o'clock Mr. and Mrs. Custance called here in their Coach and took me with them to Norwich to dine with the Bishop. I was dressed in a Gown and Cassock and Scarf. We got there to the Palace abt. 3. o'clock. . . . There were 20 of us at the Table and a very elegant Dinner the Bishop gave us. We had 2 Courses of 20 Dishes each Course, and a Desert after of 20 Dishes. Madeira, red and white Wines. The first Course amongst many other things were 2 Dishes of prodigious fine stewed Carp and Tench, and a fine Haunch of Venison. Amongst the second Course a fine Turkey Poult, Partridges, Pidgeons and Sweetmeats. Desert—amongst other things, Mulberries, Melon, Currants, Peaches, Nectarines and Grapes. A most beautiful Artificial Garden in the Center of the Table remained at Dinner and afterwards, it was one of the prettiest things I ever saw, about a Yard long, and about 18 Inches wide, in the middle of which was a high round Temple supported on round Pillars, the Pillars were wreathed round with artificial Flowers—on one side was a Shepherdess on the other a Shepherd, several handsome Urns decorated with artificial Flowers also &c. &c. The Bishop behaved with great affability towards me as I remembered him at Christ Church in Oxford. He was also very affable

Norwich Cathedral, South Transept and Cloister, *John Thirtle (1777–1839)*

and polite to all the Clergy present. . . . Nancy rec^d a long Letter from her Brother William dated the 29 June from Staten Island in North America brought by Mr. Custance's Servant from Norwich this Evening. The Letter came to 0. 2. 4. He is very well and has escaped many Dangers in America. He sent inclosed in his Letter some Continental Money Paper valued there at 10 Shillings and which he desired to be given to me.

OCT. 12. . . . Had another disagreeable Letter this morning from the Bishop's Register to preach at the Cathedral of Norwich on the Sunday Morn' Feb: 8 next. . . .

OCT. 24. [He had gone to Norwich the previous evening.] . . . After breakfast I dressed myself in my best Coat and Waistcoat and then walked down in my Boots to the Bishops Palace and had a long Conversation with the Bishop abt. many things—but what I went to his Lordship chiefly on, was my being appointed on the Combination List to preach at the Cathedral the 8. of February next, when my Name had been inserted but a few Years back. To which his Lordship replied, that as I did not then preach in propria Persona was one Reason, and the Second was that he was willing that the Pulpit at the Cathedral should be filled properly by able and beneficed Clergy, and that it was rather a Compliment conferred by him on those that he so appointed. . . .

NOV. 7. . . . We dined and spent the Afternoon with Mr. and Mrs. Custance, The Bishop [of Norwich] and his Lady Mrs. Bagot, his Lordships Chaplain Mr. Gooch, and Sr. William and Lady Jernegan. . . . Sr. Willm. Jernegan is a very fine Man, very easy, affable and good natured. Lady Jernegan is a fine Woman but high and mighty. They are both of the Romish Persuasion. It being Friday and a Fast Day of Course to them, they however eat Fowl, Pheasant and Swan and Sr. William eat some Ham. Upon the whole we spent an agreeable Day, but must confess that being with our equals is much more agreeable.

DEC. 2. [Tithe Audit Day.] . . . We had this Year a very agreeable meeting here, and were very agreeable—no grumbling whatever. Total recd. this Day for Tithe 286. 15. 0. . . . After the Company was all gone and we thought everything were agreeable and happy in my House, we were of a sudden alarmed by a great Noise in the kitchen, and on my immediately going out there found my Servant Man Will: Coleman beating about the Maids in a terrible manner and appeared quite frantic and mad. I seized him by the Collar and as soon as he was loose, he ran out into the Yard and jumped into the Pond there in a moment but he was soon taken up by Ben, which frightened us so much that we were obliged to sit up all night. We got him to bed however about 1 o'clock and after some time he was somewhat quiet—but it frightned us so much that Nancy and self did not go to bed till 6. in the morning. Ben and Jack did not go to bed at all. The reason of his being so, was on Lizzy's Account, as he wants to marry her and she will not, and he is very jealous. Am afraid however that it proceeds from a family complaint, his Father having been crazy some time. It is therefore now high time for him to leave me which I shall endeavour to do the first opportunity. It made me very ill almost instantly and made my niece very unhappy as well as ill also.

1784

JAN. 26. ... I rejoiced much this morning on shooting an old Woodpecker, which had teized me a long Time in pulling out the Reed from my House. He had been often shot at by me and others, but never could be a match for him till this Morn'. For this last 3. Years in very cold Weather did he use to come here and destroy my Thatch. Many holes he has made this Year in the Roof, and as many before. To Goody Doughty for 7 Lemons pd. 0. 0. 6.

FEB. 7. ... About 11 o'clock this morning myself, Mrs. Davy, Betsy and Nancy got into Lenewade Bridge [Chaise] to go to Norwich as I am to preach to Morrow at the Cathedral. We were obliged to have four Horses the Snow being so very deep. We got to Norwich I thank God safe about 2 o'clock. We were obliged to go round by Mr. Du Quesnes to get to the Turnpike road as soon as we could on Account of the Snow wch. was very deep indeed especially over France Green and no Tract of Wheels to be seen. We were very fearful going over that Green as it was very dangerous. It was very hard work even for the four Horses to get over that Green. It was much better on the Turnpike. The Snow in some Place was almost up to the Horses Shoulders. ...

France Green

Betsy Davy

FEB. 8. We breakfasted and slept again at the Kings Head. At 10. o'clock this morning we all went in a Coach to the Cathedral. I went full dressed and being Preacher sat next to the Sub-Dean Dr. Hammond. Whilst the Anthem was singing I was conducted by the Virger to the Pulpit and there Preached a Sermon from these Words 'Let your light so shine before Men that they may see your good Works and glorify your Father wch. is in Heaven.' After Sermon was over I walked back to the Vestry, had my Hood taken of, and then a Person came to me and gave me for Preaching 1. 1. 0. I gave the Virger for the Use of the Hood 0. 1. 0. . . .

MAR. 13. . . . Nancy brave to day (tho' this Day is the Day for the intermitting Fever to visit her) but the Bark has prevented its return—continued brave all day. Dr. Thorne and Betsy Davy with him on a little Hobby called on us this morning and stayed with us about half an Hour. . . . Dr. Thorne's Method of treating the Ague and Fever or intermitting Fever is thus—To take a Vomit in the Evening not to drink more than 3 half Pints of Warm Water after it as it operates. The Morn' following a Rhubarb Draught—and then as soon as the Fever has left the Patient about an Hour or more, begin with the Bark* taking it every two Hours till you have taken 12 Papers which contains one Ounce. The next oz. &c. you take it 6. Powders the ensuing Day, 5 Powders the Day after, 4 Ditto the Day after, then 3 Powders the Day after that till the 3rd. oz. is all taken, then 2 Powders the Day till the 4th. oz: is all taken and then leave of. If at the beginning of taking the Bark it should happen to purge, put ten Dropps of Laudanum into the Bark you take next, if that dont stop it put 10. drops more of Do. in the next Bark you

* Peruvian bark, i.e. quinine.

take—then 5 Drops in the next, then 4, then 3, then 2, then 1 and so leave of by degrees. Nancy continued brave but seemed Light in her head. The Bark at first taking it, rather purged her and she took 10 Drops of Laudanum which stopped it.

APRIL 14. I breakfasted upon some Mutton Broth about 6. o'clock and very soon after breakfast I mounted my Mare and went of [to] Norwich . . . About 10 o'clock the Market Place and Streets in Norwich were lined with People and almost all with Wodehouse's Cockades in their Hats. After breakfast I went to Mrs. Brewsters and got 6 Cockades all for Wodehouse—3 of them of blue and Pink with Wodehouse wrote in Silver on the blue, the other 3 plain blue and Pink for my Servants at home. About 11 o'clock Sr. John Wodehouse preceded with a great many Flaggs and a band of Musick, made his public Entry on horseback, attended with between two and three Thousand Men on Horseback, They came thro' St. Giles's, then thro' the Market Place, then marched on to the Shire House on the Castle Hill and there Sr. John Wodehouse with Sr. Edward Astley were unanimously chosen Members for the County. After that they had dressed themselves handsomely and were chaired first round the Castle-Hill and then three times round the Market Place amidst an innumerable Number of Spectators and the loudest acclamations of Wodehouse for ever. I never saw such universal Joy all over the City as was shown in behalf of Sr. John Wodehouse. . . .

The Market Place, Norwich, *John Sell Cotman (1782–1842)*

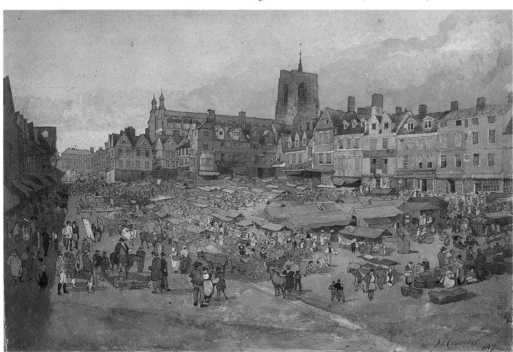

MAY 26. . . . From Church rode to Mr. Custance's but both Mr. and Mrs. Custance were gone to Norwich to see their Children now under Inoculation. I took a ride afterwards to Du Quesne's and there dined and spent the Afternoon with him, Mr. and Mrs. Priest of Norwich and Mr. Mrs. and Miss Priest of Reepham. We had for Dinner some Pike and Maccarel, a fore Qr. of Lamb rosted, Pidgeon Pye—Charter★ &c. &c. I carried Mr. Du Quesne a Cucumber in my Pocket. After Tea Mr. Du Quesne, Mr. Priest of Reepham and myself played a Game of Bowls on his Green. I lost 0. 0. 6. To some Children opening the Gate gave 0. 0. 6. I returned home to Weston about 9 this Evening. We had a most gracious Rain this Evening and it lasted.

MAY 31. . . . A smock Race† at the Heart this Afternoon, I let all my Folks go to it but Lizzy, and all came home in good Time but Will who being merry kept me up till 11 o'clock and then went to bed without waiting any longer for him, and just as I was going to sleep he came and made a Noise under my Window and then marched of and I went to sleep.

JUNE 1. . . . I gave Will notice this morning to leave me, but Nancy hearing of it prevailed on me to try him a little longer with us—but am afraid it won't do. . . .

JUNE 5. . . . Nancy recᵈ a Letter from her Brother Sam this Evening which gave her great Spirits, he having lately been introduced to the Queen and presented her a Picture of his Painting being her Son Prince Frederick. Sam talks of great things, of being soon knighted. Am very glad that his Lot fell in so fortunate a Soil—And his Merit is deserving the same. Sam's News too great to be true, am afraid.‡

JULY 5. . . . After Dinner I paid Lizzy half a Years Wages due this Day, and then dismissed her from my Service, as she is going on my recommendation to Weston House. I gave her extraordinary 0. 2. 6. I paid her for Wages 1. 6. 6. In the Evening sent Ben with a Market Cart for my New Maid who lives at Mattishall and she came here about 8 at Night and she supped and slept here. Her Name is Molly Dade about 17 years of age—a very smart Girl and pretty I think. . . .

JULY 15. . . . We were to have had Betsy Davy and Mary Roupe over from Mattishall to have spent this Day with us but Mrs. Davy's going to Pulham yesterday on a Love Affair with a Mr. Rand who went with her and came back with her, but Matters however could not be settled then. Mr. Rand is a Man of very good Fortune, keeps a Carriage and is an Apothecary and has great business—A very sensible Man, a Batchelor about 50 years of Age. And lives at Snettisham near Burnham. To a Man this morning that brought a very pretty kind of a Monkey to shew gave 1. 0ᵈ. He called it the Mongooz from Madagascar.

★ A kind of beer.
† A race for women and girls with a smock, or shift, for prize.
‡ This is Samuel Woodforde, R.A. His hopes of knighthood were not realized.

JULY 20. . . . At 4 this Afternoon I mounted my Mare and rode to Mattishall where I drank Tea and stayed till 9 in the Evening at Mrs. Davy's with her, Mr. and Mrs. Bodham, Miss Donne, Mr. Du Quesne and Nancy Woodforde—Mr. Smith was to have been there also—but went for London this morning very suddenly and much discomposed. The Cause of it is this, Mrs. Davy had a Letter this morning from Mr. Rand who is distracted after her, the Contents of which were communicated to Mr. Smith, which made him almost frantic, he immediately made Mrs. Davy an Offer to marry her after his Mothers Decease, what answer was returned I know not, but he marched from Mattishall directly. Mrs. Davy was extremely low and uneasy about it. After one Pool of Quadrille we had a Syllabub and some Rasberries with Cream and Sugar—and Wine. We all broke up about 9 o'clock rather after. At Quadrille this Evening won 0. 1. 0. To Mrs. Davy's Maid gave coming away 0. 1. 0.

AUG. 4. . . . About 10 o'clock this Night a Clergyman by name Cam[p]bell (Vicar of Weasingham in this County and formerly of Oriel Coll: Oxford and afterwards Fellow of Worcester Coll: in the same University) came to my House and he supped and slept here—himself and horse. I remember him at Oriel Coll: but not so intimate as to expect that he would have taken such freedom especially as he never made me a Visit before. He slept however in the Attic Story and I treated him as one that would be too free if treated too kindly. It kept me up till after 12 o'clock.

SEP. 22. . . . At 2 o'clock took a Walk to Mr. Micklethwaite's and there dined, spent the Afternoon, supped and spent the Evening with him, his Wife, his Father and Mother, old Mrs. Branthwaite, Captain Micklethwaite and Wife, Mr. Jonathan Micklethwaite and my Niece.—About 5 o'clock we dined. Before Dinner I publickly baptized their little Boy at home, which I did not much like, but could not tell how to refuse—He was privately named before at Norwich I believe—His Name is Nathaniel. Old Mrs. Branthwaite and old Mrs. Micklethwaite were the Godmothers—and old Mr. Micklethwaite and his Son Captain John Micklethwaite were Godfathers. We had a very genteel Dinner and Supper. Old Mr. and Mrs. Micklethwaite and his Son the Captain, the strangest kind of People I almost ever saw. Old Mrs. Branthwaite almost as strange and vulgar. Nancy was sent for in their Carriage and we returned home in it about 12 at night—very windy, very wet, and very dark; I thank God we got home however safe. I gave the Driver and the Man behind it each 1. 0.–0. 2. 0. After Tea and Coffee We got to Whist at which I won 0. 1. 0. Coming away this Evening Mr. Micklethwaite made me a present, for christening his Child, of 1. 1. 0. Upon the whole spent an odd disagreeable kind of a Day—as did also Nancy—we laughed much after we got home.

SEP. 28. . . . My Maid Betty has not been able to do any thing for this last Week owing to a bad Thumb and is still bad. Poor Molly Dade my other Maid very bad in a Cough and am afraid it is rather consumptive—She has increased it to day by easing the other Maid in helping her and she is so foolish to tell Molly that she is in a Consumption—which makes the poor Girl very unhappy.

OCT. 7. . . . Jack told me this morning that he is advised to get another Place being too old for a Skip-Jack any longer. He wants to be a Plow Boy to some

Self-portrait, *Samuel Woodforde (1763–1817)*

Farmer to learn the farming Business as he likes that best—I told him that he was very right to try to better himself, and at Lady Day next he is to leave my House for that purpose. He has been a very good Lad ever since he has been here. . . .

OCT. 15. . . . My poor Maid Molly Dade, not so well to day as I could wish her, having somewhat of a Fever on her. She is one of the best Maids that ever we had and very much liked by us both and would wish to keep her but am very much afraid it will not be in our Power tho' we are both most willing to keep her. She is one of the neatest, most modest, pretty Girl[s] I ever had. She is very young, but tall, only in her 17th year. . . .

OCT. 19. . . . I sent my Maid Molly Dade this morning behind Ben to Mattishall, to stay a few Days at home, to see if change of Air would do her Cough good. Her Sister Betty, continues in her Place. Poor Molly is as good a Girl as ever came into a House, I never had a Servant that I liked better—Nancy also likes her very much indeed—I wish to God she might get the better of her illness. . . .

NOV. 3. . . . Molly's Father called here—he gave us a very poor Account of our worthy Maid poor Molly Dade—that he believed she cannot recover. We were extremely sorry for her. He came after her Stays that were here, the others being too large for her—so much of late has she fallen away. Mr. Dade could not stay to dine with us to day. Will on his return also told us that Mr. Thorne had given poor Molly over and that he could do no more. Pray God Almighty comfort her—and with patience wait the Almighty's Will—As good a Girl as ever lived.

NOV. 17. . . . I went and saw the Dwarf Man that is at Norwich by name James Harris from Coventry—He is exactly 3 Feet high, very well proportioned in every respect—But with him, was a Girl which exceeded every Thing I ever saw—she had no Hands or Arms, and yet wonderfully cleaver with her Feet. She cut out a Watch Paper for me whilst I was there with her Toes she opened My Watch and put it in after done. Her Name was Jane Hawtin, about 22 years old. She talks very sensible and appears very happy in her Situation—She uses her Toes as well as any their Fingers. I gave her for cutting the Watch Paper 0. 1. 0. To the Dwarf gave 0. 0. 6.

NOV. 30. . . . [He has his Tithe Audit.] They were all highly pleased with their Entertainment but few dined in the Parlour. They that dined in the Kitchen had no Punch or Wine, but strong Beer and Table Beer, and would not come into Parlour to have Punch &c. I gave them for Dinner some Salt Fish, a Leg of Mutton boiled and Capers, a fine Loin of Beef rosted, and plenty of plumb and plain Puddings. They drank in Parlour 7. Bottles of Port Wine, and both my large Bowls of Rum Punch, each of which took 2 Bottles of Rum to make. Forster went away the most disguised of any. In the Kitchen they were all cheerfully merry but none much disguised—Howlett, Jn̄ Pegg and Will: Leggatt tho' Parlour Guests were rather pretty forward. Recd to day for Tithe &c. from above—234. 13. 0. Paid out of the above to Mr. Mann for Coal—0. 5. 0.

1785

JAN. 9. . . . I read Prayers and Preached this Afternoon at Weston. None from Weston House at Church being wet. Mr. Micklethwaite was at Church. I dreamt last Night that I went to Weston Church with a Corpse after me, and just as I came to the Church Yard Gate, saw another Corpse bringing from Morton Road way, and which had died of the small Pox. The corpse that I attended on seeing the other, I ordered to be carried into the Chancel, till the other was buried. When I returned to the Chancel, thought I saw a most elegant Dinner served up— particularly fish—whether I waked then or not I cannot tell, but could recollect nothing more of my dream besides. My Maid Betty Dade went to see her poor Sister Molly this morning behind Ben—they returned about 5 in the Afternoon. Poor Molly just alive and that all being in the last stage of a Consumption—she is very sensible of her approaching End and happily resigned to it. . . .

JAN. 16. . . . Mr. Custance at Church but not Mrs. Custance. I was very dull and low this Evening, having no company at all, now Nancy is from home [at Mrs. Davy's]. And not used of late to be much by myself—better soon.

JAN. 22. . . . About 1 o'clock Mrs. Davy with Nancy in Mr. Thorne's Chaise came here and Mr. Thornes Man with them. Mrs. Davy stayed here about half an Hour, would not dine here, and then set of back for Mattishall, leaving Nancy with me—Very glad she is come home. . . . Mrs. Davy did not by any means behave as she used to do towards me—was scarce civil to me.

JAN. 23. . . . Very fair and fine to day, quite a Summers Day. I read Prayers and Preached this Aft: at Weston. Mr. Dade of Mattishall came over here this morning to let his Daughter know, that her poor Sister Molly died last Night— poor Soul! I doubt not of her happiness in a future Life—She was long expected to die. Pray God bless her Spirit and comfort her Relations. . . .

JAN. 29. . . . Nancy and self had a few words this morning but soon over, poor dear, I dont wish to make her at all uneasy. . . .

FEB. 4. . . . Finished reading Roderick Random this Evening.

FEB. 26. . . . I dreamt a good deal about Jenny Woodforde Frank Woodforde's Wife, of her being dressed all in white, looked exceeding pale but very handsome. I hope my Dream portends no ill to her.

FEB. 27. . . . Harder Frost than ever with high Wind with some falling of very small kind of Snow—colder than ever. I read Prayers and Preached this morning at Weston. Very small Congregation indeed—not 20 Persons there and only two Women amongst them—Palmers Wife of Morton and the Clerk's Wife Jenny Smith. None from Weston House of any kind. . . .

Weston Longeville Church

MARCH 13. . . . I read Prayers, Preached and christened a Child by Name, Tabitha Bithia, this morning at Weston Church. Mr. Custance and Mr. Micklethwaite were at Church. Mem: Bithia is a very uncommon Name, but it was the Name of Pharoah's Daughter—See 1 Chron. iv 18. . . .

MARCH 14. . . . Poor Neighbour Clarke's Wife and 4 Children are taken down in the small Pox— Their Neighbour Gooch, his Wife, nor any of a large Family of children belonging to them, have none of them had the Small Pox.

MARCH 15. . . . Sent poor Clarkes Family a large Bushel Basket of Apples. . . .

APRIL 9. . . . To a poor deaf Man from Mattishall gave 0. 0. 1. Mrs. Custance with her 2 Children William and Fanny came here this Afternoon about 5 o'clock without the lest notice and stayed with us about an Hour and then returned back to Weston House—did not drink Tea. I had not finished my Afternoon Pipe but put it away. I told Mrs. Custance that I had been smoking and hoped she did not dislike Tobacco—and she said she liked it. . . .

APRIL 12. . . . My Servant Willm Coleman was out all the Evening till just 11 o'clock—came home in Liquor behaved very rudely and most impudently to me indeed, I told him that I was determined never more to bear with such Behaviour, and that he sh^d certainly go to Morr'. . . .

APRIL 13. . . . I got up between 5 and 6 o'clock this morning had Will before me as soon as possible, paid him his Wages and dismissed him before 8 o'clock. For a Q^{rs} Wages at Guineas p^d him 1. 6. 3. For a Q^{rs} dressing Wiggs at 10^s p^d him 0. 2. 6. For a Q^{rs} Allowance for Shoes at 12^s p^d him 0. 3. 0. For brewing-Grains 6 Coomb at 1^s 0^d p^d him 0. 6. 0. In all paid him 1. 17. 9. I threw him down a Couple of Guineas for him to have the remaining, but he would not take one farthing more than the above 1. 17. 9. Being so much hurried last night and this morning made me quite ill all Day—vomited a good deal at Night after which took a Dose of Rhubarb and was much better.

A field path near Weston Longeville

APRIL 15. ... Will: came to me to day to desire I would give him a Character if wanted, which I promised him. He seems to be rather cast down to day and at no work.

APRIL 25. ... Will: Coleman came to us this morning as we were walking in the Garden, and said that he could not be easy after his late bad behaviour, till he had spoke to me and asked pardon for it—I then told him that I would employ him as a Gardener and gave him a shilling a Day and his Board for 2 Days in a Week— but that he must get a Lodging from my House, and if he can somewhere in the Parish. He appeared then quite happy and went directly about his work in the Garden. ...

Mousehold Heath, Norwich, *John Sell Cotman (1782–1842)*

APRIL 26. ... Bretingham Scurl a new Servant came here whilst we were at Dinner, I ordered him into Parlour directly and made him wait at Table and he did pretty well. He appears to be a good-natured willing young Fellow. Will: Coleman who is gardening for me looked rather shy upon Scurl at first—We call him Briton.

JUNE 1. ... Mr. and Mrs. Custance called here about 11 o'clock and took Nancy with them in their Coach to go to Norwich. They would have taken me up also but I preferred going on horseback, about 12 therefore, I went to Norwich and took Briton with me, and we got there about 2 o'clock—but was wet getting thither. About 3 o'clock this Afternoon a violent Tempest arose at Norwich in the North East, very loud Thunder with strong white Lightening with heavy Rain— which lasted about an Hour—immediately after which Mr. Deckers Balloon with Decker himself in a boat annexed to it, ascended from Quantrells Gardens and very majestically.—It was out of Sight in about 10 Minutes, but appeared again on his Descent. It went in a South East Direction—I saw it from Brecondale Hill, and it went almost over my Head. Mr. and Mrs. Custance and Nancy were at Mackay's Gardens. They saw it also very plain from thence. A vast Concourse of People were assembled to see it. It was rather unfortunate that the Weather proved so unfavourable—but added greatly to the Courage of Decker that he ascended so very soon after the Tempest. It also bursted twice before he ascended in it, upon the filling it, if it had not, a Girl about 14 was to have went with him in it—but after so much Gas had been let out—it would not carry both. . . . Decker however has gained great Credit by it.

JUNE 8. . . . I dreamt very much last Night of Mr. Smith and Mrs. Davy and that connection entirely broke of—I told Nancy of it at breakfast.—Just as we were going to sit down to dinner, Mr. Matthews brought a Note to my Niece from Mrs. Davy—to let her know that she was in great distress, having rec^d a Letter this morn' from Mr. Smith to break of any farther connection with her—his Friends being so very averse to the Match And that he was going to leave England directly. Mrs. Davy desires my Niece to come over to her directly—but she could not go.

JULY 7. . . . Busy all Day, shewing Briton the method of brewing. It made me rather cross—Ironing being also about.

JULY 26. . . . Will: Coleman called on us this morning to take his Leave, I gave him to help pay his Expences. 1. 1. 0. Gave him also for a Deal Chest which I gave him to put his Cloaths in the Sum of 0. 10. 6. Will: was very low on the Occasion as was Nancy. . . .

AUG. 1. . . . Coming from Mr. Custance's met with a dumb Man almost naked—I gave him poor Creature 0. 0. 6. . . .

SEP. 22. . . . Mr. Custance sent us a brace of Partridges this Morn' which was very kind of him—Mr. Micklethwaite has not sent us any, tho' daily out with a Double-barrelled Gun and often in my Closes close to my House. To Largesses to day gave 0. 1. 0. J^n Pegg called on me this Morn' on account of the new Taxes★ on Male and Female Servants, Horses and Waggons &c. I entered one Male Servant Briton, and two Female, Betty Dade and Molly Peachman—and two Horses. . . .

SEP. 26. . . . Dr. Bathurst's Curate Mr. Wilson sent me a Letter this Afternoon to desire me to advance some Money to him by Dr. Bathursts desire—I sent him an Answer that it was not in my Power, but referr'd him to some of the Doctors Tenants. Mrs. Davy likewise desired Nancy to speak to me to lend her twenty Pounds—but it is not in my Power.

OCT. 1. . . . Mrs. Davy and Betsy with Mr. Ashill, in a Dereham Post-Chaise

★ The tax on menservants was imposed in 1777 by Lord North when compelled to find fresh revenue of nearly £250,000. He borrowed the idea from Adam Smith's *Wealth of Nations*, and Adam Smith had borrowed it from Holland, where the tax was in vogue. In 1785 Pitt extended the tax to maidservants.

called here this morning about 8 o'clock, breakfasted here and then took Nancy with them to a Place called Thurning about 10 Miles from Weston N.E.N. to look at a boarding Place for Mrs. Davy and Betsy—I did not like that Nancy should crowd into the Chaise with them and for no Purpose whatever—It made me rather cross. . . .

OCT. 24. . . . The Tooth-Ach so very bad all night and the same this Morn' that I sent for John Reeves the Farrier who lives at the Hart and often draws Teeth for People, to draw one for me. He returned with my Man about 11 o'clock this Morning and he pulled it out for me the first Pull, but it was a monstrous Crash and more so, it being one of the Eye Teeth, it had but one Fang but that was very long. I gave Johnny Reeves for drawing it 0. 2. 6. A great pain in the Jaw Bone continued all Day and Night but nothing so bad as the Tooth Ach. . . .

The Hart, Weston Longeville

NOV. 10. . . . About 11 o'clock this morning Mr. Press Custance called on me in a Post Chaise, and I went with him in it to Weston Church, clerically dressed, and there buried in the Church Mr. Custances youngest Daughter Mary Anne which was brought to Church in their Coach and four with Mrs. Alldis the Housekeeper and the Childs Nurse Hetty Yollop—only in it besides the Corpse. The Infant was only 16 Weeks old. After interring it—I rec^d from Mr. Press Custance 5. 5. 0. wrapped up in a clean Piece of writing Paper. I had also a black Silk Hatband and a P^r of white Gloves.

NOV. 20. . . . Nancy and her two Brothers, Willm and Saml, breakfasted, dined, supped and slept again at Weston Parsonage. I read Prayers and Preached this morning at Weston. Mr. Micklethwaite at Church—none from Weston House. It gave me much pleasure to see Nancy and her two Brothers appear so happy here—and so in each other.

The Beggar Boy, *John Sell Cotman (1782–1842)*

DEC. 12. . . . Poor Tom Twaites of Honingham who was beat by the Poachers at Mr. Townshends the other day is lately dead of the Wounds he then rec^d from them. His Skull was fractured in 2 Places.

DEC. 19. . . . The Captain [Bill] and myself took a ride to Norwich and the Servant with us. . . . After Dinner the Captain and myself, went and saw the learned Pigg at the rampant Horse in St. Stephens—there was but a small Company there but soon got larger—We stayed there about an Hour—It was wonderful to see the sagacity of the Animal—It was a Boar Pigg, very thin, quite black with a magic Collar on his Neck. He would spell any word or Number from the Letters and Figures that were placed before him paid for seeing the Pigg 0. 1. 0. . . .

DEC. 21. . . . This being St. Thomas's Day, had a great many poor People of the Parish to visit me, I gave to each of them that came, sixpence. . . .

1786

FEB. 12. . . . I sent Nancy and Betsy Davy Yesterday Morn' to Coventry and have not as yet spoke to either of them.

Norwich Cathedral from Cowgate, *David Hodgson (1798–1864)*

FEB. 13. . . . Nancy and Betsy not sent for from Coventry as yet.

FEB. 14. . . . To 53. Valentines to Day gave 0. 4. 5. Nancy and Betsy Davy called home this Aft. from Coventry. . . .

FEB. 18. . . . Mr. Smith of Mattishall sent me a note this Morn' to desire me to meet him in Weston Churchyard privately, which I accordingly did, and there I stayed with him near an Hour, talking over the Affair between him and Mrs. Davy—by which he made out that Mrs. Davy was as artful and bad as any Woman could be. It surprised me astonishingly indeed. . . .

MAR. 12. . . . I read Prayers and Preached this Morn' at Weston Church. Mr. and Mrs. Custance at Church. Neither any from my House at Church but self and 2 Servants. Mrs. Davy took on a good deal to day, and soon after Tea this Evening she took it in her head to go to bed. I had been persuading her not to go to Mattishall.

MAR. 17. . . . Mrs. Davy breakfasted, dined, supped and slept here again. Betsy Davy breakfasted here and about 12 she took leave of Weston Parsonage and went on horseback to Mr. Thorne's at Mattishall, and there she dined, supped and slept—poor dear soul—She was much hurried by her Mother on going away. Am much afraid it will be a very long time before she will be at Weston Parsonage again. . . .

MAR. 18. . . . About 1 o'clock Mrs. Thorne of Mattishall came after Mrs. Davy to spend a few Days with her and they returned to Mattishall about 2 o'clock. Our Parting was rather cool than otherwise. . . .

MAR. 23. . . . Poor Mr. Micklethwaite is gone to Lynn, and it is thought will never return again as he declines very fast in a consumptive Complaint.

MAR. 31. . . . We were to have went to Mattishall to dinner to day at Mr. Bodham's,★ but my Nephew's little grey horse being taken very ill, and obliged to send for a Farrier, prevented our going according to promise. I sent a Note to my Niece who is there on a Visit and she sent me an Answer, that Mr. and Mrs. Bodham were very angry with us. Mr. Du Quesne was asked to meet us on purpose.

MAY 30. . . . We all went to Dereham this Morning to Mr. Thomas's and there dined and spent the afternoon with him, Miss Thomas, Miss Betsy and Miss Anne Thomas, and Mr. Du Quesne—It was very hot to day. Nancy went with Briton in the little Cart, and myself and Nephew went on horseback. We returned home a little after 9 this Evening, we spent a tolerable agreeable Day there—Miss Thomas is very reserved and not handsome—Miss Betsy is very agreeable and pretty—Miss Anne very still and coarse. We had for Dinner a boiled Leg of Mutton and Caper Sauce, a green Goose rosted and Gooseberries, Veal Cutlets, Lobsters, pickled Salmon, Damson Tarts and Syllabubs. . . .

JUNE 10. . . . The Captain very busy this Morning with his Ship. . . . Just before Dinner the Captain launched his new Ship, before the Ladies and Gentlemen present but to his great Chagrin and the Company's disappointment it upset and went down to the starboard side almost immediately and took in Water and could not be righted. She was far too much overmasted. We were all exceedingly sorry on the Captains Account. We had for Dinner some Maccarel, a fore Q^r of Lamb,

---

★ Mrs. Bodham was the poet Cowper's 'my dearest Cousin', or 'my dearest Rose', of his delightful letters.

3 boiled Chicken and a Pigs Face, Pigeons and Asparagus, Lobster, Apricot and Gooseberry Tarts and Custards. After Dinner by way of Desert—A Melon, Oranges, Almonds and Raisins.

JUNE 12. . . . The Captain got up early this morning and sat of for Mattishall to my Glaziers, Hubbard, after some Lead to put on at the bottom of the Ship by way of a false Keel and returned home with it 10 o'clock, with a long piece which weighed 25 Pound—After he had breakfasted he put on the Lead to the bottom of the Vessel and then she sailed as well as our most sanguine wishes could desire.

JUNE 24. . . . We all got to London (thank God) safe and well by 3 o'clock this Afternoon . . . Nancy and her Brother walked out in the Evening by themselves, giving me the Slip, and did not return till Supper time, at which I was much displeased and gave it to them smartly, and to make it still worse soon as Supper was removed and having ordered a Bottle of Wine, they left me without drinking a drop and went to bed leaving me by myself—I sat up by myself very uneasy till about 12 and then I went.

JUNE 27. We breakfasted, dined and slept again at the Bell Savage. One George Pace, a young Man, and Mess Mate of my Nephews called on us this Morning and he dined supped and spent the Evening with us at the Bell Savage. Nancy and me walked about Town by ourselves this Morn'. The Captain and George Pace went with themselves. I shewed Nancy the Mews and the Kings Cream coloured Horses, also the Kings State Coach which she sat in. Gave to the Men that shewed us the same 0. 2. 0. For a Silver Fruit Knife for Jenny Pounsett p^d 0. 10. 6. At Charlesworths near Covent Garden for Gauze Gloves, Ribband &c. for Nancy I paid 1. 1. 0. For three Places in the Bath Coach for to Morrow Night, for part of

An early nineteenth-century engraving of Lansdown Crescent, Bath

The Baggage Wagon, *John Sell Cotman (1782–1842)*

the Fare thither p^d 3. 3. 0. In the Evening Nancy and Brother, George Pace, and myself went in a Coach to the Theatre in the Hay-Market late Mr. Footes—and there saw a Play and Farce, both performed incomparably well—it begun about 7 o'clock and not over till after 10 or very near 11 o'clock. For 4 Tickets and Coach hire back and thither I p^d 0. 15. 0. To a Barber for shaving and dressing me p^d 0. 2. 0. George Pace did not leave us till near 12 this Evening. I did not pull of my Cloaths last Night but sat up in a great Chair all night with my Feet on the bed and slept very well considering and not pestered with buggs.

JUNE 28. . . . I did not pull of my Cloaths last Night again but did as the Night before, and slept tolerably well. . . . At a Q^r before 7 this Evening Nancy and self got into the Bath Coach, and were just setting out, after some time waiting for Bill, when he luckily arrived, but it was enough to make one very mad, he was at last obliged to leave some things behind him. We had four of us in the Coach and Guard on top. It carries but 4 inside, and is called the Baloon Coach on Account of its travelling so fast, making it a point to be before the Mail Coach. We trimmed it of indeed, tho' only a P^r of Horses.

JUNE 30. We breakfasted and spent all the Morning at Bath, and about Noon we got into a Post Chaise and set forth with our Luggage for Shepton Mallet about 19 Miles from Bath, got there about 5 o'clock, had some Rum and Water at the George Inn, took a fresh Chaise and sat of for Cole to Pounsetts—thro' Ansford. . . .

AUG. 7. . . . Robert Shoard who married Farmer Corps Daughter and since the Farmer died, has continued my Estate at Ansford, called on me this Morning and paid me a Years Rent due Lady Day last past the Sum of 35. 0. 0. I paid him out of it for Poor Rates and Church 1. 12. 2¼. I paid him also for a new Gate 0. 7. 0. I gave Robert a Receipt on stampt Paper, and to let him with his Mother Law continue on the Estate. Poor Farmer Corp died just before we came down. He had over-heated himself it was said and was imprudent to drink cold Water after it. . . .

AUG. 10. . . . Nancy and self very busy this morning in making the Charter having some Company to dine with us—But unfortunately the Cellar Door being left open whilst it was put in there to cool, one of the Greyhounds (by name Jigg) got in and eat the whole, with a Cold Tongue &c. Sister Pounsett and Nancy mortally vexed at it. . . .

SEP. 21. . . . Nancy, Sister Pounsett and self went to Ansford this Morn' on foot with Nancy's Brother Willm who came over to breakfast and we all dined at Castle Cary at R: Clarkes with her, my Brother John and Wife and Juliana Woodforde and her Father—We had for Dinner, a Neck of Mutton boiled and Capers and a rost Shoulder of Pork alias mock Goose and a nice plumb Pudding. J^s Clarke spent part of the Afternoon with us. My Brother John indifferent to day being merry last Night and very near being killed last Night going home from Ansford Inn to his own House on horseback and

falling of—His face is cut but little however. . . .

OCT. 4. . . . After taking Leave of our Cole Friends, Nancy and self set forth in a Chaise from Bruton for Weston. . . . We called at Wincaunton to see Miss Tucker, but she was gone. From Wincaunton we went on to Meer and there changed Chaises and went on to Hindon—there we were obliged to bait the Horses as we could get no Chaise and then went on in the same Chaise for Sarum. N.B. At the same Inn at Hindon was Mr. Pitt the prime Minister, in the same Dilemma as we were all the Horses being engaged—He was going to Burton Pynsent. . . .

OCT. 7. We breakfasted, supped and slept again at the Angel [in London]. We dined at Bettys Chop-House on beef Stakes p^d 0. 3. 6. In the Morning we walked down to St. James's Palace and saw the Guards relieved and heard the German Band. Nancy was much frightened, being hurried at the Soldiers marching quick, and we being in their way. They however soon passed us on our standing still. After Dinner we [went] in a Coach and called on Miss Pope in Newgate Street at a Mr. Whites—who is a Hatter—there stayed till near 9 in the Evening, and it being very wet, before I could get a Coach to go back to our Inn, after walking Miles, I was wet thro' and thro'—at last did get one and got back to our Inn between 9 and 10 o'clock. For the first Coach to Miss Popes p^d 0. 1. 6. For the last Coach being very wet gave 0. 2. 6. I was pretty much fatigued this Evening being wet &c. Nancy I thank God pretty well, but very sorry for me.

OCT. 8. . . . I went by myself and saw the Guard relieved again this Morning at St. James's Palace. Miss Pope drank Tea with us in the Afternoon at the Angel—and after Tea we took Coach and went to Magdalen Chapel★ in St Georges Fields being Sunday and heard Prayers read and a Sermon. Very excellent singing at Magdalen Chapel. The Women had a thin green Curtain before them all the Time, one of them played the Organ. Dr. Milne preached from these Words 'And Nathan said unto David thou art the Man.'—Another Clergyman read Prayers—We had a first Seat. . . .

OCT. 9. . . . Nancy very ill all day, and vomited much and often. Pray God send her better—and safe to Weston. I went and saw the Guards relieved again this Morn' at St James's Palace—Horse and Foot. After that returned home to Nancy stayed a little Time with her, then walked into Bishopsgate Street, to the black Bull, and there took 2 Places in the Norwich Expedition Coach which carries 4 Passengers, and sets of from London at 9 to Mor: Night. . . .

OCT. 11. . . . Whilst we were at Newmarket and changing Coaches and Luggage, found that a small red Trunk of my Nieces was left behind in London, in which were all her principal Matters—It vexed her at first very much—but on my assuring her that I saw it safely lodged in the Warehouse, she was more composed. I would not pay the remaining part of our fare or for our Luggage till the Trunk was forthcoming. . . .

★ The Magdalen House or Hospital, for the reformation and relief of penitent prostitutes, was founded in 1758.

An early nineteenth-century view of St. James's Park from the Mall

OCT. 12. We breakfasted, dined and slept again at the Kings Head [at Norwich].
. . . Nancy but indifferent and thinking too much on her Trunk, as no Trunk was
brought by either of the Mail Coaches.

OCT. 13. . . . About 2 o'clock we got safe and tolerably well to the old Parsonage
House at Weston, found all my Servants tolerably well and things tidily . . . My
Niece seemed something better on being at home.

OCT. 23. . . . Mrs. Custance spent most of the Morning with us. Mr. Smith of
Mattishall made us a Morning Visit—he brought us a brace of Partridges. Dr.
Thorne called to see Nancy but did not stay long. He came whilst Mr. Smith was
here, but did not come into the same Room, there being rather a Coolness
between Mr. Smith and Mr. Thorne.

OCT. 28. . . . Rec^d a Letter this Evening from an old School-Fellow no less than
Mr. Thos Elbridge Rooke who is at present at a Mr. Haymans Sadler-Street
Wells, Somersett—under great distress, having lost both Feet, all his Family
Friends dead, and humbly hoping that I would contribute something to his
relief—What Changes have happened to that Family—Whilst his Father Mr.
Rooke of Somerton was alive things had every appearance of success, but his
untoward Son the Writer of the above Letter to me who spent every thing he had

and what his Father left him after he died, which was almost of a broken heart on seeing his Son going on so very badly. In my next Letter to my Sister Pounsett shall desire her to make enquiry after him, and to send him something for me— tho' little is in my Power to do, having many very near Relations that are in want.

NOV. 10. ... We dined and spent the Afternoon and part of the Evening at Weston House till after 9 o'clock with Mr. and Mrs. Custance, Mrs. Collyer Senr and a Mr. Chamberlain who is a Roman Catholick Priest and lives with Sr Wm Jernegan and Family and what is most remarkable in him is, that he was bred up a Protestant, was at the University of Cambridge, had Preferment in the Church of England to the Value of £800 per Annum all of which he has lately given up, renounced the Protestant Religion, and has been made a Monk. A very good kind of Man he appears to be and very sensible—has been in France &c. He is now Chaplain to Sr Wm Jernegan, that Family being of the Romish Persuasion. ...

NOV. 22. ... I buried this Afternoon about 4 o'clock, John Plummer an Infant aged only 5 Weeks. I knew nothing of burying the above Infant till 3 o'clock this Afternoon, then on hearing the Church Bell, I sent to Church to enquire the reason, and word was brought me, that there was a Child then at the Church Gate for Interment—It being my Dinner Time, I went as soon as ever I had finished my Dinner—Some Mistake of my old Clerk or the Father of the Child—in not acquainting me.

View of Norwich from the North-east, *John Thirtle (1777–1839)*

DEC. 10. . . . I read Prayers and Preached this Afternoon at Weston C[hurch], Mr. and Mrs. Custance at Church and a large Congregation besides at Church being fine, cheerful Weather. Nancy had two Letters from Mrs. Davy this Afternoon done up in a parcel, and with the same a little Lump of something, but what, I know not—as Nancy never mentioned a word of what it was, nor of a single word in either of the Letters—I care not for it, but shall take care to be as private myself in matters.

DEC. 26. We breakfasted, dined, &c. &c. again at home. To the Weston Ringers, their annual Gift of 0. 2. 6. To my Malsters Man a Christmas Gift gave 0. 1. 0. To my Blacksmiths Son a Christmas Gift 0. 0. 6. Mr. Girling, Mr. Custances Steward, called here this Afternoon and paid me Mr. Custances Composition for Land in hand, for Tithe the Sum of 13. 12. 6. Very sharp Frost indeed last Night and this Morning it froze the Water in my Bason this Morning that I wash in, quite over, in half an Hour after it had been brought up Stairs.

DEC. 29. . . . Had another Tub of Gin and another of the best Coniac Brandy brought me this Evening ab^t 9. We heard a thump at the Front Door about that time, but did not know what it was, till I went out and found the 2 Tubs—but nobody there.

DEC. 31. . . . This being the last Day of the Year, we sat up this Night till after 12

o'clock—then drank Health and happy New Year to all our Somersett Friends &c. and then went for Bedfordshire alias to bed.

1787

JAN. 18. ... Nancy very indifferent indeed all day—worse. Sent Briton to Reepham on foot this Morning with my Watch to be mended, the main Spring being broke, owing to my putting it forward by the Key. Briton did not return till 4 this Afternoon and then very wet and dirty, owing to the very sudden Thaw. It was quite a hard Frost when he set out, and I thought it more safe for him on foot than horseback but poor Fellow he had a terrible bad walk back being both very dirty and very wet. I gave him a glass of Gin on his return. Betty being gone to her Friends at Mattishall and Briton also out at dinner Time, I was with pleasure under the necessity of assisting at Dinner. Nancy complained a good deal in the Evening. We diverted ourselves at Cribbage this Evening at which neither won or lost.

JAN. 25. ... Nancy had a very indifferent Night and rather worse today, being still weaker. She did not come down Stairs till 2 o'clock this afternoon. However she made a good Dinner on a boiled Leg of Mutton and Caper Sauce and was better after. Rode to Ringland this Morning and married one Robert Astick and Elizabeth Howlett by Licence, Mr. Carter being from home, and the Man being in Custody, the Woman being with Child by him. The Man was a long time before he could be prevailed on to marry her when in the Church Yard; and at the Altar behaved very unbecoming. It is a cruel thing that any Person should be compelled by Law to marry. I recd. of the Officers for marrying them 0. 10. 6. It is very disagreeable to me to marry such Persons.★ ...

JAN. 28. ... I read Prayers and Preached this morning at Weston Church neither Mr. or Mrs. Custance at Church, nor above 20 People in all at Church—The Weather being extremely cold and severe with much Snow on the ground and still more falling with cutting Winds. After Service I buried a Daughter of Harrisons an Infant aged only 5 Weeks—I think that I never felt the cold more severe than when I was burying the above Infant. The Wind blowed very Strong and Snow falling all the time and the Wind almost directly in my Face, that it almost stopped my breath in reading the funeral Service at the Grave, tho' I had an Umbrella† held over my Head during the Time.

★ Under the Bastardy Act of 1733 a woman had only, upon oath before a justice, to charge any person with having gotten her with child to enable the justice, on application of the overseers of the poor, to apprehend and imprison the man charged, unless he gave security to indemnify the parish. By another clause of the Act the marriage of the woman caused the release of the man from penalty. Hence, in numerous cases, if the man could not indemnify the parish, he preferred wedlock to imprisonment.

† Umbrellas did not come into general use in England before the 1780's, and the man who first appeared with one in 1778 in London was jeered by the mob.

FEB. 3. . . . Nancy had but an indifferent night and after taking her Physick this Morning was very sick and brought up some of it, her breakfast would not stay on her Stomach also, nor anything else but a little Water Gruel, and that but a little Time, was extremely ill all the Day long till about 8 in the Evening and then was a small matter easier. The Mercury she took last Night was much too strong for her weak frame at this present. The Physic she took this morning had little or no effect, as she brought it up almost the whole, therefore she had violent griping pains in her Bowels the whole Morning without much coming from her as the Mercury only operated without the Aid of Physick to carry it of, therefore there must be a great deal of Mercury left behind—however when she went to bed, she was somewhat easier. Mr. Thorne called here this Morning accidentally having been to bleed Mrs. Custance at Weston House. He was not pleased on hearing that Nancy was so bad as not to be seen by him being above Stairs. I am afraid she caught cold, as her pain within her was so bad that she could not get from the close-Stool for near 2 Hours together. I went up to see her in the Evening, and she was very low and cried a good deal—but seemed rather easier—after she had her Tea and Toast she seemed something better and soon after came down Stairs and stayed the rest of the Evening. When she went to bed she was tolerably easy. I was very uneasy indeed the whole Day on my dear Nieces Account. 'Pray God give her more ease.' . . .

FEB. 10. . . . Nancy tolerable this morning but did not come down to breakfast, nor was below Stairs till Noon', just as she was coming down stairs Mrs. Custance came to us and stayed till near 3 o'clock. She seemed far from well, having a low nervous Fever hanging about her, and very far gone with Child. I tried to divert her as much as I could, showed her some Medals of mine &c. I was quite sorry to see her so very low and weak. Nancy dined, supped &c. below Stairs and was tolerably well and cheerful all Day.

MAR. 13. . . . Whilst we were at breakfast, Mrs. Davy from Thurning with a Servant with her, called here and drank a Dish of Tea with us, stayed about half an Hour afterwards and then went on to Mr. Thornes at Mattishall. I did not ask her to stay and dine with us. She talked of returning back to Thurning Thursday or Friday next—I did not ask her to call on her return. Nancy was highly pleased to see her. Mrs. Davy behaved as free as if nothing had been said respecting her Character by Mr. Smith. She is grown much fatter than she was. I never knew a Woman of much greater Effrontery. . . .

MAR. 18. . . . I met Mr. Custance on my return from Witchingham this Morning on the little Common, and he very genteelly desired me for the future to go thro' his inclosures by his House whenever I wanted to go to Witchingham or Lenewade Bridge, &c. as that way is somewhat nearer than the other. Nancy told me this Evening that Mrs. Davy had had an offer of marriage made her, but not said whom—also that her Daughter Betsy has had an offer also from young Walker who was lately at Mr. Thornes. The above are very great Secrets.

MAR. 27. . . . Mrs. Custance made us a morning Visit and stayed with us an Hour—She is quite hurried and uneasy on Account of her little Boy, William, having got the Measles, and herself never having them, and also that she is very near her Time of being brought to bed, having scarce a Month to go with Child.

Am exceeding sorry for poor Mrs. Custance indeed and likewise for Mr. Custance who must be very much concerned. Busy brewing some strong Beer to day.

MAY 6. . . . Soon after my return from Church, one of Mr. Custances Servants called here to let us know that Mrs. Custance was brought to bed of a Boy about 11 o'clock this Morn'. She with the little stranger as well as can be expected. I buried this Evening one Willm. Hill aged 65 yrs. . . .

MAY 29. . . . It seemed a little strange to be quite alone not being used to be so— In the Evening rather dull. Willm. Bidewell (who has taken Collisons Estate that John Pegg had from Michaelmas next, and to which Estate is annexed a publick House where Bens Father at present lives but is going out at the above Time) called on me this morning and another man with him, to ask my consent for the above public House to be continued on, and one Page (lately a Farmer and lived in this Parish, last Year and broke here) to live in it, but I said that I would never consent to it by any Means. The above Phillip Page is an old Man, had a Bastard about 3 Years [ago] by Charlotte Dunnell.

JUNE 9. . . . I went and read Prayers again this morning to Mrs. Leggatt and administered also the H. Sacrament to her—she was very weak indeed and but just alive. She was sensible and showed marks of great satisfaction after receiving the H. Sacrament. She never received it before. Pray God bless her. . . .

JUNE 29. . . . Sr. Willm. Jernegan sent me by Mr. Custance a Treatise on the Plant called Scarcity Root.★

JULY 11. . . . I was very busy all the Morning long in helping them in the Field, as we were busy carrying our Hay. We finished about 8 this Evening and then came Rain.

JULY 21. . . . Nancy very busy this morning in making some Rasberry Jam and red Currant Jelly. She made to day about 8 Pd. of Currant Jelly and about 9 Pound of Rasberry Jamm. This Evening as we were going to Supper, a covered Cart drove into my Yard with 3 Men with it, and one of them, the principal, was a black with a french Horn, blowing it all the way up the Yard to the Kitchen Door, to know if we would [like to see] a little Woman only 33 Inches high and 31 Years of Age. As we did not give our Dissent, she was taken out of the Cart and brought into our Kitchen, where we saw her and heard her sing two Songs. I dont think she was any taller than represented, but rather deformed, seemed in good Spirits, sang exceedingly high with very little Judgment and was very talkative. She was called by the black Polly Coleshill of Glocester. The Black told me that he formerly lived with the Earl of Albermarle I gave him 0. 1. 0. . . .

AUG. 10. . . . About 1 o'clock this Morning there was a most violent Tempest— very much Lightning and the most vivid, strong and quick I think I ever saw before—Not so much Thunder but very loud what there was—The Rain was some time before it came but then it was very heavy, the Rain did not last long.

★ The mangel-wurzel, which was first brought into notice in England in 1786 by Sir Richard Jebb, a distinguished doctor and scientist.

The Wind in the Trees, *John Sell Cotman (1782–1842)*

We were much alarmed, the Maids came downstairs crying and shrieking at 1 o'clock. I got up immediately and thinking when I went up Stairs to bed last Night that there was likelihood of a Tempest being so hot, I had lighted my little Lamp, and only laid down on my Bed with most of my Cloathes on and was just dozing when I heard the Maids all of a sudden shrieking at my Door. We lighted some Candles. Nancy had one in her Room, they were much frightned. It continued incessantly lightning from before 1 till 4 this Morning—then it abated and then I went to bed and slept comfortably till 9 o'clock. Thank God Almighty, for preserving us all safe from so violent a Tempest. May all others escape as well. It was most dreadful to behold the Lightning. . . .

AUG. 28. . . . My Greyhounds being both very full of fleas and almost raw on their backs, I put some Oil of Turpentine on them, which soon made many of them retire and also killed many more. . . .

SEP. 4. . . . About 11 o'clock this Morning walked to Weston Church to christen Mr. Custance's last little Boy . . . Mr. Custance very genteelly made me a present for christning the Child, wrapped in White Paper of the Sum of 5. 5. 0. In the Morn' I sent a Dozen of very fine Anson Apricots to Weston House which were on the table after Dinner and all eat, but not a word mentioned from whence they came, therefore suppose that neither Mr. or Mrs. Custance knew anything of the Matter.

Great Witchingham Church

OCT. 2. . . . Nancy went in her little Cart with Briton, and I on my Mare to Witchingham about 1 o'clock and there we dined and spent the Afternoon at Mr. Jeanes's with him, his Wife, Mr. Du Quesne, Mr. and Mrs. Priest of Reepham with their two Daughters, Rebeccah and Mary. We had for Dinner a Couple of small Chicken boiled, and a Tongue, one stewed Duck, a fine Haunch of Venison and a baked Pudding. Mr. Du Quesne fell backward from his Chair in the Afternoon and bruised himself much. The Ladies were not in the Room at the time. We returned as we went directly after Coffee. Mr. Du Quesne went with me, he complained a good deal of his Fall when on horseback in giving him much Pain. Mr. Du Quesne should have went in his Carriage especially as Mr. Jeanes desired him, and to take up my Niece with him in the same, and which he might have done. We spent a very agreeable Day and did due justice to the Venison which came out of the New Forest from Mr. Jeanes's Father.

OCT. 17. ... St. Faiths Fair to day. I would not let any of my Servants go to it, on Account of a very bad Fever of the putrid kind, raging there and of which many have died there already. To 2 Dozen fresh Herrings paid 0. 1. 0.

NOV. 12. ... Soon after breakfast I walked out a Coursing and took Ben and the Boy with me, did not return till near three, afternoon, we had tolerable Sport, coursed one Hare and a Couple of Rabbitts, all of whom we killed, it was a very large Hare. I think I never knew so pleasant a day so far in November, it was more like Summer than Autumn. I was very indifferent the whole Day, could eat but very little for Dinner being over fatigued and likewise my Spirits but very bad.

NOV. 14. ... To a poor Man of Easton having lost a Horse, 0. 1. 0. Poor Neighbour Downings Wife bad in a Fever.

1788

JANRY. 25. ... Of Nancy for not being below Stairs for 2 Mornings before 10 o'clock, forfeit each time 6^d recd. 0. 1. 0. ...

FEB. 1. ... Mr. Carter of Ringland sent me a Note this Morn' before breakfast, to desire my Sentiments on a particular Question relating to the tolling of a Bell for a Child that died without being baptised at its decease, at any time from thence to its being interred and at the putting of it into the ground. I sent an Answer back to Mr. Carter, that as the Funeral Service could not be read over it, the tolling of the Bell at any time to be inadmissable. ...

FEBRY. 6. ... Very busy all the Morning being very fine Weather in trimming up my young Scotch Firs.

FEB. 11. ... Nancy not being below Stairs this morning before the clock had done striking 10 forfeited—0. 0. 6.

FEB. 29. ... Mr. Taswell sent early to me this morning that he would take a Family Dinner with us to day and desired us to send to Mr. Custance that they might not wait dinner for him. ... At 11 o'clock this Morning I sent Briton to Weston House to let them know that Mr. Taswell was to take a Family Dinner with us to day, Briton returned pretty soon and informed us that Mr. and Mrs. Custance, Lady Bacon and Son and Master Taswell would also come and partake of the Family Dinner, and they sent us some Fish, a wild Duck and a Sallad. It occasioned rather a Bustle in our House but we did as well as we could—We had not a bit of White bread in House, no Tarts whatever, and this Week gave no Order whatever to my Butcher for Meat, as I killed a Pigg this Week. We soon baked some white bread and some Tartlets and made the best shift we could on the whole. ... We gave the Company for Dinner some Fish and Oyster Sauce, a niece Piece of Boiled Beef, a fine Neck of Pork rosted and Apple Sauce, some hashed Turkey, Mutton Stakes, Sallad &c. a wild Duck rosted, fryed Rabbits, a plumb Pudding and some Tartlets. Desert, some Olives, Nutts, Almonds, and

Still Life, *Emily Stannard (1803–85)*

Raisins and Apples. The whole Company were pleased with their Dinner &c. Considering we had not above 3 Hours notice of their coming we did very well in that short time. All of us were rather hurried on the Occasion.

MARCH 15. . . . I made a bet with Nancy on Wednesday last of 2ˢ/6ᵈ, that it rained before 8 o'clock this Evening which it did not till about 7 this Evening, as she lost her bet on so near gaining it, I not only omitted receiving the same, but gave her besides 0. 2. 6.

APRIL 2. . . . I took a walk to a Cottage just by Mr. Bodhams to see one Mary Brand an old Woman of 80 who belongs to Weston and to whom I send Mony every Year out of the Charity belonging to poor Widows of Weston. She lives with her Daughter, Wife of Jos. Bruton and a Tenant to Mr. Bodham, I found her spinning by the fire tho' she almost is blind. I gave her to buy Tobacco as she smokes 0. 1. 0. . . .

APRIL 19. . . . Recd. . . . a very short Letter from my Brother Heighes informing me that his Daughter Juliana is entirely given over by the Faculty—poor Girl— Nancy recd. also a very melancholy Letter from her Brother Willm. concerning poor Juliana, that she was at the last stage of Life, and to desire Nancy to come down immediately into Somersett. Am afraid by this time that poor Juliana is no more. Nancy was half distracted almost on the Account. She cried incessantly the whole Evening, I sincerely pity her—no two Sisters could love one another more. . . .

APRIL 21. . . . He [Mr. Du Quesne] brought for Nancy a little Parcel from her poor Sister and gave it to her—which she opened on her return home. It was a small roundish red Morrocco Purse with a small silver lock to it and in it was a new half guinea of 1787 and 2 Queen Anne's Sixpences. It made her very uneasy and unhappy for a long time after, was rather more composed before she went to bed. It made my heart ache to see her so miserable. . . .

MAY 8. . . . Sent Briton to Norwich early this morning for things wanted from thence, he returned by dinner, and brought a Letter for Nancy from her Brother Willm. upbraiding her for not coming to see her Sister, who is still alive and that is all—poor Girl I am sorry for her but am not pleased with Willm. for such a Letter to her Sister, as it made her very unhappy and very ill, vomited a good [deal] and could eat nothing at all for Dinner. Instead of condoling with her about her poor Sister and sorry for her not being able to go into the Country he rebukes her with want of humanity &c. It is quite cruel and unfeeling of him I think. His Letter was composed of a great many fine Epithets and sentimental thoughts.

MAY 12. . . . Merry doings at the Heart to day being Whit Monday plowing for a Pʳ of Breeches, running for a Shift, Raffling for a Gown &c.

MAY 17. . . . He [Ben, his servant] . . . brought me 2 Letters—One from My Sister Pounsett and the other from my Brother Heighes both which brought the disagreeable news of Nancy's Sister's Death, poor Juliana Woodforde, she died on Monday Morn' last about 11 o'clock. Poor Nancy greatly affected on hearing of the same. . . .

JUNE 11. . . . We had a very excellent Dinner [at Mr. Jeanes's house], that is to say, a fine Piece of fresh Salmon with Tench and Eel, boiled Ham and Fowls, the best part of a Rump of Beef stewed, Carrots and Peas, a fore Qr. of Lamb rosted, Cucumbers and Mint Sauce, a Couple of Ducks rosted, plain and Currant Puddings. After Dinner 2 large Dishes of Strawberries, some Blanched Almonds with Raisins and Aples. We were much crowded at Table, rather unpleasant. Major Lloyd with his 2 eldest Daughters joined us at the Tea Table in the Evening which made the whole Company than consist of 18 in Number. After Coffee and Tea we had two or three Songs from Miss Kate Lloyd who sings delightfully indeed. It was sometime after 9 o'clock before we got back to Weston—we returned as we went. Upon the whole we spent a very agreeable Day. Mr. Jeanes Senr. is a mighty cheerful good natured plain downright Man. Mr. Locke a very neat well looking old gentleman, and Country Esq. fond of Hunting, keeps 16 fox Hounds, talks plain Hampshire and Delights also in farming. Mr. Charles Springer a very modest young Man about 17 or 18 yrs, in some branch of Trade belonging to the India House.

JULY 7. . . . Mr. Custance sent me a Melon and with it a Note to inform us that Mrs. Custance was this morning about 2 o'clock safely delivered of another Son and that both Mother and Child were as well as could possibly be expected in the time. Mr. C. also desired me (if perfectly convenient) to wait on him in the afternoon and name the little Stranger. After Dinner therefore about 5 o'clock I took a Walk to Weston House and named the little Infant, in Lady Bacons dressing Room by name, Neville. The Revd. Mr. Daniel Collyer of Wroxham was with Mr. Custance when I first went in but he soon went. . . .

JULY 29. . . . In the Evening took a ride to Norwich and Briton with me, and there I supped and slept at the Kings Head. In the Evening before Supper I walked into St. Stephens and saw the Polish Dwarf, Joseph Boruwlaski and his Wife who is a middle sized Person, he is only three feet three Inches in height, quite well proportioned everyway, very polite, sensible and very sprightly, and gave us a tune upon the Guitar, and one Tune of his own composing. The common price of admittance was one Shilling, but I gave him rather more 0. 2. 6.

JULY 30. I got up this morning about six o'clock and before breakfast mounted my Mare and sat of for Bungay and Briton with me, went three Miles at least out of our Way to find out Ellingham where Mr. Hall is Rector . . . Such a Parsonage House and Garden and in so low a place, close also to the River which often overflows, besides Ellingham Mill so close that the Sound of it is continually heard. Such a House and Situation I think very far from being agreeable. Mr. Hall however is fitting of it up in a shabby Manner and at present sleeps there of nights, no Man, Maid, Horse, Dog, or any living Creature but himself there— The House very small indeed. . . .

AUG. 16. . . . Mrs. Davy with one Harris in a Cart called here, this Evening about 5 o'clock and drank Tea here in her road from Norwich to Foulsham. Soon after Mrs. Davy came also Mr. Walker and with him another young Man by name Viol, both almost wet thro' and they drank Tea also here in their road from Norwich homewards, so that my House was more like an Inn this Evening than anything else.

SEPT. 25. . . . Nancy, Mrs. Davy and Betsy breakfasted here and as soon as they had done breakfast, they went of for Norwich in a Norwich Chaise from the Kings Head. And at 10 o'clock I mounted my Mare and sat of for the same place and my Servant Man Ben went with me to carry my Portmanteau. My Servant Man Briton went with the Chaise and sat with the Driver before the Chaise. Going into Norwich about a Mile from it I met Mr. Smith of Mattishall coming from Norwich we just spoke to each other and that was all. . . .

SEPT. 26. As I only laid down on the Bed last Night with some of my Cloaths, I got up pretty early (considering we did not go to bed till near 2 this morning) and I took a Walk in the City, went to Bacons and got Tickets for the Oratorio this morning at St Peters Church . . . Soon after breakfast, Mrs. Davy and Betsy, Miss Walker, my Niece, and Mr. Walker went in a Coach to St. Peters Church to the Oratorio of Judas Maccabeus,★ I walked to the House of Mr. Priests and there waited for Mr. Custances Coach . . . the Coach called about 11, with Mr. and Mrs. Custance in it, and I went with them to St. Peter's Church and there heard the fine Oratorio of Judas Maccabeus which was performed very capitally— Madame Mara also performed her part very well indeed. There was supposed to be present 1200 People. The Church was quite full, I got as near to my Party as I could. Mrs. Davy during the performance made some little disturbance, fainting away, but she soon came to herself again, quite a fine Air. Betsy Davy did not mind it at all, as she knows her well. The Oratorio was not over till 3 this Afternoon. . . . I thank God, got home safe and well after my Hurry without being either much fatigued or heavy. I left my Party at Norwich, as they all go to the Assembly this Evening in Chapel Field, I desired Mr. Walker to settle all Accounts at Norwich and that I would reckon with him at home. . . . I was highly entertained by the Musick. . . . Scarce ever seen so much Company at Norwich. Lodgings scarce to be got and some exceeding dear indeed—two Rooms it was said, was let at 10 guineas. Almost all the principal Families in the County there.

SEPT. 27. . . . Between 2 and 3 o'clock this Afternoon there came to my House in a Post-Chaise from Norwich Mrs. Davy, Betsy, Miss Charlotte Quarles and my Niece, and they all dined and spent the Afternoon here. . . . Mr. Walker and me settled our Norwich Accounts. . . . It was a dear Frolick but nevertheless I should have been sorry that my Niece had not went to it. It also gave me pleasure to attend at it, and would have given more to all parties if Mrs. Davy had not been so full of strange Vagaries expecting so much Court and Attention from everyone. There was not one of the Party pleased with her. We all went to bed in tolerable good time to night. Miss Charlotte Quarles is a great Beauty and exquisitely genteel without the lest affectation but very affable and very agreeable.

OCT. 27. . . . Mr. Walker went out early this Morning a hunting and did not return the whole day. Poor Betsy Davy could eat no Supper and obliged to go to bed, her heart ached so very much. Mr. Walker sent over a Messenger from Mattishall this Evening to inform us that he sleeps at Mattishall.

★ Composed by Handel in 1746.

St. Luke's Chapel, Norwich Cathedral, *John Sell Cotman (1782–1842)*

OCT. 29. . . . Recd. this morning by Mr. Custance's Servant Richd. brought by him from Norwich from the Post Office a gilt Card enclosed in a Cover from Mr. and Mrs Coke of Holkham, containing an Invitation to me and my Niece the fifth of November next to a Ball and Supper at Holkham. The Card was printed all but our Names and in these words. Mr. and Mrs Coke desire the honour of Mr. and Miss Woodford's Company the 5th of November, at eight o'clock to a Ball and Supper, in Commemoration of the glorious Revolution of 1688. Holkham, Oct. 1788. The Favour of an Answer is desired. My Servant, Briton, paid for the same 0. 0. 8. N.B. a general Invitation throughout the County. . . .

NOV. 3. . . . My poor old Spaniel Bitch Mab was hung this Morn' she being very old and almost blind. I had her hanged out of Charity.

NOV. 5. . . . Soon after breakfast (young Rose called here and desired me to lend him my Greyhounds, having found a Hare sitting) Mr. Walker and self took a Walk with the Greyhounds and saw the Hare coursed which gave great Sport indeed, but was killed at last. I never saw a better Course. I let Mr. Rose have the Hare for a Friend of his. After we had killed that Hare we went after another and found one in about an Hour, but we had very little Diversion with her, the Greyhounds scarcely seeing her, She soon got of. Saw never another tho' we stayed out till 3 o'clock. Mr. Walker almost knocked up by walking so long, we were out from 11 till 3 in the Afternoon. . . .

NOV. 8. . . . Mr. Walker breakfasted, and spent the Morning with us, and at 1 o'clock set of for Norwich to go in the Mail Coach this Afternoon at 4 for London.

NOV. 11. . . . Reported this Day at Norwich that our good King was dead, pray God it might not be true.★

NOV. 13. . . . We returned home about ½ past 9 o'clock and on our return found Mr. Walker at Weston Parsonage, who is returned from London in pursuit of his Portmanteau which is at present lost. He supped and slept here. . . .

NOV. 14. . . . After breakfast Nancy, and Betsy Davy would go to Norwich with Mr. Walker, and there they dined at the Kings Head and returned home to Tea about 6 o'clock and Mr. Walker instead of going to London as proposed returned with them. A pretty expensive and foolish Scheme indeed—I was not pleased . . . Mr. Walker paid me what I lent him at Cards 0. 2. 6.

NOV. 15. . . . Mr. Walker breakfasted here and then sat of for Norwich in my little Cart and Briton with him, who is to bring back News &c. Mr. Walker goes by the Mail Coach this Aft. for London. Briton returned about 5 o'clock this Afternoon. . . . Briton . . . said that Mr. Walker did not go to London this Day neither, and that he would return to my house again this Evening, which he did to Supper and also slept here again. It was after 12 before I got to bed this Night. Mr. Walker brought us a brace of Pheasants.

NOV. 16. . . . I prayed at Church for our most gracious and truly beloved Sovereign King George the third. I did it out of my own head, no prayer yet arrived.

A view of Norwich from Crown Point, *John Joseph Cotman (1814–78)*

★ It was on 5 November that George III's illness, insanity, declared itself
beyond all possibility of question.

NOV. 18. . . . Soon after breakfast Mr. Walker took a ride to Norwich to take a place in the Mail Coach for this Afternoon for London—but he returned to us this Evening between 7 and 8 o'clock and it being very dark, he hired a Man to come with him on another horse—Joe at the Kings Head. After Joe had refreshed himself and Horse also he returned back to Norwich. Mr. Walker said that there was no Place in the Coach but all that is nothing, his inclination was to stay. Betsy Davy's Birth Day now 18 Years of Age.

NOV. 19. . . . Mr. Walker breakfasted here, and then sat of once more for Norwich to go in the Mail Coach this Afternoon for London—I still think it rather dubious where [whether?] he goes or not this Day. On his taking leave he went up to Nancy and wished her well shaking her by her hand, and then went to Betsy and did the same, but to me (altho' in the Room at the same time) he never said one word or took the lest notice of me (tho' I also helped him on with his great Coat) after he was mounted and just going out of the great Gates then he said good Morning and that was all—very slight return for my Civilities towards him of late and which I did not expect. It hurt me very much indeed. Mr. Walker did not return however this Day to us.

NOV. 21. . . . Mr. Walkers Birth-Day now 21 Years of Age.

NOV. 22. . . . Sent Ben early this Morning to Norwich after News and other things from thence, he returned about Dinner time. No Letters for us. Betsy Davy had a Letter from Mr. Walker from Thetford and with it a Parcel in which was nothing but a Fox's Brush or Tail.

DEC. 6. . . . Sent Ben to Norwich on horseback after News &c. He returned home to dinner with the same. Betsy Davy had a Parcel and a Letter from Mr. Walker in Town. The Parcel contained a very handsome red Morocco Almanack and Pocket Book, gilt with a silver Clasp to the same—quite new fashioned. Nancy also had a Letter from Mr. Walker and a Barrel of Oysters sent her by him also.

DEC. 20. . . . Received a Letter by him [Briton] from Mr. Walker in which he mentions having sent me 2 Gallons of English Gin, but he mentioned nothing of when it was sent, by what Conveyance, or where left.

DEC. 23. . . . Just as we were going to Dinner a Man came express from the Kings Head at Norwich, with a Letter for Betsy Davy from Mr. Walker at London to desire her to meet him at Norwich at the Kings Head on Christmas Day next Thursday and that Nancy would accompany her. He mentioned in his Letter that he had ordered a Post-Chaise from the Kings head to be at my House for them in the Morning. Very wild, unsteady, and thoughtless Work indeed.

DEC. 25. . . . Before I went to Church this Morning Nancy and Betsy Davy went of in a Norwich Chaise which came to my House by 7 o'clock this morning for Norwich to meet Mr. Walker at the Kings Head, and there they dined, but returned home to Tea in the Afternoon and Mr. Walker with them. Mr. Walker supped and slept here. . . .

1789

JAN^{ry} 1st. ... About 12 Mr. Walker went to Norwich in a Chaise that he had ordered from thence. ... Mr. Walker returned to us by Tea time this Aft. At Cards this Evening won 0. 2. 0. So that Nancy owes me now 0. 7. 0. Bitter cold this Evening and a very hard Frost. N.B. Fox's Brush &c. made me quite sick and tired.

JAN^{ry} 2. ... As cold today as it has been yet. ... Mr. Walker's Cough somewhat better. Nancy, Betsy Davy, and Mr. Walker are all confederate against me and am never let into any of their Schemes or Intentions &c. Nancy I think ought not to be so to me.

JAN^{ry} 3. ... Did not get to bed till near 1 o'clock—being very uneasy. The treatment I meet with for my Civility this Christmas is to me abominable.

JAN^{ry} 4. ... Mr. Walker breakfasted, and spent the Morn' here. At 12 he went from my House in a Chaise for Norwich to go for London this Afternoon. ...

JAN. 6. ... Bitter cold day again with high wind, it froze in all parts of the House. Sent Ben round my Parish with some money to the Poor People this severe Weather, chiefly those that cannot work at this time, some 1 Shilling apiece—some at 1^s/6^d apiece. In all, Ben gave for me this Day 1. 14. 6.

JAN. 24, SATURDAY. ... Sent Briton early this morning on horseback to Norwich after News &c. returned home by Dinner. Brought a Letter for Nancy from Mr. Walker. An old Man came express from Foulsham with a Letter for Betsy Davy from Mr. Walker in Town. Betsy gave the old Gentleman for coming over with it 1^s/6^d. I gave him some Victuals and Drink. The Wind was so high in the Night that I got up about 2 o'clock but did not come below. Went to bed before 5 o'clock.

 N.B. Not a Word mentioned to me by either Betsy or Nancy concerning anything in the Letters sent by Walker. Betsy very busy all the Evening writing since she recd. Walkers Letter—but to who not one Word to me. They are both artful.

JAN. 25, SUNDAY. ... Nancy and Betsy went to bed exactly at 10 to night.

MARCH 8, SUNDAY. ... I read Prayers and Preached this Afternoon at Weston Church—Also read with the greatest Pleasure a Prayer composed on the Occasion on the restoration of his Majesty's Health, which I received this Morning. I return also to thee O Lord my private but most unfeigned Prayer of Thanksgiving for the same, And may so good a King long live to reign over us— and pray God that his amiable and beloved Queen Charlotte may now enjoy again every happiness this World can afford, with so good a Man, and may it long, very long continue with them both here and eternal happiness hereafter.

This is the ardent and most fervent Prayer of one of their most sincere subjects for the best of Kings and Queens. Neither Mr. or Mrs. Custance at Church. The Weather, I suppose, being so very Cloudy with Snow. Nancys Birth Day to day she is now entered into her 32. Year.

MARCH 17, TUESDAY. ... This morning settled Money Matters with my Niece for the last year—paid her the balance in ready Cash—which was—4. 4. 0. The whole that I had paid for her and gave her the last Year—amounted to 31. 2. 9. Brewed some strong Beer to day. Nancy very discontented of late, and runs out against living in such a dull Place.

MARCH 18, WEDNESDAY. ... Great Rejoicings at Norwich this Evening on the happy restoration of his Majesty's Health. I gave to our People in the Kitchen on the Occasion a Bottle of Gin to drink the King's Health, this Evening after Supper, and the Queens to Morrow.

MARCH 28, SATURDAY. ... I took a Walk to Weston House this Morning to see Mr. Custance who is ill in a swelled Face. I stayed with him an hour and half and returned home to dinner. Mr. Custance pressed me much to dine with him as he was alone, and Mrs. Custance at Raveningham, at Sr Edmund Bacons, but I could not as I expected a Letter from the West by my Servant, Briton, who went to Norwich this morning after News &c. and which in all probability would be

most unwelcome to me and likewise to my poor Niece—accordingly when I returned which was about 3 o'clock to my House, Briton was returned, and with him brought a Letter sealed with black Wax to me, which on opening I found to be from my Brother John, informing us, that my dear Brother Heighes died on Sunday last the 22 Instant about 11 o'clock in the Morning from a violent inflammation in the urinary passage which finally terminated in a Mortification in a very short time, pray Almighty God that he might be more happy in a future State than he has experienced in this, and all his frailties in this Life forgiven. We heard nothing of his being ill till Tuesday night last, and now gone, O Lord make us wise to think on futurity. . . . Pray God comfort my Nephew Willm in his great distress. . . .

APRIL 19, SUNDAY. . . . I read Prayers, Preached, and publickly christened a Child this Afternoon at Weston Church. Neither Mr. or Mrs. Custance at Church this Afternoon. There was a very full Congregation at Church this Aft. Read a Royal Proclamation for a general thanksgiving day to be observed on Thursday next upon the late great and wonderful recovery of our most gracious and truly beloved Sovereign King George the third. If he had not recovered God only knows, what troubles England might have been involved in just at this time. Thanks be to God! Between 7 and 8 this Evening Mr. Walker and Betsy Davy came to my House they were on horseback. They stayed and drank Tea and at 8. sat of for Foulsham, as I was determined not to offer them beds. . . .

Weston Hall

APRIL 23, THURSDAY. . . . Mr. Custance went for London yesterday I heard. He is to stay a Week in Town it is reported. Mr. Custance being one of the Gentlemen of the privy Chamber to his Majesty, I apprehend is the Occasion of his going, as this Day the King goes publickly to St. Pauls to return thanks, both

Houses of Parliament attend him etc. It is to be a grand Procession thither. It is to be a great day of rejoicing every where almost. We heard firing of Guns from many Quarters ab^t Noon. There was nothing at all done at Weston in that way.

The Royal Procession in St. Paul's Cathedral on St. George's Day, 1789, to give thanks for the recovery of George III

The Lord Mayor presenting the City Sword to George III on his procession to St. Paul's Cathedral, 23 April 1789

APRIL 29, WEDNESDAY. . . . As I was putting on my Boots in the Kitchen this morning to go to Mr. Bodhams, Mr. Walker and Betsy Davy called at the Kitchen Door on horseback, to whom I went out to speak to with only one boot on. I asked them to unlight and have some refreshment but they neither would. They both looked very cool on me, particularly Betsy Davy who scarce deigned to cast a look on me when I spoke to her, they behaved with great reserve. . . .

MAY 3, SUNDAY. . . . I read Prayers and Preached and christned a Child by name Joseph this afternoon at Weston Church. None from Weston House to day at Church. Mr. Custance not returned home as yet. Rec^d a letter this Evening from my Niece at Mattishall to let me know that she goes to Morrow to Mr. Thorne's to spend a few days with Mrs. Thorne &c. Betsy Davy and Mr. Walker are I believe there. I was very much displeased at it and shall send for her home to Morrow early. I am almost continually vexed and tormented by her connection with the Davy's &c. They have almost alienated my regard for my Niece.

MAY 4, MONDAY. . . . I got up at 6 o'clock this morning and sent of Briton after Nancy as soon as I could. . . . Nancy returned with Briton which was very good of her about 2 o'clock and she dined and slept at home.

MAY 9, SATURDAY. . . . Mr. Custance returned home from London this Evening. I sent to Weston House this Evening to enquire. I read the Letter which Nancy rec^d from her Brother William last Wednesday and which she gave me. I think William talks at present in too high Strains rather disrespectful both of the Living and the dead. No Compliments from either him or his Wife to us. A very long Letter but full of egotisms. He also desires his Sister to write to her B[rother]. Sam on the disagreeable News of his Fathers Death &c.

MAY 20, WEDNESDAY. . . . Mr. Walker with Betsy Davy behind him, called here about 2 o'clock and after staying with us about half an Hour Mr. Walker mounted his horse and went of for Foulsham leaving Betsy Davy behind to spend the Day and the Night with us, and she therefore dined, supped and slept here. She looks very poorly and is very bad again in her old Complaint the palpitation of the heart and Cramp in her head. Too much raking about has been I think the cause of her being so ill again, much beyond her Strength.

MAY 28, THURSDAY. . . . I had a very odd Dream last Night, I dreamt that I should die the Friday before the fifth of Nov^br next; not my Will o Lord but thine be done, if it be thy good pleasure thus to fulfil the same. And may thou O Good God forgive me all my Sins.

JUNE 1st MONDAY. . . . To a decayed old Schoolmaster gave 0. 1. 0. . . .

Parson Woodforde and Nancy set off for Somerset on June 9th and stayed with Sister Pounsett till Sept. 8th. Mr. Du Quesne visited them while they were there.

JUNE 29, MONDAY. . . . Old Mr. Dalton and son John called on me this Morning stayed half an Hour with us. I did not know old Mr. Dalton at first as he now wears his Hair.* . . .

JULY 11, SATURDAY. . . . Sister Pounsett and Daughter, my Niece Nancy and self with Mr. Du Quesne dined and spent the Afternoon at Ansford, at Mr. Frank Woodfordes with him and his Wife, at Ansford Parsonage the Place and House in which I was born and lived many Years but had not been in it before this day, for almost fifteen years, owing to a disagreement between us, which now I hope will be ever done away. The House and Garden greatly altered for the best. . . .

AUG. 4, TUESDAY. Dies Memorabilis. I breakfasted, supped and slept again at Cole. I rose this morning at 6 o'clock, shaved and dressed, and at 7 I went in a Bruton Chaise and my Niece Jenny Pounsett with me, to my Brothers at C. Cary and there we made a second breakfast, after that my Brother and Wife, Mrs. Richd Clarke and Nancy, a Dr. Brodum who is a German Doctor, Mr. James Clarke and Wife and the latters Brother Mr. Willm Dawe, all sat of about 9 o'clock for Sherborne to see the Royal Family . . . We got to Sherborne about 11 o'clock,

---

* Wigs had been going out for some time now. Soon only the clergy would be faithful to a fashion which had been universal in Europe since the second half of the seventeenth century.

had some White Wine Negus at the Antelope, and then we all went down to Lord Digby's Park, and there walked about till about 12 o'clock, at which time, the King, Queen, Princess Royal, Princess Elizabeth, and Princess Augusta arrived in the Park in three Royal Coaches with 4 Horses to each. We were very near them as they passed by. After they had taken some refreshment, they all walked upon the Terrace before the Crowd. We were all very near indeed to them, the King looked very red and is very tall and erect, The Queen and Princesses rather short but very pleasing Countenances and fair. After the Royal Family had walked round the Garden, they returned into Lord Digby's for a time. The King walked first with Lord Digby who held his hat in his hand, The Kings Hat was on, then the Queen with her Lady in waiting, then the Princess Royal and her Attendant Lady, then Princess Elizabeth and her Attendant Lady, then Princess Augusta and her attendant Lady. The King was in his Windsor Uniform, blue coat with red Cape and Cuffs to the Sleeves, with a plain round Hat with a black Ribband round it, The Queen was in a purple Silk, and white Bonnett, The Princesses all in Pink Silk and white Bonnetts. After they had been within Doors about an Hour They all came into the Park, the King on horseback, The Queen and Princesses and their Ladies, in two open Carriages, and they all passed thro' the Multitude, I was close to them as they passed. They took a ride quite round the Park, and were I suppose in performing it near 3 Hours. The King returned to the House by Water—The Queen and Princesses returned in their Carriages. They then went to Dinner at Lord Digbys. It was 5 o'clock this Afternoon before they got into Lord Digbys. Our Company then made the best of our way to our Inn to dine also. Nancy and the other Ladies bore the fatigue pretty well, we were obliged often to sit on the grass in the Park, being there almost 6 Hours. It was a most delightful Day, thank God for it. . . .

On Tuesday, Sept. 15th, the Diarist and his niece reached Weston in safety—'found all our People well and all things in very good Order and Harvest all in'.

OCT. 16, FRIDAY. . . . Sad News from France all anarchy and Confusion. The King, Queen and Royal Family confined at Paris. The Soldiers joined the People, many murdered.

NOV. 13, FRIDAY. I breakfasted, dined, supped and slept at Norwich. Nancy breakfasted dined &c at Norwich. About 11 o'clock this Morn' our Somersett Friends my Brother [John] and Wife and Mrs. Richd Clarke arrived at Norwich from London in the Expedition Coach after travelling all night. We were very happy to see them arrived safe thanks be to God for the same, considering their great fatigue they all looked very well. . . .

NOV. 14, SATURDAY. We all breakfasted and spent the Morn' at Norwich. At about 2 o'clock my Brothers Wife, Mrs. Richd Clarke and Nancy got into one of the Kings Head Chaises, and my Brother and self into another, and sat of for Weston to which Place we got safe and well 'thank God' to the Parsonage House about 4 o'clock where we dined, supped and slept. . . . Saw Mr. Walker this morning at Norwich he looked very poorly . . . I think my Brother is grown very fat of late.

NOV. 20, FRIDAY. ... Mr. and Mrs. Jeanes made us a morning Visit. I asked them to dine with us but they would not, I asked them also to dine with us on Tuesday next to meet Mr. Du Quesne, but Mrs. Jeanes said it was inconvenient, tho' she had the assurance to invite us the Wednesday following without once offering to send their Carriage for the Ladies. We declined accepting the Invitation immediately.

NOV. 27, FRIDAY. ... Mr. Custance very kindly called on me this Morn to enquire how I did, he did not stay long as he was going on to Mr. Townshends on a Visit. I thank God had a better night of rest than I have had the 3 last Nights. Had no Cramp at all. My Brother recommending me last Night to carry a small Piece of the roll Brimstone sewed up in a piece of very thin Linnen, to bed with me and if I felt any Symptom of the Cramp to hold it in my hand or put it near the affected part, which I did, as I apprehended at one time it was coming into one of my legs, and I felt no more advances of it. This I thought deserving of notice, even in so trifling a book as this is. ...

DEC. 28, MONDAY. ... Rec^d of Edwd Gooch this morning for Tithe 0. 6. 0. To one Willm Mason of Sparham who goes about at Christmas playing on 10 Bells gave him 0. 1. 6. To my Malsters Man James Barrett Xmas Gift 0. 1. 0. I walked to Church about 2 o'clock this afternoon and buried poor John Gooch who has left a Wife and several Children but most of them out. He was lately a near Neighbour of ours for some Y^{rs}. I thought that he had been older only 48 Y^{rs}. At Quadrille this Evening lost 0. 0. 6.

1790

JAN^{ry} 8, FRIDAY. ... Mr. Walker came here about 1 o'clock in a Fakenham Chaise and he stayed and dined, supped and spent the Evening with us. About 10 o'clock this Evening he went in the same Chaise to Lenewade Bridge Inn to sleep. Mr. Walker looked very bad indeed and made us low. ...

JAN^{ry} 13, WEDNESDAY. ... Was taken very ill [this] morning in bed about 4 o'clock with a violent pain in my Stomach, which I apprehend proceeded from gouty Wind there and likewise from Bile. I continued ill all the whole Day, could not eat any Dinner &c. In the Afternoon was taken with a vomiting, and afterwards was some matter easier. I took a small Dose of Rhubarb and Ginger going to bed to night, as did my Brother also. Pray God! I might be better to Morrow, as it adds to my Uneasiness to make my Somersett Friends not enjoy themselves as well as I could wish. My poor old Clerk, J^s Smith is very ill, he dined with our Folks in Kitchen to day but looks very bad. It was very wet this Evening but quite warm.

JAN^ry 14, THURSDAY. . . . Was I thank God! some small matter better this morning, tho' but an indifferent night of rest. Mem. The Season so remarkably mild and warm that my Brother gathered this morning in my Garden some full blown Primroses. . . .

Norwich Castle, *Michael Angelo Rooker (1746–1801)*

JAN^ry 28, THURSDAY. . . . Mr. Custance shewed me a Letter when at Du Quesnes from Mr. Walkers Uncle of Woodstock to a Mr. Barker, Wine Merchant, at Norwich informing him that Mr. Walker was a profligate abandoned young Man, and to guard Barker from trusting him with any more Money or any one else, that he should allow him 30 P^d per Annum to keep him from starving provided he made a better Use of it than he has hitherto done, and if he did not, he should even withdraw that. Mr. Custance also told me that he had made use of his Name, Sr Thos Beauchamps and mine to get money raised for him at Norwich particularly the above Mr. Barker of whom he has had 300 P^d, besides many others. Among the others Hylett, Hostler at the Kings Head to whom he owes 50 P^d. Also Mr. Custance told me that Walker should say that he was coming over to my House for a few Days, was to be married to Betsy Davy very soon, that I was her Guardian and he was to have her fortune of me directly on the Marriage &c. I was astonished to hear such things, but not so much as I should otherwise, had I not been an eye-witness in some degree of his profligacy and extravagance. I have a long time given him up, his behaviour to me last Winter made me despise him utterly. Nancys encouraging him to come to my House after such behaviour has greatly lessened my esteem for her, as she shewed no regard for me. . . .

JANry **30, SATURDAY. . . .** Walker is talked of very much at Norwich, there are two Writs out against him, he is gone of but is supposed to be at Thetford at an Inn. . . .

FEB. 4, THURSDAY. . . . My poor Cow very weak indeed not able to get up. My poor Greyhound Patch died in the Night in her Kennel, she had fresh strained herself a Day or two ago, and hurt herself so much that she could not stand at all and groaned very much. Mr. Du Quesne made us a long Morning Visit and brought over his Violin and played a good deal. . . .

FEB. 5, FRIDAY. . . . My poor Cow rather better this morning, but not able to get up as yet, she having a Disorder which I never heard of before or any of our Somersett Friends. It is called Tail-shot, that is, a separation of some of the Joints of the Tail about a foot from the tip of the Tail, or rather a slipping of one Joint from another. It also makes all her Teeth quite loose in her head. The Cure, is to open that part of the Tail so slipt lengthways and put in an Onion boiled and some Salt, and bind it up with some coarse Tape. . . .

FEBry **27, SATURDAY. . . .** Briton heard at Norwich to day that Mr. Walker was not in the Castle neither could he be found out. He also said that it was reported that he was near £1500 in debt.

Yarmouth Jetty, *Alfred Stannard (1806–89)*

MARCH 3, WEDNESDAY. . . . Nancy had a Letter by Mr. Cary from Mrs. Davy of Foulsham relating almost the same bad Actions that Walker had been guilty of &c. I wish now to break of every Connection with Mrs. Davy and all her long train of Acquaintance. I desired Nancy to drop her Acquaintance by all means, which if she does not (after their Characters are so well known) she will disoblige me as much as she possibly can do, and so &c. Mrs. Davy in her Letter desires her to look for a House to board at in her Neighbourhood as she intends leaving Foulsham very soon. N.B. I dont think Nancy has had a Letter from her before for the last twelvemonth. Nancy's Character (being too intimate with Miss Davy) is not talked of so well: as she used to go with Betsy Davy and Walker to Norwich &c by themselves. They all spent the Day and slept at Mrs. Davy's at Foulsham when Mrs. Davy was gone from home. Betsys Character is entirely ruined by her indiscreet ways, many times out by themselves, suffered herself to go for his Wife at public Places &c. Walker even boasts (as people say) of his behaviour to Betsy and says the worst of things of her. He now proves to be one of the most profligate, wicked, artful, ungrateful and deceiving Wretches I ever heard of, I never liked him. I believe both Mother Davy and Daughter also to be very cunning, close and not without much Art. I never wish to meet them again at my House none of the 3.

APRIL 27, TUESDAY. . . . Rec^d a Note this Morning from Dr. Thorne informing me of the death of his Nephew Walker, and that he should be glad to have him buried at Weston on Thursday next. I returned an answer to it.

APRIL 29, THURSDAY. . . . Between 1. and 2. o'clock this Afternoon walked to Weston Church and buried Mr. Thorne's Nephew Robert George Walker, aged 23 Years. He was brought in a Hearse with 4 Horses, but from whence I know not. Dr. Thorne was present, and a young Man Son of Mr. Thorne of Kimberly, and a short Man (at whose house) Walker was at, were all that attended. My Brother walked with me to Weston Church. I had a black silk Hatband and a pair of Beaver Gloves. And the Dr. also gave me 1. 1. 0. There was not the least Description on the Coffin or any kind of Ornament, quite plain and uncoloured. At Quadrille this Evening won 0. 1. 0.

MAY 12, WEDNESDAY. I breakfasted, dined, supped and slept again at the Angel Inn at Yarmouth, as did likewise My Brother and Wife, Mrs. R. Clarke and Nancy. . . . In the Evening I called on Lady Bacon who is in Lodgings near the New-Chapel Yarmouth. I stayed with her about half an Hour. To a small Box Compass pd. 0. 1. 0. To a small Book with some Poems of Goldsmith 0. 0. 9. At a Pot-House on the Quay with my Brother amongst some jolly Tars, for Porter 0. 0. 4. For some Cakes at a Confectioners pd. 0. 1. 0. At a Hospital for old Sailors gave 0. 1. 0.

MAY 19, WEDNESDAY. . . . Mr. Love the Painter dined with our Folks to day in Kitchen, he being painting my Weather-cock.

MAY 26, WEDNESDAY. . . . Memorandum. Had the Weather-Cock erected in my Garden this Morning, and a very good effect it has there, looks very well indeed and handsome. The Pole painted a dark-green, and the Weather-cock black and gold. It is put in the middle of the first Clump of Firs on the right hand

Lady Bacon, Mrs Custance's sister

from the front Door of the House. . . .

JUNE 2, WEDNESDAY. . . . Mrs. Clarke very indifferent indeed, breakfasted in bed. Mrs. Custance made us a short morning Visit and took leave of our Somersett Friends. Mrs. Clarke rather worse this Afternoon—her Disorder is the Mumps or swellings of the Chaps. She could eat no Solids only spoon-victuals all day. I took a Walk this Evening with my Brother to Mr. Howletts and Mr. Girlings, but none were at home, so the Compliments are paid.

JUNE 4, FRIDAY. . . . My Brother and Wife, and Mrs. Clarke, breakfasted and dined with us at the Kings Head [at Norwich], and at 3. o'clock, this Afternoon, after taking leave of us, they went of for London in the Expedition Coach, from the Kings Head—a double-Coach. Mrs. Clarke but very indifferent with a swelled Face. It being the Kings Birthday St. Peters Bells rang most part of the Day and at 1. o'clock Lord Heathfields Light Horse were drawn up in the Market Place and fired 3. Vollies in honour of the Day. We also saw St. Andrews Hall and likewise the Mayor and Aldermen go from thence full dressed to the great Church to Prayers and a Sermon this Morning about 11. I gave to a Man at St. Andrews Hall 0. 1. 0. Shewed the Ladies also Bunns Rural Gardens and the Iron-Foundery this Morning. At parting we were all very low on the Occasion. Pray God send them a safe Journey into the West. . . . At 7. o'clock I took Nancy with me in one of the Hackney Coaches down to Bunns Gardens to hear a Concert and see some Fireworks. We stayed there till near 11. o'clock—the Concert was midling, the Fireworks very good. . . . There was very little genteel Company there, but as Nancy never saw any publick Gardens before, she was well pleased with the sight. Lord Orfords droll-dressed Militia Men at Norwich, red Cloth Slops and long white Trowsers. . . .

JUNE 7, MONDAY. . . . To Ross Bean, losing a good Horse, gave 0. 10. 6. Mr. Du Quesne gave him the same as did Mr. Custance.

JULY 15, THURSDAY. . . . To a poor Woman from Dereham by name Hall with a small Child with her was taken very ill with a violent Pain within her by my great Gates and was laid down in the road, I went out to her and gave her a good Glass of Gin and gave her sixpence to go to the Inn, but she did not go there but returned back towards Dereham. She is a Widow and belongs to the House of Industry near Dereham. I hope she is no Impostor. . . .

Lodge Gates, Weston House

Lane Scene, *John Middleton (1828–56)*

JULY 22, THURSDAY. ... Nancy very pert and saucy this morning.

AUGUST 3, TUESDAY. ... I thank God, had a tolerable good Night last Night. I drank but very little Wine Yesterday or to day only 2. or 3. Glasses. I used myself before and all last Winter to near a Pint of Port Wine every Day and I now believe did me much harm.

AUG. 28, SATURDAY. ... In shearing Wheat this Afternoon Briton cut off part of his left hand Thumb with the Sickle, owing in a great Measure to his making too free with Liquor at Norwich to day, having met his Uncle Scurl there who treated him with Wine. It bled very much I put some Friars Balsam to it and had it bound up, he almost fainted.

SEPT. 8, WEDNESDAY. ... Norwich Musick Festival begun this Morning. I did not go having had enough of the last Musick Meeting in September 1788—at which I experienced a great deal of uneasiness and for which it cost me besides about 7. 0. 0. It was a very good day for the Harvest.

SEPT. 17, FRIDAY. ... The young Woman Spincks (who lately had a Bastard Child by one Garthon of Norwich) called on me this morning to acquaint me that her Child is dead, died last night, owing it is supposed to her [having] given him a Sleeping Pill which she had of her Neighbour Nobbs whose Husband is very ill and had some composing Pills from Mr. Thornes, one of which Nobbs wife advised her to give her Child to put him to sleep whilst she was out. The Child slept for about 5 hours, then he waked and fell into convulsion fits wch. continued for 4 Hours and half and then died in great Agonies. If the Child died owing to the effects of the Pill, I believe it not intentionally given to destroy the Child as she always had taken particular care of him and looked remarkably healthy. I advised her to make herself easy on that respect. Mr. Peachman and Mr. Buck also called on me this morning soon after and talked with me a good deal on the death of the Child. They both think that the Childs Death was owing to the Mothers giving the Pill to it. I had no objection I told them of burying the Child without the Coroners Inquest, as It was possible the Child might have died without taking the Pill, however it ought to be well considered on for the public good. . . . I walked to Mr. Bucks and advised him and the Woman Spincks to inform the Father of the Child of its death and to send for Mr. Thorne to have his Opinion whether the Childs Death was owing to the Pill being given it, as Mr. Thorne made them. Mr. Buck sent immediately to Mr. Thorne. . . .

SEPT. 18, SATURDAY. . . . Mr. Thorne called here about Noon having been to see the dead Child and said that its Death was owing to the Mothers giving it part of the Pill. Soon after the Doctor went, the Mother of the Child Eliz. Spincks came here to know what to do, I told her to go to the Overseer (Emery) to send for the Coroner and inspect the Body before I could bury it. . . .

SEPT. 19, SUNDAY. . . . Few Farmers at Church this Afternoon on Account of an Inquest being taken by a Coroner from Norwich on the Body of Eliz. Spincks Boy. They were from 1. till near 5. on the above business. The Jury brought in their Verdict—not intentionally given by the Mother to her Child. This Evening between 6. and 7. I buried the Child (by name Garthon Spincks) in the Churchyard. . . .

NOV. 20, SATURDAY. . . . I buried about 2. o'clock this Afternoon poor Lydia Betts, Widow of the late old Richd. Betts. I did not know that she was ill, till she was dead. She was above 70. Years of Age, I was told. The Corpse was carried by my House, and what was remarkable a recruiting Party with a Drum and fife and Flag flying, passed just before all by chance—Drum beating and fife playing. They came from Lyng, Lyng fair being Yesterday in pursuit of a young Fellow who had listed Yesterday and had run away, and who shd. that young Fellow be but Barber, Mr. Hardy's the Mason's Lad, to whom I gave a Shilling to last Saturday, hearing he was a good sober Lad and particularly kind to his aged Mother. . . .

NOV. 25, THURSDAY. . . . Nancy repeated to me this Evening seventy two Verses taken out of a Magazine of some of the Kings of England from 1066 the time that William the Conqueror began to reign till 1737 when George the 2nd succeeded his Father George the 1st. She repeated them without missing one Word. I sent Ben after breakfast round the Parish to let them know that my Tithe Audit will be Tuesday. He returned about 4. in the Aft. pretty full of Liquor. Every Farmer almost asked him to drink.

DECEM. 9, THURSDAY. . . . About one o'clock took a Walk to Weston-Church and buried poor Henry Nobbs and Eliz. Atterton a great many People attended at their Funerals. Eliz. Atterton I buried first, the other Corpse not being brought, as soon as I had buried her, the other Corpse was brought to the Church-Yard Gate, and I went thro' the whole Service again after the first. Eliz. Atterton, was 56. Years old. Henry Nobbes, was only 25. Years old. Pray God they may be both happy in Heaven. May Almighty God everlastingly reward poor Henry Nobbes for his very, very great Sufferings here. His poor aged Mother attended at the Funeral and came to see me after with Tears in her Eyes to thank me for what I had done for him. But O Lord! not unto me but unto thy divine Goodness be ascribed all the Praise. . . .

DECM. 11, SATURDAY. . . . Gave Nancy this morning a green silk damask Gown, that was formerly my poor Aunt Parrs. . . .

DECEM. 13, MONDAY. . . . When I came down Stairs this Morning could hear no tidings of Ben at all, which still made me more uneasy. I then sent for Willm Large and sent him on horseback after him. And about 2. o'clock Ben with Willm Large returned and I thank God safe and well. Ben went Yesterday in the Afternoon with a Mr. Watson Steward to Sr. John Woodhouse to Kimberly Hall, where having made too free with the Baronets strong Beer, fell of his Horse coming home and lost her, so that he walked about all the Night after her and did not find her till about Noon, she was found at Kimberly in a Stable of Mr. Hares, a boy happening to see and put her in there. I ordered Willm Large to dine here and to have 2^s/0^d. Thank God! that Matters turned out no worse. Windy and wet and my Study Chimney smoak[ed]. . . .

Kimberley Stables

DECEM, 25, SATURDAY and Christmas Day. ... I read Prayers and administered the H. Sacrament this morning at Weston Church being Christmas Day. Gave for an Offering, 0. 2. 6. Mr. and Mrs. Custance at Church and at the Sacrament. Mr. Custance's two eldest Sons were at Church and during the administration of the H. Sacrament were in my Seat in the Chancel to see the whole Ceremony by Mrs. Custance's desire. My old Clerk J^s Smith, old Tom Cary, old Nat. Heavers, old John Peachman, and old Christ. Dunnell dined at my House on rost Beef and Plumb Pudding. I gave also to each to carry home to their Wives 1^s/0^d, 0. 5. 0. Sent old Tom Carr not being able to come as being ill, his Dinner, and with it, 0. 1. 0. I lighted my large Wax-Candle being Xmas Day during Tea-time this Afternoon for abt. an Hour. It was very mild thank God to day for this time of the Year tho' wet and very dirty walking. Nancy having herself new made the late green Silk Gown I gave her, wore it this Day for the 1st time.

1791

JANUARY 1st 1791, SATURDAY. ... We did not set up last Night to usher in the New Year, as it migh[t] be as well omitted and by the blessing of God hope that this Year may bring more pleasant Days than the last Year to me. Since our Somersett Friends left us in June last my Niece hath been almost daily making me uneasy by continually complaining of the dismal Life she leads at Weston Parsonage for want of being more out in Company and having more at home, tho' I enjoy no more than herself. It was not so in 1780. ...

FEB. 20, SUNDAY. ... I read Prayers and Preached this Afternoon at Weston Church—Mr. and Mrs. Custance at Church. I was rather out of temper this Aft. on Account of my Maid's (Nanny Kaye) Banns being not published this Afternoon by me, as she never mentioned it to me before I went to Church. Pray God! forgive me.

FEB. 22, TUESDAY. ... A Mary Noller of Felthorpe about 25. Years of Age and who lived with Major Lloyd one Year at Michaelmas last, came to offer here. She has a Mother and 7. or 8. Brothers and Sisters. I did not agree with her, but If I did take her I would let her know in a Week, if she did not hear from me, then I should not take her—I did not like her Appearance being of a bold Masculine Cast—Neither her home or Family. ...

FEB. 27, SUNDAY. ... I published the Banns for the first time between my Maid Nanny Kaye and Willm Spraggs of Attlebridge. recd. for publishing the same 0. 2. 6 which I gave to my Maid (Nanny) on my return from Church, and at the same time told her that I hoped she might repent not of what she was about to do. She is about 34. and he about 20. with an indifferent Character.

MAR. 7, MONDAY. ... Washing Week at our House and a fine Day. The small-Pox spreads much in the Parish. Abigail Roberts's Husband was very bad in it in the natural way, who was supposed to have had it before and which he thought also. His Children are inoculated by Johnny Reeve, as are also

Cottages with Washerwoman, *John Sell Cotman (1782–1842)*

Richmonds Children near me. It is a pity that all the Poor in the Parish were not inoculated also. I am entirely for it.

MAR. 8, TUESDAY. . . . Gave poor Roberts one of my old Shirts to put on in the small-Pox—His, poor Fellow, being so extremely coarse and rough, that his having the small-Pox so very full, his coarse Shirt makes it very painful to him. I sent his Family a Basket of Apples and some black Currant Robb.★ There are many, many People in the Parish yet [who] have never had the Small-pox. Pray God all may do well that have it or shall have it. . . .

MAR. 11, FRIDAY. . . . Mem. The Stiony on my right Eye-lid still swelled and inflamed very much. As it is commonly said that the Eye-lid being rubbed by the tail of a black Cat would do it much good if not entirely cure it, and having a black Cat, a little before dinner I made a trial of it, and very soon after dinner I found my Eye-lid much abated of the swelling and almost free from Pain. I cannot therefore but conclude it to be of the greatest service to a Stiony on the Eye-lid. Any other Cats Tail may have the above effect in all probability—but I did my Eye-lid with my own black Tom Cat's Tail. . . .

★ Syrup produced by boiling.

MAR. 16, WEDNESDAY. . . . Mr. Custance came (walking) to my House about six o'clock this Evening, he found us walking in the Garden, he drank Tea with us and left us about 7. o'clock. He gave me a Guinea to pay for the Inoculation of Harry Dunnells Children 6. in Number, which was extremely kind and good of him—The Parish refusing to pay for the same, tho' at the same time they agreed to the inoculating Case's Family and have had it done, tho' a Farmer and better off. All Mr. Custances Actions to the poor assimulate with the above, every one of them generous and charitable to the highest. Mrs. Custance just the same. . . .

APRIL 15, FRIDAY. . . . Quite a Summer's Day to day. All Nature gay. Turnips quite a dead Load upon the Land. Many are obliged to throw them into Ditches &c. I am obliged to carry many off from Carys Close.

APRIL 16, SATURDAY. . . . Mr. Cary brought my News &c. from Norwich. A Reward of 100 Pound offered on one of the London Papers for apprehending one Richard Perry (eldest Son of John Perry that formerly kept Ansford Inn) for running away with a Miss Clarke (about 14 Years of Age) from a boarding School at Bristol. Her fortune great £6000 per Annum.

JUNE 5, SUNDAY. . . . We had Green Peas for Supper this Evening being the first pulled this Season by us. Also cut the first Cucumber and gathered the first Strawberries.

JUNE 29, WEDNESDAY. . . . The News of to day, is, that the French King and Queen &c. are retaken and carried back to Paris. I hope that it is not true, tho' on Lloyds Paper.

JULY 21, THURSDAY. . . . Shocking Accounts on the Papers of dreadful Riots at Birmingham, Nottingham &c. on Account of commemorating the French Revolution the fourteenth of this Month. The Presbyterian and Independent Meeting Houses pulled down to the Ground and the inside furniture burnt, many of the Dissenters Houses destroyed, amongst the rest Dr. Priestlys, both Town and Country Houses burnt.

AUG. 2, TUESDAY. . . . My Servant Maid Nanny Golding had another Fit this morning, screamed out most hideously and so loud that Ben heard her in a Field beyond the Cover, where he was hoeing Turnips. I never heard so frightful a Shriek or crying out. She continued in the fit near an Hour and then went to bed with a violent headache, and there lay all Day and night. It frightned us all. I must part with her at Michaelmas. . . .

AUG. 7, SUNDAY. . . . Poor Love the Painter who lived with his Father at Norwich was buried Yesterday, he had been in a low way some time owing to his being very deaf, and one day last Week cut his Throat—pray God forgive him. He was a great Support to a very infirm and aged Father, and afraid that he might be reduced to want. He was a young Man of good Character and much respected, he used to be much at Weston House, and has painted some Rooms for me, and gilded my Weather Cock the last thing he did for me. I am sorry for him.

AUG. 14, SUNDAY. . . . I read Prayers and Preached this Afternoon at Weston Church. Sr Edmd. Bacon was at Church and the only Person in Mr. Custances Seat. There was a large Congregation at Church. Poor old Js. Smith my Clerk made a shocking hand of it in singing this Afternoon at Church, much laughed at. Dinner to day, Fillett of Veal rosted.

SEP. 12, MONDAY. . . . Gave my Servant-Maid, Nanny Golding, warning this Morning to leave my Service at Michaelmas next, on Account of her being subject to bad fits. I was sorry to do it, as she was or at least appeared to be, a very good Servant. I should have been glad to have kept her—if I could, but fits are dreadful, they are so very alarming and come on so suddenly. . . .

OCTOB. 12, WEDNESDAY. . . . I paid my Maid Nanny Golding this Morning her half Years Wages due Oct. 10, 2. 12. 6. And about 2. o'clock this Afternoon her Mother came after her and she returned with her to her own home. . . . Pray God! she might get better of the fits. Since she has taken Assafœtida Drops by my desire she has not had a fit since. I gave her the remaining part of a bottle to carry home. My new Maid Winfred Budery came home this Evening about 5 o'clock. I hope she will do. Dinner to [day] a Couple of rost Chicken and Piggs Face and a broiled blade bone of Veal.

NOV. 6, SUNDAY. . . . I privately named a spurious Child of Mary Younges by John Bridges this Morn' at my House. I read Prayers and Preached, christened a Child of John Hubbard's, and buried one James Thacker of the Parish of Lyng, this Afternoon at Weston Church. I had a very large Congregation at Church. Mr. Custance with his two Daughters at Church. I did not take any thing for burying the young Man, tho' he did not belong to the Parish, his Father being poor and willing that his Son should lie near his Mother. I would not even take the duty on Burials, but pay it myself. Neither did I take the duty for christening Hubbards Child. It was near five o'clock this Afternoon before I could get to dinner. We had for Dinner to day, Calfs Feet boiled and a Loin Veal rosted.

DEC. 6, TUESDAY. . . . This being my Tithe Audit Day the following People waited on me, paid me their respective dues and dined and spent the remaining part of the day with me, they left me about 12 o'clock at night, well pleased with their entertainment. Mr. Girling and Son, Mr. Peachman, Mr. Howlett, John Baker, Jonas Silvey, Henry Case, Js. Pegg, Robt. Emeris, Stephen Andrews, Hugh Bush, Willm. Bidewell, John Buck, John Norton, Thos. Reynolds Junr., John Culley, Charles Hardy, Henry Rising, Thos. Cary, and John Heavers. Widow Pratts Son James came soon after dinner and paid me for his Mother. He came quite drunk and behaved very impudently. Stephen Andrews and Billy Bidewell rather full. Billy Bidewell paid me for a Calf which he is to have of me in a few Days, 0. 10. 6. Recd. for Tithe to day about 285. 0. 0. I gave them for Dinner a Surloin of Beef rosted, Sliff-Marrow-Bone of Beef boiled, a boiled Leg of Mutton and Caper-Sauce, a Couple of Rabbits and Onion Sauce, Some salt Fish boiled and Parsnips, and Egg Sauce with plenty of plumb-Puddings and plain ditto. They spoke highly in favour of my strong Beer, they never drank any better they said. Paid Stephen Andrews for Carr[iage] of Coal, 0. 15. 0. Paid Ditto, for 1½^d Rate to the Church 0. 2. 0. Recd. of Ditto, my last Visitation Fee,

0. 2. 6. Mr. Howlett was very dull and dejected. There was drank, six Bottles of Rum which made three Bowls of Punch, four Bottles of Port Wine, besides strong-Beer. No Punch or Wine suffered in Kitchen. . . .

DEC. 12, MONDAY. . . . Norton and Bush had some Words I heard to day at my Tithe Audit in the Kitchen, which was never mentioned to me before or known by me till Norton himself came and told me this Morn' he having applied to Mr. Custance for a Warrant against Bush for assaulting him. Mr. Custance told him to come to me. I advised him to make it up with Bush. Norton is in one of his crazy fits. It vexed me to hear of it. I thought all was harmony and Mirth that Night in the Kitchen.

DEC. 25, SUNDAY and Xmas Day. . . . This being Christmas I walked to Church this Morning and read Prayers and administered the Holy Sacrament to 22 Communicants. Gave for an Offering at the Altar 0. 2. 6. None from Weston House at Church this Morn' the Weather being very cold, wet and windy and extreme bad Walking, being all Ice under [foot]. My Foot extremely painful, hard Matter to get to and from Church, but thank God I went thro' it all better than I expected. . . .

Pastoral Scene, *George Vincent (1796–1831)*

The River Wensum, Norwich, *Henry Ninham (1793–1874)*

1792

JANY. 1ST, 1792, SUNDAY. . . . My Foot (blessed be God for it) is much better. I walked to Church quite trig, but have not as yet left of my great Shoe lined with bays [baize] and still sleep with a worsted gauze-Stocking on that foot, which I think have done good. . . .

JANY. 3, TUESDAY. . . . Master Custance with his two Brothers, George and William made us a morning Visit, stayed about half an Hour with us, and then I took a Walk back with them to Weston House and there privately baptized Mrs. Custance's last Child (Born on Christmas Day last) by name Charlotte. I was ready dressed and just going to take a Walk to Weston-House as the young Gentlemen came. Poor Mrs. Custance still extremely ill, not able to move. Mr. Custance most unhappy abt. it tho' Mr. Martineau says, he sees no danger. Pray God Almighty restore her to her former Health soon, is the earnest Prayers and Wishes of her many many Friends, particularly to her dearest Friend and deservedly so, my much ever respected Squire Mr. Custance. It is my daily, Morning and Evening Prayer, that she might get over it and that soon. Poor Lady Bacon I sincerely pity on her Sister being so ill. I never knew two Sisters in all my life testify more regard one to another more than Lady Bacon and Mrs. Custance, and I believe them to be as good Women in every respect as England ever produced. . . .

JANRY. 10, TUESDAY. . . . Mrs. Custance still mending for the better, thank God. Much better I am this morning, and had a good Night but am far from well nevertheless. Paid my Servants this morning their Wages, viz.

To Ben Leggatt a Yrs.	Wages due	Janry 6,	10.	0.	0
To Bret. Scurl	ditto	ditto	8.	0.	0
To Billy Downing	ditto	do.	2.	2.	0
To Eliz. Dade	ditto	do.	5.	5.	0
To Winfred Budery, a Qrs.	Wages due	Janry 6	1.	6.	6

... Paid Ben, Betty, and Briton with Norwich B[ank] Bills. Ben and Betty took them without the lest hesitation but Briton refused to take one, which hurt me, however some time after, he complied and took it.

FEB. 3RD, FRIDAY. ... I am neither well or ill, have at times strange feeling about me, cold streams running over my Shoulders &c. at times, and restless Nights.

FEB. 15, WEDNESDAY. ... Mrs. Custance sent her Coach and four after Nancy this morning to spend an Hour with her in her Room which she did and returned about 1 o'clock. She found Mrs. Custance better than she expected but nevertheless so bad as to be unable to move herself in bed or likely to do so perhaps for the next two Months, owing it is supposed to some violent strain in the back-bone on Child-bearing. In every other respect very well, can eat and drink heartily and now in tolerable good Spirits. ...

APRIL 24, TUESDAY. ... Mr. Jeanes called here this morning in his way to Mr. Du Quesnes, but did not dismount. A most gracious and gentle Rain in the Afternoon. Had a Tub of Gin brought this Evening.

APRIL 26, THURSDAY. ... We dined and spent the Afternoon at Weston-House with only Mr. Custance at dinner with us. We drank Coffee and Tea in the Octagon Room alias Mrs. Custances dressing Room, and Mrs. Custance being finely drank Tea with us, she looks very well considering her long Confinement. Tho' she is now able to sit up in a Chair, yet she cannot walk a step without great Assistance. This is the first time that I have seen her for the last four Months, No Gentlemen besides those of the Families have as yet been admitted to her presence, I was the first. ...

MAY 21, MONDAY. ... Sent Briton this Evening after Nancy [who had been staying a day or two with the Jeanes's] in my new little Curricle, she returned safe and well ab^t 8 o'clock, she met with a Storm on her Journey. She supped and slept at home. She gave me a worse description than ever of the bad management in

Farm buildings at Hockering

Mr. Jeanes House and dirtier than ever. Had not Miss Lloyd been there Nancy would not have liked it at all. Mrs. Jeanes more affected. Miss Lloyd told Nancy that she could not endure being there, as she is treated by them like almost unto a Servant, being ordered about so—And as for Mrs. Jeanes Brother Springer she never saw or heard so poor a *Honey*. . . .

MAY 30, WEDNESDAY. . . . Great Rejoicings at Weston House &c. Bells ringing, Guns-firing &c. on Account of Mrs. Custance coming down Stairs for the first time for the last 5 Months. I gave my People on the Occasion a bottle of Gin to drink this Evening in Kitchen. I am most heartily glad that Mrs. Custance is so much recovered, hope she wont make too free. . . .

JUNE 26, TUESDAY. . . . A little before 12 I walked to Church and publickly presented Miss Charlotte Custance in the Church—present Mr. and Mrs. Custance with all their eight Children, and Lady Bacon, the Sponsors were represented by their Proxies Lady Bacon for Miss Hickman, Mrs. Custance for Mrs. George Beauchamp, and Mr. Custance for Mr. Willm Beauchamp. Immediately after the Ceremony Mr. Custance very genteelly presented me with a five Guinea Note from Gurney's Bank at Norwich. We dined and spent the Afternoon at Weston-House with Mr. and Mrs. Custance, Lady Bacon and Mrs. Press Custance. We went and returned in the Coach. Dinner boiled Tench, Peas Soup, a Couple of boiled Chicken and Pigs Face, hashed Calfs Head, Beans, and rosted Rump of Beef with New Potatoes &c. 2nd Course rosted Duck and green Peas, a very fine Leveret rosted, Strawberry Cream, Jelly, Puddings &c. Desert— Strawberries, Cherries and last Years nonpareils.★ About 7 o'clock after Coffee and Tea we got to Cards to limited Loo at which, lost 0. 6. . . .

JULY 9, MONDAY. . . . Mem. A Stalk of Wheat (from a field that was formerly a Furze-Cover) I measured this Morning, and it was in Length six feet seven inches and about a barley corn. . . .

SEPT. 1ST, SATURDAY. . . . Mr. Custance made us a long morning Visit, he was on foot. He made us very uneasy by what he told us, which was, that they were going to leave Weston-House and reside at Bath in about a Month from this time, that their Children might be educated there. . . .

SEP. 15, SATURDAY. . . . Had a Tub of Rum brought me this Evening.

SEP. 16, SUNDAY. . . . We were much agitated this Evening about what I had brought me Yesterday. Bad reports about the Parish.

SEP. 17, MONDAY. . . . I got up very early this Morning and was very busy all the Morn in very necessary business.† . . . Mem. J^n/o Norton is supposed to have informed against his Neighbour Buck.

★ A variety of apples.
†Presumably hiding, perhaps even burying, his smuggled rum. By clause xxii of 19 Geo. III, c. 69, he was liable to a forfeit of £10 for each offence of buying smuggled goods, while the village blacksmith, as supplier, was liable to a fine of £50.

Fruit, *Eloise Harriet Stannard (1829–1915)*

OCTOB. 7, SUNDAY. . . . Our very good and worthy Friends Mr. and Mrs. Custance with five of their Children with two Nurses and Rising the Butler, left Weston this morning about 10 o'clock and gone for Bath. They had their own Coach and four, and a Post-Chaise. As we were walking in the Garden at the time Nancy saw them at the opening in Church Street, I heard them very plain. Their own Horses carry them to Attleborough, and there the Horses return with their Servants the drivers back to Weston House. Pray God bless them and theirs, and may every thing turn out to their most sanguine wishes. It made us quite low all the whole Day. It is a great, very great loss to us indeed. . . .

OCT. 12, FRIDAY. . . . John Buck, the blacksmith, who was lately informed against for having a Tub of Gin found in his House that was smuggled, by two Excise Officers, was pretty easy fined. Dinner to day boiled Tongue and Turnips and a fine Couple of Ducks rosted.

OCT. 23, TUESDAY. . . . Had a Tub of Brandy and a Tub of Rum brought this Evening. Gave one of the Men that brought it 1/0.

OCT. 27, SATURDAY. . . . To a Man of Bargewell (by name Brighton whose Father and Mother lately kept the Bell Inn at Billingford) who escaped this Morning out of Bargewell's Poor House being hardly kept alive there, the Allowance so very short, the House being farmed out at $1^s/6^d$ per Week for each

poor Person—I gave him as he appeared to be a very civil spoken Man and as one that once knew better days 0. 1. 0. He was going for London he said to his Wife who is a Housekeeper to some Person in Town.

NOV. 1, THURSDAY. ... My right foot worse this morning than yesterday. Mr. Jeanes was here this morning before I was stirring, tho' was down Stairs before 8 o'clock. ... Mrs. Jeans, two Daughters and Nurse were left at Weston Parsonage and there dined, supped and slept. Mrs. Jeans slept with Nancy in the best Chamber, with Miss Jeans on a Mattress on the floor of the same Room, and the youngest about 7. Months old with her Nurse, Susan Harrison in the Attic Story. We had for Dinner to day, some boiled Skaite, a Leg of Mutton rosted and Damson Tarts. For Supper one rosted Partridge &c. It is
rather disagreeable to be so lame just at this time—but
thank God! it is no worse.

NOV. 9, FRIDAY. ... No tidings of Mr. Jeans [who went to London on Nov 1] as yet, how long they stay with us cannot tell, they only begged to be taken in for 3. or 4. Days and now it is more than a Week— The Children particularly the smallest very great trouble, continually a fire above Stairs, washing, &c. &c.

NOV. 10, SATURDAY. ... As my Servant Lad, Billy Downing, was going to Lenewade Bridge after some flour for the House, he saw Mr. Jeans with a young Lady in a Post-Chaise, going to Witchingham, and the Chaise

Witchingham Parsonage

went thro' our Parish. Mr. Jeans asked him if his Wife was gone home, to which the Boy answered, no—however they went on for Witchingham Parsonage, and about 3 o'clock or rather after a Note came to Mrs. Jeans from Mr. Jeans with a Servant Boy and a little Cart to convey Mrs. Jeans and Children home. Accordingly as soon as they had dined, Mrs. Jeans with her two Children got into the Cart and went for Witchingham. The Nurse, Susannah Harrison was sent for afterwards by the same convenience, tho' rather dark when she went. I cannot say, but it was by no means genteel in Mr. Jeans to go thro' the Parish and not call. That they are gone, neither myself or Niece much lament—as the Children gave much unnecessary trouble, and Mrs. Jeans too much affected. . . .

NOV. 28, WEDNESDAY. . . . Much talking about Mobs rising in many parts of the Kingdom especially in Norfolk and in Norwich, a great Number of Clubs about the County and City, who stile themselves Resolution-Men alias Revolution-Men. A great many rich People it is said back them. It was also rumoured that there was to be a meeting of the County Mobs this day at Norwich. That

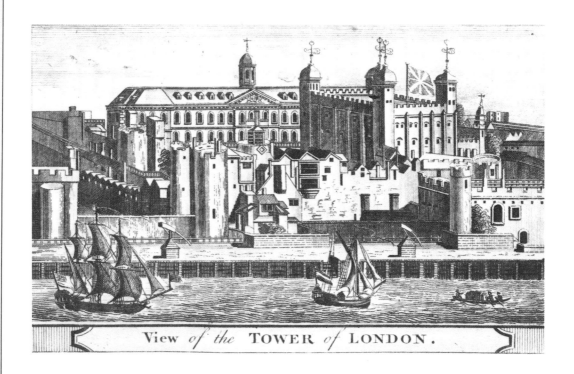

View *of the* TOWER *of* LONDON.

there were also great disturbances at present in London. . . .

DEC. 8, SATURDAY. . . . Alarming Accounts on the Papers, Riots daily expected in many parts of the Kingdom, London &c. &c. A fresh Proclamation from the King on the present Affairs. The Tower of London putting in Order— Double Guard at the Tower and at the Bank ordered. Some People unknown sent to the Tower for high Treason. Meetings held in London by the Lord Mayor Aldermen and Magistrates, at Norwich the same. Militia ordered to be embodied the ensuing Week. Meeting of the Norfolk Magistrates on Tuesday next at Norwich. Norfolk Militia to meet on Monday next, One Division at Yarmouth, the other at Lynn. Every appearance at present of troublesome times being at hand, and which chiefly are set on foot by the troubles in France. Pray God! however prevent all bad designs against old England and may we enjoy Peace. Parliament meets on Thursday next.

A view of Norwich Castle in the 1750s

DEC. 15, SATURDAY. . . . The Meeting at Norwich on Tuesday last was a very full one, almost all the Magistrates in the County attended, and very active measures taken to prevent any public disturbances from the different Societies or Clubs, respecting their late levelling behaviour. The Kings Speech in the House of Lords, a very long one, but very good one, much liked. Most parts of the Kingdom have had general Meetings respecting the present threatening and levelling Principles, and fully attended. And proper measures taken to prevent any bad consequences from the levelling doctrines, dispersed among the poorer sort of People, by seditious publications &c. of late so much spread abroad every where. Every thing carried on at Norwich at the above meeting without the lest appearance of Riot or Disorder, and in other places the same, tho' it was rumoured about that it was the intention of many riotously disposed People, to have a rising of them this Week at Norwich, thank God it did not.

DEC. 25, TUESDAY. . . . The following old Men dined at my House to day being Christmas Day. . . . It pleased me much to see the old Folks so happy as they were.

DEC. 29, SATURDAY. . . . Revolution Clubbs every where much suppressed and Constitutional Societies daily increasing all over the Kingdom. Levelling Principles and Equality almost discarded.

1793

JAN^ry 26, SATURDAY. . . . The King of France Louis 16 inhumanly and unjustly beheaded on Monday last by his cruel, blood-thirsty Subjects. Dreadful times I am afraid are approaching to all Europe. France the foundation of all of it. [France declared war on England on Feb. 1st.] The poor King of France bore his horrid fate with manly fortitude and resignation. Pray God he may be eternally happy in thy heavenly Kingdom. And have mercy upon his Queen, 2. Children and their Aunt Princess Elizabeth, all of whom by the Papers are very ill indeed in their confinement. Their lives are in great danger now of being taken away by the French Assassins or Ruffians.

JAN^ry 28, MONDAY. . . . Nancy not over nice this Evening.

FEB. 7, THURSDAY. . . . Mr. Custance arrived this afternoon about 4. o'clock at Weston House from Bath. . . .

FEB. 8. . . . Mr. Custance was so kind as to make us a long morning Visit tho' rainy most of the Morning. Mrs. Custance and Family he left well at Bath. Mrs. Custance sent Nancy by Mr. Custance a small present of Tunbridge Ware, a kind of Vice with a Cushion to pin work to at a Table. Also a large wooden Spoon and a four-pronged wooden Fork for dressing up a Sallad, quite fashion. Mr. Custance looked tolerably well after his Journey. . . .

MAR. 22, FRIDAY. . . . Got up this morning with a comical kind of a sore throat, not much pain, had something of it Yesterday, rather worse to day—

The Custances' town house in Bath

made use of Port Wine Yesterday pretty freely . . . Mr. Custance was so kind as to drink Tea and Coffee with us this Afternoon, and stayed till near nine in the Evening, he sets off for Bath soon. Whilst Mr. Custance was here, was seized with a violent pain in the small of my back, which continued the whole Evening, could not move from my Chair without great pain. . . .

APRIL 5, FRIDAY. . . . Mr. Peachman called on me this morning to shew me what was collected already on the Petition that I drew up for poor Peachman and his Wife on the late Fire. There was collected upwards of 7. 0. 0. Rec^d of my Butcher, Stouton, for Tallow, 1. 6. Called this morning at Mr. Carys, and found the old Gentleman almost at his last gasp. Totally senseless with rattlings in his Throat. Dinner to day boiled Beef and Rabbit rosted. Poor old Mr. Cary died this Afternoon.

APRIL 22, MONDAY. . . . Between eleven and twelve this Morning I drove Nancy over to Mr. Du Quesnes in my Curricle and we spent an Hour with him at Berries Hall and returned home to dinner. Mem. Not asked to Dinner, tho' we should not if so. We found Mr. Du Quesne tolerably well considering he has been ill lately. . . .

MAY 2, THURSDAY. . . . Mr. Du Quesne made us a long morning Visit in his one horse Chaise, came to meet Mr. Priest of Reepham as per Note to him, and from hence Mr. Priest was to return with Mr. Du Quesne to dinner. Mr. Priest however never came and Mr. Du Quesne returned to his own home to dinner, though we asked him to dine with us more than once. He complained much of being terribly shook about in his Chaise by the badness of the roads more particularly those of his own Parish. Mr. Du Quesne is very far advanced in Years but he will not own it. He is by no means fit to drive a single Horse Chaise. His Servant Man that came on horseback with him, was afraid that he would overturn coming along, he cannot see the ruts distinctly, he will not however wear Spectacles at all. He cannot bear to appear old, but must be as young in anything as the youngest Person.

JUNE 26, WEDNESDAY. We breakfasted, dined, supped & slept at the Angel Inn [in London]. Soon after breakfast Mr. Saml. Woodforde joined us and being fine Weather we all walked to Leicester Fields, and there saw the Panorama, a fine deception in painting of the British & Russian Fleets at Spithead in the Year [?]. It was well worth seeing indeed, only one Shilling apiece, I pd. 0. 3. 0. We stayed about an Hour there, Company continually going to see it. We called at Samuel's Lodgings in Tavistock Row, Covent Garden, and saw his Paintings—very good Picture of Caractacus &c. At Reeves Hosiery Warehouse in the Strand early this Morning for a pair of Boot Stockings, pd. 0. 4. 6. For a brown travelling worsted Cap, pd. 0. 4. 0. For a Cotton & worsted shaving Cap, pd. 0. 2. 3. For a Silk Purse at the same Shop, pd. 0. 2. 0. For a Caracature of Charles Fox, pd. 0. 2. 0. Mr. Saml. Woodforde dined, supped and spent the Evening with us at the Angel. After Coffee and Tea this Evening we walked to the Theatre in the Haymarket and there saw performed a Comedy called Ways and Means, with the Entertainment of Peeping Tom of Coventry, for 3 Tickets pd. 0. 9. 0. We sat in the Pit and had very good places. It was near 11 o'clock before it was all over.

Nancy Woodforde

Tavistock Row, Covent Garden

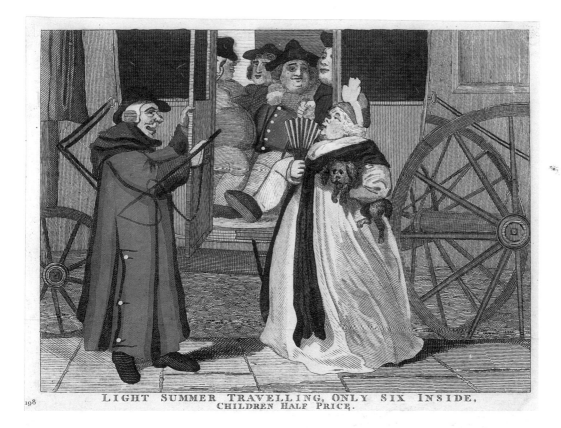

LIGHT SUMMER TRAVELLING, ONLY SIX INSIDE,
CHILDREN HALF PRICE.

JUNE 28, FRIDAY. We got up about 4 o'clock this morning and at 5 got into the Bath Coach from the Angel and set off for Bath. Briton on the top of the Coach. The Coach carries only 4 inside Passengers. We had a very fat Woman with a Dog and many band boxes, which much incommoded us, and also a poor sickly good kind of a Man that went with us.

JUNE 29, SATURDAY. We breakfasted at the Hart and after breakfast paid at the Inn for our Suppers last Night . . .

JULY 3, WEDNESDAY. We breakfasted at Roubelles and spent the Morning at Bath. About 1. o'clock we all set off from Bath in two Post-Chaises for Cole. Myself and 2. Nieces in the first Chaise. Mr. Pounsett & Sister in another. . . .

AUGUST 14, WEDNESDAY. . . . Had an unpleasant Letter this Evening from my Maid Betty Dade at Weston Parsonage in Norfolk, informing me that my other Maid Winifred Buderoy has turned out very bad, was with Child and so near her time that she was paid her Wages & sent away from my house which was very well managed by Betty. Poor Mr. DuQuesne rather worse than better.

SEPT. 26, THURSDAY. . . . We were sorry to see on this Days Paper from Bath that our very valuable and worthy Friend the Revd. Mr. DuQuesne of Tuddenham was no more. It is a very great Loss to us, but I hope to him, Gain. Pray God he may be eternally happy. . . .

The Mishap, *John Sell Cotman (1782–1842)*

OCT. 11, FRIDAY. . . . About 11. o'clock this morning we took our leave of our Cole Friends, got into one of Bruton Chaises and went off for Frome, got to Frome by one o'clock . . . About 2. o'clock we got into a Frome Chaise for Bath, but had not gone above 500. Yards from the Inn, going up Frome Hill, when on a sudden turn up the Hill we met with a large tilted London Waggon with eight Horses in it and very heavily loaden, and it being very narrow where we met it, the Driver of the Chaise in backing his Horses to avoid being drove over overturned the Chaise, but very providentially blessed be Almighty God for it! we received very little Injury, Nancys Face was a little bruised. It was a wonder that we escaped so well, as we were afraid that the Waggon would have crushed us. Briton got off his Horse & stopped the Horses in the Waggon, The Waggoner being rather behind. The Chaise Windows & pole were broke, we therefore walked back to the Inn, stayed about half an Hour till the Pole was mended, and then set off in the same Chaise for Bath. . . . [They stayed at Bath till Oct. 16.]

OCT. 16, WEDNESDAY. . . . About 8 o'clock this Evening we got safe & well to Oxford (blessed be God for it) to the Angel Inn in High Street, where we supped & slept. . . .

High Street, Oxford

OCT. 17, THURSDAY. . . . I called at New-College about 2. o'clock this Afternoon saw Caldecot and Mr. Cook who was last Year presented to the Living of Hardwiche, and also saw Mr. Sissmore who behaved very kindly to me. They desired me much to dine at College to Morrow. Caldecot shewed me the improvements making in the Chapel, which when finished will be one of the finest Sights in the whole University. . . . The high Street of Oxford greatly improved since I last saw it all paved like London, and I think is one of the finest Streets in the Kingdom.

On Oct. 19th the Diarist and Nancy proceed to London which they left on Oct. 22nd for Norwich via Bury.

Barn at Weston Longeville

OCT. 23, WEDNESDAY. . . . We drank Tea, supped and slept once more at our old House, Weston Parsonage. Whilst we were at Norwich I wrote a Letter to my Sister Pounsett informing her of our safe arrival at Norwich, & put it into the Post Office myself. Accept O Almighty God! my sincere & unfeigned thanks for thy great goodness to us, in our late long Journey into the West & back again, and all the dangers we have escaped, particularly for that great & providential escape near Frome in Somersett. Lord! ever make us thankful, and may thy divine goodness ever protect us. Travelling Expenses and others from June 23, 1793 from the time we left Weston to our return back again this Evening to Weston, amounted in the whole—78. 19. 7.

NOV. 4, MONDAY. . . . After breakfast I drove Nancy over to Witchingham being fine Morn' to Mr. Jeans's and spent the remaining part of the Morn' with him & his Wife. We met with Mr. Jeans in our Parish coming to us. Mrs. Jeans is far advanced in pregnancy. We stayed there till almost 2. o'clock, they pressed us much to dine with them, but there being no Moon and likewise some Rain falling we could not, but borrowed an Umbrella and Mr. Jeans's french Cloke for Nancy & returned home by three o'clock. It rained tho' very gently all the way. Dinner to day Knuckle of Veal boiled & Pigs face and a Neck of Pork rosted with apple Sauce. Mrs. Jeans was pressing for us to dine with them more than was agreeable. It was rather beyond the Line of being pleasing.

NOV. 25, MONDAY. ... Mr. and Mrs. Bodham made us a long Morning Visit, it gave us much pleasure to see them. Mr. Bodham looked poorly & complained much. Mrs. Bodham appeared rather thinner than usual. They were so kind as to bring us a profile Picture of our late worthy Friend Mr. DuQuesne. They eat a Biscuit with us & drank a Glass of Wine. I am much afraid that poor Mr. Bodham is not long one of this World, he is much altered. ...

DEC. 11, WEDNESDAY. ... My poor old Spanish Dog, by name Spring, was found this morning dead and stiff, under the hay Stack, worn out with age, being 14. Years old. He has looked very thin and poor some time. ...

DEC. 25, WEDNESDAY also Christmas Day. We breakfasted, dined, &c. again at home. This being Christmas Day I walked to Church this morning, read Prayers and administered the Holy Sacrament, gave for an Offering 0. 2. 6. Had a very respectable Appearance at the Altar to partake with me of the H. Sacrament, 2. Rails. The Singers sang the Christmas Anthem and very well, between the Litany & Communion. The following poor People dined at my House or had their Dinner sent them & one Shilling each—Widow Case, my Clerk Tom Thurston, Christopher Dunnell, John Peachman, Tom Carr and Nathaniel Heavers. Nat. Heavers & Tom Carr had their Dinners sent them being ill. Gave to the above People in all 0. 6. 0. Dinner to day, a boiled Rabbit and Onion Sauce, Surloin of Beef rosted, plumb Puddings and Mince Pies.

1794

JAN. 19, SUNDAY. ... Nancy made me very uneasy this Afternoon and does very often, by complaining of the dismal Situation of my House, nothing to be seen, and little or no visiting, or being visited &c. If we have of late lost our best Friends, by the removal of Mr. Custance's Family to Bath, and the Death of Mr. DuQuesne, must it not be affected by me as well as her? In short my Place has been too dull for her I am sorry to say for many Years.—As things are so— infoelix!★

JAN. 25, SATURDAY. ... The Barometer about 4. o'clock this Afternoon was down to 28—4, the lowest I ever remembered. The Wind so high that it greatly alarmed us. Part of my Barn uncovered by it, Thatch blown off, Many Tiles from my House blown down &c. Pray God: preserve all that are exposed to it particularly all poor Souls on board Ships. Dinner to day a Couple of Rabbits boiled and Onion Sauce, some beef Steakes &c. But the Wind was so very tempestuous at dinner time, that we made a very poor dinner. The Wind rather somewhat abated towards the Evening but still very high. Glass rather rose. I sat up in my Study the whole Night.

JAN. 28, TUESDAY. ... Thank God! had some tolerable Sleep last Night. Very severe frost indeed, freezes sharp within doors and bitter cold it is now.

★ Alas.

Tombland, Norwich, *John Thirtle (1777–1839)*

Two Women froze to death Saturday last going from Norwich Market to their home. . . .

JAN. 30, THURSDAY. . . . Had a very indifferent Night of sleep scarce any at all. . . . A Frost again but not so sharp as Yesterday. It did not freeze within doors last Night. Recd. for Butter this Evening at 1ˢ/0ᵈ, 0. 2. 6. It froze also in the Afternoon, and the Barometer still rising, but in the Evening it thawed and some Rain fell. I was saying before dinner that there would be alteration of Weather soon as I a long time observed one of our Cats wash over both her Ears—an old observation and now I must believe it to be a pretty true one. . . .

FEB. 10, MONDAY. . . . Between 11. and 12. o'clock this morning we took a Walk to Hungate Lodge, and paid our respects to Mr. and Mrs. Carbould, who came there to reside on Thursday last and were married that Morning at Talcolneston by Mrs. Carbould's Father the Revd. Mr. Warren, and was the first time of our ever seeing either of them. They behaved very friendly to us as well as politely and appear to be very agreeable, pleasant People. We were treated with Chocolate & Wedding Cake. Mr. Carbould is a Clergyman and Son of a Mr. Carbould, many Years an Hatter at Norwich of whom I have had many a Hat. He has retired from business about 5. or 6. Years, and with a fortune of at least 15. Thousand Pound. He has only two Children one Son & one Daughter. . . .

FEB. 11, TUESDAY. ... Mr. Custance arrived at Weston House this Aft. from Bath, after being absent almost a whole Year. I sent to enquire for him in the Evening. To a poor Man of N. Tuddenham out of work and a very cleanly old Man, gave this Morn' 0. 0. 6.

MARCH 7, FRIDAY. ... Sent a Note this Evening to Mr. Carbould at Hungate Lodge to invite him, Mrs. Carbould & Miss Carbould to dinner on Wednesday next. Recd. a Note back that they would wait on us. Note shockingly bad wrote.

MARCH 8, SATURDAY. ... Busy this morning in bottling off Moonshine. ...

APRIL 11, FRIDAY. ... One of my Greyhounds, young Fly, got to Betty Cary's this morning and ran away with a Shoulder of Mutton undressed & eat it all up. They made great lamentation & work about it. I had the Greyhound hanged in the Evening. ...

APRIL 12, SATURDAY. ... A County Meeting held to day at Norwich concerning voluntary contributions for the internal defence of the Country in the present Crisis in case of a french Invasion, or any Riots &c. I did not go to it, neither did Mr. Custance.

APRIL 22, E. TUESDAY. ... Hearing Yesterday that Mr. Mellish, who succeeded Mr. DuQuesne was come to reside at Tuddenham, I drove over to the old House and paid my respects to him this morning, stayed about half an Hour with him and returned home to dinner. Mr. Mellish is quite a young Man, fair with flaxen hair, rather short & lisps, very much of the true Gentleman in his behaviour. ...

APRIL 23, WEDNESDAY. ... It being a very fine pleasant Morning I drove my Niece over to Mattishall to Mr. Bodhams and made them a long Visit, but we returned home to dinner. Mr. Bodham is I think better, but worse than ever with regard to his temper, for ever scolding & finding fault.

MAY 31, SATURDAY. ... Mr. Custance made us a Morning Visit to take his leave of us, being going to Bath very soon. He seemed very low on the thoughts of quitting Weston. I was quite sorry to see Mr. Custance so dejected. I believe he goes from Weston to Morrow Morning.

JUNE 4, WEDNESDAY. ... It being the Kings Birth-Day, I put the Ship into the Lagoon in my Garden, full dressed ...

JUNE 11, WEDNESDAY. ... Sent Ben early this morning to Norwich with my great Cart, after my new Garden Roller of Cast-Iron. He returned home with it before two o'clock and brought some Maccarel which we had for dinner with a very nice small Neck of Pork rosted &c. It is a very clever Roller and is called the ballance Roller, as the handle never goes to the Ground. It is certainly very expensive but certainly also very handy. The Roller amounts in the whole to 4. 0. 0. viz.: Cast-Iron 2 cwt.—2 qrs.—26 lb., at $2\frac{1}{2}^{d}$ per lb. 2. 17. 6. Hammer'd-Iron, 40 lb. at $6\frac{3}{4}^{d}$, do. 1. 2. 6. ...

JUNE 18, WEDNESDAY. . . . Mr. and Mrs. Carbould called on us this Evening between Tea & Supper & stayed an hour or better with us. They came home from Norwich to dinner to day. They told us a good deal about the Guild as they were at it—A great many People but very few great folks. Mrs. Corbould met with a sad Accident at the Assembly last Night during Tea-Time. A Tea Kettle of boiling Water was by some Accident or another overturned into Mrs. Corboulds lap, but providentially did not scald her, she was obliged to leave the Assembly Room directly, and did not return any more to it.

JULY 17, THURSDAY. . . . Soon after Eleven this Morning I drove Nancy over to Mr. Mellishs at East-Tuddenham and paid our respects to Mr. Mellishs Mother and his Sister, we stayed near an Hour with them and then returned home to dinner—They are very genteel, and fashionable Ladies. . . .

JULY 25, FRIDAY. . . . I told Briton this Morning that I should by no means keep him after Michaelmas—He did not care for he could get a Place he did not doubt, if not, he had a home to go to, his Fathers. After breakfast, he walked into the Garden to work singing out very loud, which was very impudent.★ . . .

AUG. 21, THURSDAY. . . . Finished Harvest this Evening. I cracked my Parlour Bell this Evening by giving it a very gentle Touch with my little Stick, and which I had done many times before without hurting it. It fretted me a good deal, but not at all abt. the value.

AUG. 30, SATURDAY. . . . We made some Cheesecakes to day, the first we ever made and exceeding good they were indeed. . . .

SEPT. 1ST, MONDAY. . . . Herring, & his Nephew, Tuttle of Norwich & Peachman beat very early this Morning for Partridges all round my House, before

The Assembly Rooms, Norwich

★ Briton did not go at Michaelmas after all, though he continued in his bad habits.

The Cloisters, Norwich Cathedral

anybody else, shot several times, and about Noon came again & did the same, went thro' my Yard, but never sent me a single Bird. . . .

SEPT. 2, TUESDAY. . . . Herring sent me this Evening a brace of Partridges.

SEPT. 15, MONDAY. . . . Took a ride this morning in my little Curricle to Mr. Mellish's at E. Tuddenham, to make him a Visit after his return from London on Friday last, after the very late melancholy Event in his Family, the Death of his Mother, who was taken off very soon indeed, by a very violent Fever, she is much regretted by all that knew her. We never saw her but twice, once at Mr. Mellish's & once at my own house and that not above two Months ago, and then she appeared as well & in as good Spirits as I ever saw any Person. Pray God! she may be happier and send Comfort to her much distressed Family—As so good a Parent must occasion on her decease such sorrow as is not to be described or felt but by those that have experienced it—The Loss of my dear Parents I feel to this Moment, and never can forget it during Life. . . .

OCT. 7, TUESDAY. . . . It being a fine cheery Morning tho' cool, we got up at 7. o'clock, dressed ourselves, and about 8. we got into my little Curricle, and I drove Nancy over to Witchingham to Mr. Jeans's where we made a second tho' late breakfast with Mr. & Mrs. Jeans, the Bishop of Norwich Dr. Charles Sutton and his Chaplain, Mr. Thoroton a young Man, and half Brother to the Bishop

Landscape – A View through Trees, *James Stark (1794–1859)*

who married his Sister. We had for breakfast, Chocolate, green & brown Tea, hot Rolls, dried Toast, Bread & Butter, Honey, Tongue and ham grated very small. The Bishop did not come to Mr. Jeans's till 10. o'clock having mistaken the road. He and his Chaplain came in a Post-Chariot & four, with three Servants. About a Quarter before 11., we attended the Bishop to Reepham to Mr. Priest's, and when the Bishop had robed himself we attended him to Church in our Gowns, where he confirmed about 200. People. Mr. Priest, Mr. Jeans & self were with the Bishop in the Church, arranging the People in order as they came & the Chaplain recd. the Tickets at the Church Gates. It was all finished by two Clock, and the Bishop walked back to Mr. Priests, we attending him, and after drinking a Dish of Chocolate, the Bishop with his Chaplain drove back to Norwich to a late Dinner. A great Many Clergy attended on the Occasion, in their Canonicals, who most of them after their return from Church, went for their respective homes. . . . About 5. o'clock we left Reepham and drove to our respective homes. We left Mr. Jeans at Witchingham, did not get out being likely for Rain, which it did a little on the road from Mr. Jeans's, and lucky we had not more, for our Umbrella was clung so fast that we had a hard matter to open it when at home. . . . We got home safe & well, thank God for it before seven o'clock. The Rain that fell Yesterday rose the Water at Foxford & at Eads Mill quite high, Nancy very much alarmed & frightened therewith as it came almost into our little Cart. Every thing however passed over exceeding well to day and all conducted well throughout. Miss Woodforde much pleased with her Excursion and mightily so with the Bishop's very agreeable and affable, as well as polite & sensible behaviour.

OCT. 27, MONDAY. . . . Betty, both the Washerwomen as well as ourselves say that our Maid Molly is with Child, but she persists in it that she is not.

NOV. 2, SUNDAY. . . . I read Prayers & Preached this Aft. at Weston-Church. Had a pretty full Congregation at Church. My Maid Molly has declared herself with Child, more than half gone. Molly is with Child by one Sam. Cudble, a Carpenter of the Parish of Coulton, and he says that he will marry her—The Man bears a fair Character—However, in her Situation, it is necessary for me to part with her as soon as possible. To Morrow therefore I intend at present to dismiss her. She is a very poor, weak Girl, but I believe honest. . . .

NOV. 3, MONDAY. . . . After breakfast, I talked with Molly, paid her three Quarters of a Year and one Months Wages, which amounted in the whole to 4. 7. 0 and after packing up her things, about one o'clock she left my House, and walked off for Coulton where she is to be at Cudble's Father's, till such time that they are married. She says that Cudble made not the least objection to marrying her, she foolishly denied being with Child till the middle of last Week, and then obliged to, the Work becoming too much for her present Situation. I don't think that she is far from lying in by her appearance. For my own part, I have long thought her breeding. . . .

NOV. 17, MONDAY. . . . Mr. Maynard Rector of Morton called on me this Morning to ask my Advice, about one of his Parish by name Fisher, doing a kind of Penance next Sunday for calling Mrs. Michael Andrews, a Whore. He shewed me the form issued out of the Bishops Court. It is called a Deed of Retractation. A foolish kind of Affair between the parties, and the expences of which to both must be high. . . .

View towards Reepham

NOV. 30, SUNDAY. . . . Mem. a Primrose in my Garden in full bloom, seen by myself and my Niece.

DEC. 16, TUESDAY. . . . Brewed a Barrell of common Beer to day. Mr. Symonds of Reepham, cleaned both my eight day Clocks to day, almost the whole day after them, he breakfasted & dined with our folks. When he went away, which was in the Evening I paid him a Bill for cleaning Clocks & Watch from October, 1789, to Dec. 1794 1. 0. 6. cleaning my Clocks to day included in it. I did not take any change of him out of a Guinea. . . .

DEC. 25, THURSDAY, Xmas Day. . . . It was very cold indeed this Morning, and the Snow in many Places quite deep, with an E. Wind. About 11. this Morning I walked to Church and read Prayers & administered the Holy Sacrament. Had but few Communicants the Weather so bad. Gave at the Altar for an Offering 0. 2. 6. Immediately after the Morning Service so far as before the administration of the H. Sacrament I was attacked with an Epileptic Fit, and fainted away in my Desk, but thank God! soon recovered and went through the remaining part of my duty. Mr. & Mrs. Girling, Mr. & Mrs. Howlett, Mr. St. Andrews, Mr. Hardy &c. &c. were much alarmed and were very kind to Me, during the fit and after. The Weather being so severely cold, which I could never escape from feeling its effect at all times, affected me so much this Morning, that made me faint away, what I always was afraid off for some Winters past, having often had many fears. Mr. Howlett after Service, very kindly offered to drive me home in his Cart, but as I was better I declined it, however hope that I shall not forget his civility. . . .

DEC. 26, FRIDAY. . . . Thank God! had a pretty good Night last Night, and I hope am something better, but rather languid & low. Could eat but very little for dinner to day. Appetite bad. To Weston Ringers, gave 0. 2. 6. To Christmas Boxes &c. gave 0. 4. 0. Dinner to day, Calfs Fry & a Rabbit rosted. I drank plentifully of Port Wine after dinner, instead of one Glass, drank 7. or 8. Wine Glasses, and it seemed to do me much good, being better for it.

Furze Lane towards Witchingham

1795

JAN. 15, THURSDAY. . . . Got up this morning very bad indeed in the Gout in my right foot, could scarce bare to put him on the ground, and so it continued the whole Day and night, not free one Minute from violent pain. The Weather Most piercing, severe frost, with Wind & some Snow, the Wind from the East and very rough. We had some boiled Beef & a Hare rosted for dinner. I could eat but very little indeed for dinner to day. I had my bed warmed to night & a fire in my bed-Room. I never was attacked so severe before in my life. Obliged to put on my great Shoe, lined with flannel. The Weather very much against me besides.

JAN. 21, WEDNESDAY. . . . The last Night, the most severest yet, extreme cold. So cold that the Poultry kept in the Cart-Shed and obliged to be driven out to be fed. . . .

JAN. 23, FRIDAY. . . . The Weather more severe than ever, it froze apples within doors, tho' covered with a thick carpet. The cold to day was the severest I ever felt. The Thermometer in my Study, with a fire, down to No. 46. Very lame to day in both feet, but not very painful. Mr. Corbould made us a Morning Visit, very friendly. Dinner to day, odds and ends &c. Mr. Buck the Farmer brought us this Morning as a present an uncommon bird, shot by Mr. Emeris this Morning in Weston, not good to eat, called by what we could find out, a Pippet-Grebe, remarkable for the beautiful Feathers on his breast, like the finest white Sattin, with uncommon feet, about the size of a duck, only much longer Neck with a long sharp pointed bill, something of the Moor-Hen species, a smutty back.

Winter Landscape, Norfolk, *Edward Seago (1910-74)*

JAN. 25, SUNDAY. ... The French have taken all Holland, and the Stadt-holder the Prince of Orange with his Princess and Family, landed at Yarmouth & Harwich, last Tuesday & Wednesday, and are all gone to London.★ Dread & terrible times appear to be near at hand. Pray God! deliver us and send us an happy Peace. The Ice in the Pond in the Yard which is broke every Morning for the Horses, froze two Inches in thickness last Night, when broke this morning.

Yarmouth Jetty, *John Crome (1768–1821)*

FEB. 5, THURSDAY. ... Mr. Custance arrived at Weston House last Night from Bath. ...

FEB. 8, SUNDAY. ... Weather much altered, very foggy and a cold Thawe, with very small Rain, all the whole Day. I hope to God that now We shall no more have any very severe Frosts this Year. Barometer fell, Thermometer rose. No Service this Afternoon at Weston Church. ...

★ The frost was so intense in Holland that the French Hussars rode over the ice and captured the Dutch fleet in the Texel.

The Effect After Rain, *Henry Bright (1810–73)*

FEB. 13, FRIDAY. ... Whilst Mr. Corbould was with us this Evening, Mr. Girling and Mr. Howlett called on me and stayed about an Hour with us, they came to talk about disposing of the Money collected for the Poor. The whole Sum collected, amount to 43. 12. 0. which was very great indeed—Mr. Custance gave 10. Pounds—Mr. Howlett 5.£—Mr. Corbould 3. Guineas—Mr. Girling 3. Guineas—Mr. Emeris 3. Guineas, and many others 1. Guinea apiece.

FEB. 18, WEDNESDAY. ... Very hard Frost with strong Easterly Winds, a black Frost. Every Vegetable seems affected by it. As cold this day almost, as any this Winter. I felt it before I got up this Morning, pain within me. It froze very sharp within doors all the day long. Dinner to day odds and ends, but very good. Had a fire again in My bedchamber to night, tho' I had left it off some time, bitter cold to night.

FEB. 20, FRIDAY. ... This Day is said to be the most cutting this Winter. It snowed the whole Day, but small & very drifting. The cold this day affected us this day so much that it gave us pains all over us, within & without and were even cold tho' sitting by a good fire. ...

FEB. 22, SUNDAY. ... Severe, cold Weather still continues, froze again within doors. In the Afternoon some Snow. I am afraid now that we shall have more of it—The New Moon being now three Days old, and no appearance of a change. Gout much better. I fully intended to have gone to Church and done my duty this Afternoon at Weston-Church, but the Weather still continuing so very severe, and much Snow on the Ground, I thought too dangerous for me to venture to go into a damp Church and Walking upon Snow, having not left off my flannel lined second Gouty Shoes, therefore sent word to my Parishioners, that there would be no Service. ...

MARCH 13, FRIDAY. . . . Ground covered with Snow this Morning, having a great deal of Snow in the Night. The Morning was fair but Air very cold. A 4th Winter. . . .

MARCH 28, SATURDAY. . . . I slept very well (thank God) last night, my Ancle a little painful in the Morning early but not much. It looked in a fair way when dressed this Morning. . . . Mr. Thorne waited on me again this morning and looked at my Ancle, applied a Caustic to it just touching the part with it with a small kind of fine hair Pencil in a Quill-Case. He much recommended again the resting of it. . . .

MAY 15, FRIDAY. . . . Mr. Wilson, Curate of Ling, who has a Wife and a large Family, being exceeding poor and owing entirely to his own indiscretion & dissipation, called on me this morning to borrow 3. or 4. Shillings of Me. I let him have immediately a Guinea 1. 1. 0. Dinner to day—boiled Pork & Greens, Souce, &c. Sent Mr. Custance this Evening some Rasberry Puffs and some small Cakes, having baked to day. Sent Mr. Corbould about 2. Hndrd. of Hay this Even'.

Mattishall Church

JUNE 3, WEDNESDAY. ... I drove Nancy over to Mattishal to day about Noon, and we dined & spent the Afternoon at Mr. Bodhams, with him, Mrs. Bodham, & Miss Anne Donne, Daughter of the late Revd. Castres Donne who is about thirteen Years of Age, a very nice Girl. We found Mr. Bodham very bad indeed, much altered. As helpless almost as an Infant, being led about and also fed, besides being almost blind. He looks fresh, and eats and drinks heartily, he complains at times of violent pains, and very sleepy by day, but very restless at nights, is had out of bed often in the Night. Poor Mrs. Bodham does everything for him, poor Woman I heartily pity her, she bears it up wonderfully well. We had for Dinner a few Maccarel, some Veal Cutlets and a small Green-Goose & Asparagus, and some Gooseberry Tarts. No Potatoes, Greens &c. Mr. Bodham is very hasty & often swears at People. He is certainly at times deranged & talks wildly. Tho' he has been so ill & so long, yet is continually having Workmen about him & spends great Sums that way, in building up and pulling down, besides buying Carriages to go out in, but will get into none of them. We saw a prodigious handsome new full-bodied Coach, sent from London half a Year ago. He behaved very civil indeed to us & glad to have us. ...

JUNE 16, TUESDAY. ... After breakfast I got into my Curricle and drove to Norwich, taking Briton with me. We got [there] about Noon—And it being Guild-Day when the new Mayor is sworn in, there were great doings, the Court going in Procession to the great Church and from thence to the Guild-Hall, & then to St. Andrews Hall to dinner. Old Mr. Alderman Ives is the new Mayor, and it is the second Time of his succeeding to that Office. Some of the old time doings exhibited to day such as he did the last Time of being Mayor—A fine & curious Triumphal Arch of green Box intersped with many Flowers & variegated Lamps hung in the Centre of the Arch, near Mr. Ives's House and by St. Clements Church near Fye Bridge. At the Mayors Door there was a similar Arch with three golden Crowns on it and the Prince of Wales's Feather in the middle, of Gold, with a continual Firing of Cannon & Guns. Flaggs flying through-out the Mayors Parish &c. A vast Number of People at Norwich to day indeed. ...

JUNE 24, WEDNESDAY. ... About 9. this Evening we got into the London Coach from the Angel Inn [at Norwich] & went off for London. Briton went in the outside. We had four inside Passengers besides: one very stout Man of Norwich by name Hix, a Grocer, one Single Lady, and a comical Woman and a little Boy her Son—The Child sick most part of the night as was the single Woman. We dropped the Stout Man at Bury & took up a very agreeable one. We travelled all Night some Rain.

The Diarist and Nancy spent four nights in London and two at Bath where they dined with the Custances—and reached Sister Pounsett at Cole on July 1st.

JULY 15, WEDNESDAY. ... My Sister P. complains a good deal, more so than I think she ought. She eats too gross things, too rich for her Stomach.

AUG. 6, THURSDAY. ... My Sister Pounsett is greatly altered to what she used to be, she is vexing, fretting & complaining all the day long. Nothing can please her. The Folks busy in making Cheesecakes &c. to day. ...

AUG. 21, FRIDAY. ... This morning I partly settled Accounts with my Sister Pounsett, of Monies received and paid by her for me during the last two Years— She had received for me in all 95. 15. 6. Paid in all 44. 3. 8¾. Balance due to me

Triforium, Norwich Cathedral, *John Thirtle (1777–1839)*

from her 51. 11. 9½. Recd. of her in Bills & Cash the Sum of 42. 1. 3½. Remaining due from her to me 9. 10. 5¾. Dinner to day, Knuckle of Veal boiled, rost Beef &c. At Quadrille this Evening after Tea, lost 0. 0. 6. We had a very heavy Storm of Rain with Thunder and Lightning about dinner Time, but soon over.

AUG. 28, FRIDAY. ... After breakfast, I desired Willm. [Woodforde] to drive me over in his one horse Phaeton to Sandford-Orcas, where I have a small Estate which I have not seen for many Years ... We got thither about 12. o'clock, and viewed all the Premises. Farmer John Downe has taken to it, and has let one of the Tenements to one Thomas Marks, a Husbandman, and the other Tenement to one Saml. Bullen, a Carpenter. The whole has been put in very sufficient repair,

A late eighteenth-century map of Norwich

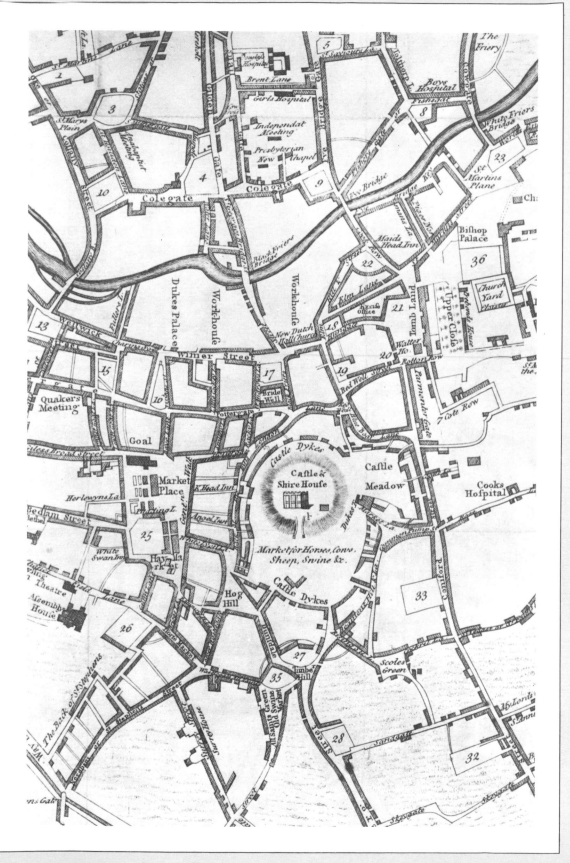

and a new blacksmith's Shop erected upon it, all done by the above Farmer John Downe, the Orchards near the Tenements have been dug up and set to Potatoes, which should not have been done. I did not see either the Farmer or his Tenants. I have recd. no Rent for the above Premises since Lady Day, 1787. Last Lady Day therefore had eight Years Rent due from my Estate at Sandford. . . .

SEPT. 8, TUESDAY. . . . Jane [his niece] behaved quite rude this Evening, I never saw a Girl in my Life of such a Disposition, she is never easy, & always disturbing other People.

A lane near Castle Cary

SEPT. 14, MONDAY. ... Farmer John Downe of Sanford Orcas my Tenant came to Cole about 2. o'clock this Afternoon to settle some Matters with me. ...

OCT. 3RD, SATURDAY. ... Caught a very large Bitch Otter in the Garden to day with a large Gin.

OCT. 14, WEDNESDAY. ... Sam. Pounsett told us three very remarkable facts this Evening of some wonderful Men. The first was, that he saw a Man who was a Soldier eat a hind-Quarter of Veal that weighed eighteen Pounds, a sixpenny Loaf of Bread, and drank three Quarts of Beer, at one Meal for a Wager. The Second was that there were two Men, that eat a Leg of Beef, bone and all, one eat the Meat and the other eat the bone. The third was, of a Man drinking half Pint Tumbler Glass of Beer and eat the Glass after it.

OCT. 15, THURSDAY. ... Had a very restless Night indeed last Night, very little Sleep and frightfull Dreams but short. Dreamt that I took out three of my Teeth, and my Sister Pounsett had taken out two of hers, likewise that my Brother John was terribly bruised. It was very hot in the Night, with Thunder, and Lightning and heavy Storms of Rain. ...

OCT. 26, MONDAY. I breakfasted & spent part of the Morn' at Cole—As did also Miss Woodforde. Sister White, my Brother & Wife & Mrs. R. Clarke also breakfasted with us at my Sister Pounsetts. About Eleven o'clock this Morning, Nancy and self took leave of our Friends at Cole, and sat off for Bath. ...

OCT. 27, TUESDAY. We breakfasted, supped & slept at the White-Hart. I took a long Walk early this Morning about Bath. ... About 2. o'clock I walked with

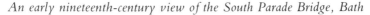

An early nineteenth-century view of the South Parade Bridge, Bath

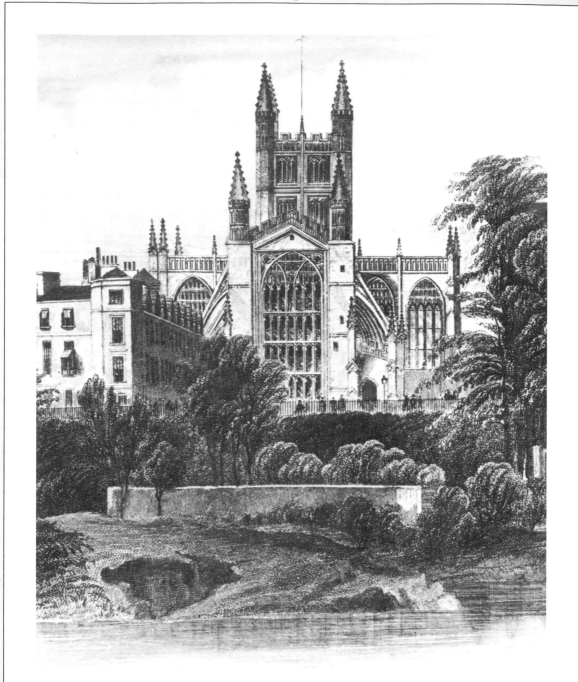

An early nineteenth-century view of Bath Abbey

Nancy to Portland Place where we dined & spent the Afternoon with Mr. & Mrs. Custance, their Children, Willm., Miss Custance, Emily, John, Neville & Charlotte. Poor Nancy was greatly chagrined & mortified going up to Portland Place which stands very high & the Wind much Power. The Wind was unluckily very high with some Rain just before we got thither, and directly opposite Mr. Custance's Front Windows, the Wind took Nancy's riding Hat & Feathers with a green Vail entirely off and was blown some little way, and her Hair tho' but just dressed, quite destroyed, the Family at Portland-Place, seeing it all. The Family were extremely glad to see us. . . .

OCT. 28, WEDNESDAY. . . . At four we got into the London Coach, and had two Gentlemen with us, one of them was a Counsellor Bragge Member for Monmouth & a Co-temporary of mine at New-College, as he did not acknowledge me, I did not him. It turned out a very fine Afternoon & Evening.

OCT. 29, THURSDAY. . . . At one o'clock I walked with Nancy to St. James's Park about half a Mile, where at two o'clock or rather after we saw the King go in his State Coach drawn with eight fine Cream-Coloured Horses in red Morrocco-leather Harness, to the House of Lords. The Park was uncommonly crouded indeed, never was known a greater Concourse of People before, and I am very [sorry] to insert that his Majesty was very grossly insulted by some of the Mob, and had a very narrow escape of being killed going to the House, a Ball passing thro' the Windows as he went thro' old Palace-Yard, supposed to be discharged from an air Gun, but very fortunately did not strike the King or Lords. On his return from the House to James's Palace he was very much hissed & hooted at, and on his going from St. James's to the Queens Palace in his private Coach, he had another very lucky Escape, as the Mob surrounded his Coach and one of them was going to open the Door but the Horse Guards coming up very providentially at the Time, prevented any further danger. The State-Coach Windows going from St. James's to the Mews were broke all to Pieces by the Mob, but no other damage done to the Coach. We had very difficult work to get out of the Park, the Croud still increasing, however at about 4. o'clock we got out thro' a narrow Passage between Marlborough House and St. James's Palace into Pall-Mall, and when we got to Charing-Cross in going up the Strand We Met such a Mob of the lowest Class that quite alarmed us, they were going to the Park. We crossed the Street under the Heads of Horses that were in the Coaches which stood quite close one to another all up the Strand. The Mob was composed of the most violent & lowest Democrats. Thank God the King received no Injury whatever, neither did we as it happened. Every Person attached to his Majesty was very much alarmed and concerned for him to-day. It was said that there were near two hundred thousand People in St. James Park about 3 o'clock. I never was in such a Croud in all my Life. By the Horse Guards the whole Area of the Parade was entirely filled up and all the Park quite to the Queens Palace very much crouded besides. Soon as ever the King got thro' the Horse Guards the Gates were shut as he went & as he returned. We were glad to get back to our Inn safe. Dreadful Work was expected to be done to night. Three or four of the Rascals that insulted the King were taken into Custody & had before Parliament. Both Houses of Parliament were very busy almost the whole night in consultation concerning the shameful Insult his Majesty received,★ but nothing done as we heard off when we went to bed which was very late to night. Dinner to day, Whitings & some Veal Cutlets.

The attempt on King George III's life, 29 October 1795

OCT. 31, SATURDAY. . . . His Majesty with the Queen and most of the Royal Family were at Covent Garden last Night, and very graciously received, God Save the King was played six Times—Every thing pleasant. Thank God! that they met with nothing disagreeable.

★ This scene of mob violence followed on a mass meeting on October 26th in Copenhagen Fields to present remonstrances on the state of the country. Prices had risen steeply and in the autumn and winter reached famine level.

A concert in the Covent Garden Theatre

NOV. 4, WEDNESDAY. We had I thank God! a good night of Weather all last night, good Lights to our Coach the beginning of the Night, and a good Moon early in the Morning. . . . About 11. o'clock this Morn' we got to Norwich safe & well, blessed be God for it. We stayed at Norwich at the Kings Head about an Hour then off in one of their Chaises for Weston and got home to Weston Parsonage between 3. and 4. o'clock in the Afternoon, and found all my Family well & all things in order—accept O Lord my Thanks for the same. . . . We drank Tea, supped & slept at our comfortable quiet, happy, thatched Dwelling. Our People had been expecting us some time.

NOV. 16, MONDAY. . . . Mr. and Mrs. Corbould made us a late Morning Visit. I engaged Mr. Corbould this Morning to be my Curate for the ensuing six Months, to begin on Sunday next, at the rate of thirty Pounds per Annum with all Surplice Fees. . . .

NOV. 22, SUNDAY Mem: . . . Mr. Corbould read Prayers & Preached for me this Morning at Weston Church, for the first time on being appointed by me for my Curate. He called on us as he rode to Church. We did not go to Church this Morning. Dinner to day, Neck of Veal rosted &c. Mr. Smith of Mattishall sent over his Servant Lad this Morning to enquire for us after our Journey. It is somewhat strange, as he has not sent a Servant to enquire after us for Years—No Note.

DEC. 1ST, TUESDAY. We breakfasted, dined, &c. again at home. This being my Tithe-Audit Day—The following Farmers &c. paid me their respective Composition and dined at my House afterwards . . . They all behaved remarkably well, and were all happy & well pleased with the Frolic. . . . Mr. Howlett was very indifferent indeed and went away very early, could neither eat or drink, appeared very feaverish all the time. His usual flow of Spirits quite gone. My Company to day, at least most of them did not leave my House, till after 2. in the Morn' but all parted then in very high Glee—Stephen Andrews, John Buck Senr., and Hugh Bush, very much disguised in Liquor. . . . Small Beer & strong, Punch & Wine as much as they pleased to make use off—Strong Beer amazingly liked and drank in great Quantity, six Bottles of Rum made into Punch, one Dozen of Lemons, and about five Bottles of Port Wine drank to day. They were all extremely well pleased with their Entertainment and very harmonious. . . .

DEC. 25, FRIDAY, Christmas Day. We breakfasted, dined, &c. again at home. This being Christmas-Day, the following poor People dined at my House & had each one Shilling apiece given to them by me 0. 6. 0. Old Tom Atterton, Ned Howes, Robin Downing, old Mrs. Case, old Cutty Dunnell, and my Clerk Tom Thurston. They had each a Glass of strong Beer after they had dined. The Holy Sacrament was administered this Morning at Weston Church by Mr. Corbould. It hurt me to think that I could not do it myself, but suffering so much the last Christmas Day by the cold, am afraid since to go to Church during the Winter Season. Nancy might have gone, but did not. It turned out a very fine Day indeed, no frost. Dinner to day, a Surloin of Beef rosted, a fine Fowl boiled & Bacon, & plumb Puddings.

At Weybourne, *John Middleton (1827–56)*

1796

1796, JANRY. 1ST., FRIDAY. ... Gave Nancy this Afternoon being New Years Day her annual Gift of the Sum of 10. 0. 0 but her pleasing me to day I added to it 0. 10. 0 which made it ten Guineas.

FEB. 5, FRIDAY. ... Mr. Custance arrived this Evening at Weston House from Bath. Mrs. Custance &c. left at Bath. ...

Squire Custance and his wife with Hymen, *Benjamin West (1738–1820)*

FEB. 9, TUESDAY. ... Widow Greaves Junr. who in the last Summer lost a Cow, waited on me this morning with the Petition that was drawn up for her on the Occasion with the List of the Subscribers. She had collected near Six Pounds, had bought another Cow for four Pounds, so that she was a great Gainer by her loss. I gave her, this Morning (as I happened not to be at home at the time) 0. 5. 0. ...

FEB. 15, MONDAY. . . . To one John Turner an old decayed Fisherman with a petition, gave 0. 1. 0. He was the Man that brought me once some very indifferent Spratts. . . .

MARCH 8, TUESDAY. . . . Very indifferent to day again, especially abt. Noon, very cold & trembled much, had a hard matter to shave myself to day.

MARCH 9, WEDNESDAY. . . . Very ill this morning, having had little or no Sleep all last Night, so very cold. A general Fast this Day. Mr. Corbould read Prayers only this morning at Weston-Church. Mr. Custance at Church, we were not. . . .

APRIL 3, SUNDAY. . . . Mr. Corbould called here this Morning in his way to Weston Church. I walked with him to Church, where Mr. Corbould read Prayers and administered the Holy Sacrament at which I was present. I gave for an Offering 0. 2. 6. It gave Me Much pleasure & Satisfaction in my Attendance this day on Divine Service. It was ever my greatest Pleasure to pay that homage to our great Creator which even only from Gratitude, it demands. It gave me also pleasure to see so many Communicants—25 or 26—present. . . .

APRIL 11, MONDAY. . . . Very cold, barren, growless Weather still.

APRIL 20, WEDNESDAY. . . . At 3. o'clock I drove Nancy over in my little Cart to Mr. Mellishs, and did not get there till 4. o'clock, owing to Briton's being on foot. Mr. Corbould overtook us near Mouses House and went with us, he being going to dine there. The Party we met there was Mr. Mellish, Mr. and Mrs. Eaton, Mr. and Mrs. Howman and Mr. Corbould. All the Company met within ten Minutes of each other. Dinner was soon announced after our Arrival, which consisted of the following things, Salmon boiled & Shrimp Sauce, some White Soup, Saddle of Mutton rosted & Cucumber &c., Lambs Fry, Tongue, Breast of Veal ragoued, rice Pudding the best part of a Rump of Beef stewed immediately after the Salmon was removed. 2nd. Course. A Couple of Spring Chicken, rosted Sweetbreads, Jellies, Maccaroni, frill'd Oysters, 2. small Crabs, & made Dish of Eggs. N.B. No kind of Pastrey, no Wheat Flour made use of★ and even the melted Butter thickened with Wheat-Meal, and the Bread all brown Wheat-Meal with one part in four of Barley Flour. The Bread was well made and eat very well indeed, may we never eat worse. . . . About half past eight we all took our Leave of Mr. Mellish and returned to our respective homes as we went, we got home about half past nine, as we went very slowly on Account of Briton's walking, who muttered very much about walking and when he got home was very impudent indeed, but I believe he had been making too free with Mr. Mellishs Beer &c. Mr. & Mrs. Howman are both high and consequential, the Latter remarkably so, if a Dutchess (by which name she is by some called) could not give herself more consequential Airs. Mr. Mellish is a very worthy Man I verily believe. No Affectation or Pride, but seems to have every good Quality that can belong to Man. I neither won or lost at Cards this Evening. Nancy lost 1ˢ 6ᵈ.

> ★ Probably this was a patriotic effort of Mr. Mellish's. Pitt was said to have
> suggested that people should eat meat to save bread—which was excessively
> dear.

MAY 6, FRIDAY. ... Billy Gunton, Brother to my Maid, and who at present lives at Michael Andrews being in a low way—I had some talk with him on it at the desire of Michael's Wife.

MAY 8, SUNDAY. ... By particular desire of Billy Gunton, & which I promised him on friday last, as this day to administer the H. Sacrament to him, himself with his Mistress Mrs. Michael Andrews, came to my House about 11. o'clock this Morning and I then had them into the Parlour and there administered the H. Sacrament to them and which I hope will be attended with due effects both to him, Mrs. Andrews & myself. I put on my Gown and Band on the Occasion. Mrs. Andrews appeared to pay as much Attention to Billy Gunton, tho' her Servant, as if it was really her own Son—very good of her. It gave me great pleasure, tho' far from well in doing what I did, as it will ever give me pleasure to do any thing in my power, that may give any satisfaction or ease to any person whatever, especially to the distressed. ...

MAY 10, TUESDAY. ... On going to bed to Night, our Boy Tim Tooley who was supposed to have been gone to bed was not to be found—All his Cloaths gone also. It is thought that he is gone to Norwich to enlist himself, as his Head has long run on a Soldiers Life. His being at Norwich last Saturday & then offered ten Guineas if he would go for a Soldier, determined him.

MAY 16, MONDAY. ... My late Servant Lad, Tim Tooley, called on us this Morning. He came from Norwich with a Cockade in his Hat, and says he has entered himself in the thirty third Regiment of Foot. Poor Fellow, he appeared happy & looked well. I paid him what Wages were due to him and half a Crown extraordinary, in all 17. 6. ...

MAY 26, THURSDAY. ... We took a Walk to Weston House about Noon and spent an Hour with Mr. Custance who is very low on the thoughts of leaving Weston very soon and going to Bath till next Year. ... Mr. Custance very genteelly and very earnestly desired that we would send at any time and the oftner the better for any thing whatever his Garden produced. Next to his Brother, he desired that we might be served. ...

MAY 27, FRIDAY. ... Tim Tooley, late a Servant of ours, but now a Soldier gave us a Call this Morning, he still continues at Norwich and continues firmly attached to the Army. ...

JUNE 4, SATURDAY. ... Still very rough, tempestuous Weather, not quite so much Rain. We are quite flooded in the Yard. I promised to send for Nancy this Morning from Norwich, but the Weather proving so very bad prevented me, tho' I wish for her home. I told Nancy before Miss Corbould on Thursday last, that I would send for her on Saturday. Miss Corbould was totally silent on the Occasion, did not express the least desire of Nancy's staying any longer. Miss Corbould they say, is like her Father, rather penurious and stingy. ...

JUNE 15, WEDNESDAY. ... I ... called at Mr. Corboulds, went in, but saw only a Servant, Mrs. Corbould and Miss Corbould were at home but above Stairs, but did not make their appearance, sending word down that they were

The Mill, *John Sell Cotman (1782–1842)*

dressing. Mr. Corbould Junr. was just walked out, it was said. Old Mr. Corbould I knew was at Weston. I never saw any thing at all of them all the time I was at Norwich which was till 5. in the Afternoon. I was obliged to go many times by their Door, my Cart being put up almost directly opposite their House, which is in St. Giles's. . . .

JUNE 25, SATURDAY. . . . This Morning about 9. o'clock, got into my Cart and drove to Mattishall to attend at the funeral of Mr. Bodham, an old acquaintance. I got thither about half past ten o'clock, and there stayed at the House till near half past two in the Afternoon before the Corpse was carried to Church. It was a very handsome Funeral indeed. Two mourning Coaches and four, one Mourning Chariot and pair, two Post Chaises, besides other Carriages. The Pall-bearers, were Mr. Smith, Vicar of Mattishall, Mr. Edwards, Rector of Hethersett, myself; Mr. Shelford, Rector of N. Tuddenham, Mr. St. John Priest, of Scarning, and Mr. Howman Rector of Hockering. We each of us had a rich black Silk Scarf & Hatband, and a pr. of  Beaver Gloves. Poor Mr. Bodham was fifty five Years of Age. Mr. George Smith, Curate of Mattishall, buried him. A great Number of People attended indeed. Chocolate, cold Ham, Veal &c. at the side Tables in the Room we were in, the best Parlour. . . . We returned back to the House after the interment, took some little refreshment, and then each went to their respective homes. I did not get home to Weston to dinner till 5. o'clock this Afternoon. I took Briton with me. He had a black Silk Hatband and a pair of Gloves. I brought Nancy a pair of the best white Kid Gloves which was orderd by Mrs. Bodham. Nancy had saved me for Dinner a few green Peas & Bacon, and some rost Chicken. I was quite jaded when I got home and very hungry. I was very glad when I got home, for I much dreaded the Day, my Spirits being but indifferent, thank God however, I got thro' it extremely well.

JULY 18, MONDAY. . . . Drew my great Bason in the Garden this Morn' after breakfast, and caught one very fine Silver Eel, which weighed two Pounds, drew out also several small Carp all which I threw back again. Not one Tench seen. In all probability The Eel eat the Tench. . . .

AUG. 7, SUNDAY. . . . Mr. Corbould read Prayers & Preached this Morning at Weston Church. Mrs. Corbould at Church as were Miss Woodforde & self. Mrs. Corbould was so frightened at Church by a Bat flying about the Church, that she was obliged to leave the Church. Nancy went out also to attend her. They went to the Parsonage where Mrs. Corbould stayed till we returned. Mrs. Howlett was at Church and exhibited for the first time, a black Vail over her Face. Mem. Times must be good for Farmers when their Wives can dress in such stile. . . .

SEPT. 10, SATURDAY. . . . We finished Harvest this Afternoon, and thank God! had a fine Time for it, & all well. . . . The Austrians have beaten the French smartly of late, killed 5000, and taken 2000. Serious apprehensions are entertained by many in high rank of the French invading England some time this Autumn. Preparations are making.

SEPT. 12, MONDAY. . . . I dreamt last Night that I was at an Entertainment given by Mr. Coke at his House, amongst other Dishes there was a Faun rosted but cold, and plenty of Hares rosted, and cold also, &c. Mr. Coke very civil to me, on coming away I lost my Hat, some one had taken it, & I thought a Soldier. I thought however that I bought a second hand one of old Mr. Corbould, with many other things, all forgot. A Raven fled over my House this Morning. All which tokens are said to bode no good. . . .

SEPT. 24, SATURDAY. . . . The Morning was cool. Afternoon fair. Evening cold with a kind of Scotch Mist. Dinner to day, Bullocks Cheek stewed, and a Neck of Mutton rosted &c. James Pegg brought our News for us to day, & likewise two Letters, One for me from my Niece Jane Pounsett, and one for Nancy from her Brother Saml. now at Stourhead. Miss Pounsett informs me that she and Mother had been lately at Weymouth for six Weeks, during the Time of the Royal Family being there, and that my Sister Pounsett was much better by going. And also she acquainted me that during her stay at Weymouth, a Mr. Grove a young Man & a Clergyman (and a quondam Admirer of Janes) had again paid his Addresses to her, and that she accepted of him & hope it will meet my Approbation. . . .

The Parson's Great Pond

OCT. 14, FRIDAY. . . . Mr. Girling with one of the Chief Constables by name Copeman called on me to subscribe my name to an agreement, to prevent Riots or any publick disturbances that may happen by being active in suppressing such. I told them that I heartily concurred in it, and would do all in my power, but did not think it consistent with the Character of a Clergyman to put his name to it, therefore I did not.

OCT. 28, FRIDAY. . . . Gathered in my keeping Apples this Morn' had but very few Nonpareils or Pearmains but a good many large Russetts, and seven Bushel-Baskits of the old true Beefans, so peculiar to the County of Norfolk. Willm. Thorogold, Gardner, here to day, to trim up, my Fig Trees & Vines, against rough Winds. Dinner to day, rost Breast of Mutton &c. Had one of my little Pigs killed, to have it rosted. Quite a cheeery Day but Air cool.

NOV. 6, SUNDAY. . . . The general talk is now concerning an Invasion from the French—Mr. Pitt having Mentioned in the House of Commons that he had substantial reasons for believing it, but such as at present improper to mention. As Mr. Pitt is prime Minister, it is much credited throughout the whole Country, and creates a general alarm. The Militia are to be doubled, and new Cavalry to be raised. . . .

NOV. 7, MONDAY. . . . There being a Justice Meeting to day at Reepham, respecting Militia Men, and those inrolled concerning this Hundred in defence of it, against any Riots or disturbances that might happen—I sent my two Men, Ben and Briton (whose Names were put down some time back) this Morning to

Reepham Church

Interior of a Barn, *Miles Edmund Cotman (1810-58)*

Reepham & there stayed all Day but returned in good Time in the Evening abt. six o'clock, with two black Staves in their Hands with a black Leather-Guard for the Hand, and on the Staff were painted these Letters in white and figures 58, 59. E. H. L. A., viz.: Eynesford Hundred Loyal Association.

NOV. 19, SATURDAY. ... No good News upon the Papers but rather the contrary on Account of the late Act for augmenting the Militia—Riots talked of very much about it—Rebellion said to be in Ireland, & the French at the bottom of it. ★

DEC. 24, SATURDAY. ... We were obliged to have Hulver-branches† without berries to dress up our Windows &c. against Christmas, the Weather having been so severe all this Month, that the poor Birds have entirely already stript the Bushes.

DEC. 25, XMAS DAY, SUNDAY. ... Mr. Corbould read Prayers & administered the H. Sacrament this Morning at Weston Church. ... He said the cold at Church was so great as to make him tremble again. ... My Appetite this very cold Weather very bad. The Cold pierces me thro' almost on going to bed, cannot get to sleep for a long time, We however do not have our beds warmed. Gave the People that dined here to day before they went, to each of them 1. Shilling 0. 6. 0. After they had dined they had some strong Beer.

DEC. 31, SATURDAY. ... Tho' very unfavourable the present aspect of public Affairs throughout Europe, at the Conclusion of the Year 1796—May God so direct the Minds of Men before the Conclusion of the ensuing Year, that a general Peace and every blessing attending it, may be felt in every Nation of Europe & over the whole World and whenever such Blessings arrive, May we all with one Heart & one Mind give our Most hearty thanks to that God for the same, and not unmindful of him Now or for ever.

1797

JAN. 15, SUNDAY. ... Mr. Corbould read Prayers & Preached this afternoon at Weston-Church, he called on us as he went, and told us that one of his Pointer Dogs, by name Tony, was gone mad and had got out in the Night when confined by making a Hole in the door, after loosening his Chain, and went over great part of the Parish & the Parish of Ling, biting many dogs, Pigs, &c. But was killed this Morning at Mr. Corboulds, as he returned home. Mr. Corbould hung all his Greyhounds & other Dogs immediately, except a favourite Pointer by name Juno, which is close confined & Antidotes given her, and is to be removed to Bracon, soon. The mischief done by the Dog, as known, is this, 2. Piggs of Mr.

★ There was no actual rebellion in Ireland at this time, but the country, specially Ulster, was seething with discontent.

† Holly.

Howletts, Michael Andrews Yard Dog, Mr. Girlings ditto. 2. Pigs of Cases, and what is worse than all, is, that Jermyn's Son was bit in the hand—so far known, but what other Mischief has been done, God knows. I hope we shall not hear of much more. Mr. Corbould is very uneasy about it. We did not go to Church, being rather dirty —c. . . .

FEB. 3, FRIDAY. . . . To a poor French emigrant Woman, very short, who came to my House this Morning to ask Charity, being in very great distress— gave 0. 1. 0. and also a Mince Pye & some Beer. She told me as far as I understood her (as she talked but little English) that her Husband with 2. or 3. Children were killed in the late Bloody Commotions in France. . . .

MARCH 1, WEDNESDAY. . . . Mr. Custance with his Son Willm. made us a Morning Visit, informed us, that a Proclamation from the Privy Council had been issued, to stop paying in Cash at the Bank of England for some time, fearing that if not stopped, there would not be soon enough to transact necessary & urgent business. On that Account, All Country Banks have done the same, and are at present shut up.★ . . .

MAR. 16, THURSDAY. . . . There being little or no Cash stirring and the Country Bank Notes being refused to be taken, create great uneasiness in almost all People—fearful what Consequences may follow. Excise Officers refuse taking Country Notes for the payment of the several Duties. Many do not know what to do on the present Occasion having but very little Cash by them.

MAR. 29, WEDNESDAY. . . . Mr. Thorne came to see Nancy [who had been suffering from a 'feverish complaint'] this Morning. He strongly recommends Port Wine and to drink rather More than less. She drank to day between a Pint & a Quart without having the lest effect upon the Brain. She has not drank less than a Pint for many Days. . . .

APRIL 10, MONDAY. . . . Very cold, strong E. Wind & cloudy—colder a great deal than Yesterday, the Wind being high. Last night I had but indifferent Night of Sleep, having very hurrying & frightful Dreams at times. Dinner to day, Peas Soup & some Beef Steaks.

MAY 13, SATURDAY. Had a very indifferent Night last night. This Morning taken very ill, could scarce get down Stairs. Sent for Mr. Thorne, who ordered me immediately to bed, having had a fit in the last Night and there I laid all night in a very bad State scarce sensible all the Night long. In the Night had a Blister put between my Shoulders which discharged very much indeed in the night and which made me soon better. But before that was put on was all but dead quite senseless. Nancy & Betty up with me most part of the night.

★ The banking crisis of February 1797 was due to a variety of causes: large advances to finance the war, made by the Bank of England to the Government, the critical state of affairs at home and abroad—on February 4th news reached Pitt of Napoleon's victory at Rivoli—the fear of invasion, which caused farmers and others in different parts of the country, specially on the coasts, to withdraw their money from the banks and hoard it.

The Gnarled Oak, *John Sell Cotman (1782–1842)*

MAY 20, SATURDAY. Had a good Night again last night thank God and got up very early. N.B. Sally [his maid] a bad Sitter up at Nights. My Brother & Wife from Somersett, came to us just before Dinner to day, and they dined, supped & slept there. They were much fatigued indeed. I was very glad to see them. Nancy had very properly informed them of my Illness. Dr. Thorne called on me again to day, found me better. Briton & Betty sat up with me to night.

MAY 22, MONDAY. . . . Somewhat better to day thank God had a tolerable night.

Memorandum. Ben Leggatt & Sally Gunton sat up with me last Night.

The next four lines are crossed out but are just decipherable and read as follows: 'N.B. I have a particular reason for making this remark★ which made me uneasy—not to sit up with me on any account. Time will shew the cause of my Uneasiness and Suspicion.' The last line of the day's entry is not scored through and simply reads: 'Slept but very indifferent all the night long—rather uneasy.'

MAY 31, WEDNESDAY. . . . My Brother & Wife, & Willm. Woodforde breakfasted, dined &c. here again. Somewhat better, thank God this Morning, but very weak yet. I find by my Niece that I have been very dangerously ill indeed, quite senseless some times. I have been blistered and I do not know what I have suffered. Quite senseless at times, and in very great danger indeed. Dr. Thorne with me very often indeed & did me great Service.

JUNE 13, TUESDAY. . . . Mr. & Mrs. Custance with all their Family from Bath arrived at Weston-House about 5. o'clock this Afternoon. They went by our House in a new Coach & four Horses and a Post-Chaise with Servants attending on the same. Great Rejoicings on their Return to Weston made on the occasion. . . .

JUNE 19, MONDAY. . . . Very much vexed indeed on going up to Weston H. to see a Clay Pit of mine in the Field in the path thro which we go thither (occupied at present by Jn̄ Baker) so much Clay having been of late taken from thence by him & carried away, as to make the foot path very dangerous indeed for Passengers, in some places the foot path entirely taken away. I sent to him directly to leave that Glebe at Michelmas next—It greatly hurt me. In Parlour & Kitchen to day we had 14 People at Dinner. I was quite tired out almost before I got to bed to Night. Dinner to day, Maccarel & fore Qr. of Lamb rosted &c.

JULY 20, THURSDAY. . . . I find myself rather getting strength but very slow indeed. Have at times uncommon sinkings within me—tho' I constantly take Cake and a Glass of Port Wine every Morn' about 11. o'clock and strengthening Cordial twice a Day the first thing before breakfast and at 2. in the Afternoon being an Hour before Dinner—which I have constantly been taken for the last Month if not longer. Finished my last Dose this Afternoon and now am to drop it. . . .

★Presumably the remark about Ben and Sally.

AUGUST 12, SATURDAY. . . . Holland the Chimney Sweeper, swept my Study Chimney, Parlour ditto—and their Chamber Chimneys, with Kitchen and Back-Kitchen ditto—in all six. He had a new Boy with him who had likely to have lost his Life this Morning at Weston House in sticking in one [of] their Chimnies. I gave the poor Boy a Shilling. . . .

SEP. 20, WEDNESDAY. . . . Soon after breakfast this Morning, I made my Brother a Present of a twenty Pound Bank of England Note 20. 0. 0. I also desired him to accept of a ten Pound Bank of England note for Mrs. Woodforde to spend in Town 10. 0. 0. . . . I put on a flannel Waistcoat under my other, for the first time during my Life—and hope it will do me good.

OCTOBER 5, THURSDAY. . . . My Brother & Wife breakfasted with us and about 10. o'clock set off in one of the Kings Head Chaises from Norwich (wh. came here about 8. o'clock this Morning) for their return into Somersett. . . . Pray God! they may have a good and safe Journey to Castle-Cary. . . .

OCTOBER 10, TUESDAY. . . . Dinner to day boiled Fowl & Pork &c. Brewed a Barrel of Table Beer to day. Very weak indeed to day. No Appetite whatever. Unless I get better soon I cannot long survive it. Pray God! have mercy on me a poor, weak Creature. . . .

OCTOBER 15, SUNDAY. . . . Weaker this Morning than I have been yet. Scarce able to make a Walk of it to day. No Appetite still. Mr. Corbould did duty this Afternoon at Weston Church. . . . I eat some plumb Pudding for Dinner but nothing else. In the Evening thought Myself a little better. The Medicine that Mr. Thorne sent me seem to do good. For the last two days I have been very bad indeed not able to put on some of my Cloaths or pull them off. Great News on the public Papers, Admiral Duncan having completely beaten a large Fleet of the Dutch.★

NOVBR. 17, FRIDAY. . . . Thank God! found myself rather better this Morn' not so bewildered or so weak as Yesterday, Senses better & stronger—still however very, very poorly. Appetite better, made a very good Dinner considering what I have done of late. Eat pretty hearty of a fresh boiled Tongue & mash Potatoes. Smoked my Pipe this Afternoon better than of late. . . .

DECBR. 3, SUNDAY. . . . A smart Frost this Morning which rather affected me, but upon the whole think myself rather stronger than of late. Dinner to day, Neck of Veal rosted &c. The present times seem to prognosticate e'er long very alarming circumstances. No appearance of Peace, but on the contrary the French reject every Proposition of it and so inveterate are they against our Government, that they are determined to make a descent on England & the Taxes therefore on the above account are talked of being raised trebly to what they were last Year.†

★ The battle of Camperdown, fought on October 11th.

† On October 26th, 1797, the Directory had named 'Citizen General Bonaparte' commander-in-chief of the 'Army of England', and the troops already assembled on the western coasts of France were to be supplemented by reinforcements from the Army of Italy.

Street Scene near St. Laurence's Church, Norwich, *Henry Ninham (1793–1874)*

DECMBR 17, SUNDAY. . . . I found myself rather weaker to day than of late; but very little. I can eat pretty well and thank God sleep very well. Mr. Cotman [his new curate] did duty this Afternoon at Weston Church. It grieves me much that I am rendered unable to do it myself or to attend at Church being so very infirm. . . .

1798

JANRY. 15, MONDAY. . . . After breakfast I paid my Servants their Year's Wages due Janry. 5th. 1798 as follows.

To Benj. Leggatt, my farming Man pd. 10. 0. 0.
To Bretingham Scurl my Footman pd. 8. 0. 0.
To Betty Dade, my House-Maid pd. 5. 5. 0.
To Sally Gunton, my Cook & Dairy Maid pd. 5. 5. 0.
To Barnabas Woodcock my Yard-Boy pd. 2. 2. 0. . . .

FEBRY. 3, SATURDAY. . . . Sent Briton this Morning to Norwich in my old Cart after many things. He returned home about 4. in the After. brought a Letter to Nancy from her Aunt J^n_o Woodforde announcing the Marriage between my Niece Jane Pounsett and the Revd. Frederick Grove to have taken place on Thursday the 25th. Day of January last past, at Pitcomb Church in Somersett. . . . Mrs. Woodforde's Letter also mentions that the Settlement on Jane Pounsett is a very bad one & a very cunning one for in case she dies without Issue, every thing whatever goes to Grove immediately on her demise. . . .

FEBRY. 16, FRIDAY. . . . Paid John Reeve for 2. doz. of Port Wine 3. 6. 0. 13. Quart Bottles to the Dozen—an amazing Price indeed, 33^s/0^d per Dozen. In the Year 1774 we had Port Wine at New-College at 1^s/6^d per Qt. Bottle. A Pipe of Wine★ then to be had at about £30. pr. Pipe. Now it cannot be had under near £70. . . .

FEBRY. 19, MONDAY. . . . Michael Andrew's Wife called on me this Morning upon Mrs. Mann's Account she being dangerously ill and informed me that she was desirous of having the Sacrament administered to her on Wednesday next. I sent to Mr. Maynard directly to desire him to do it. A more officious, busy-bodied, Woman in all Cases relating to other People's Concerns I know not. More particularly when ill—a true Jobish Friend. . . .

FEBRY. 28, WEDNESDAY. . . . My poor Dog Rover, a Most sagacious & sensible Dog as I ever had, was found dead this Morning near his kennel, supposed to be poisoned, as at this time of the Year, Farmers lay Poison, on Account of their Lambs. It vexed me much, he being a favourite of my Dairy Maid, Sally Gunton, she could not help crying for him—she was very fond of him. He was as sensible a Dog if not more so, than I ever had.

★ A cask containing 105 gallons.

A Fine Day in February, Weybourne, *John Middleton (1827–56)*

MARCH 27, TUESDAY. . . . Gave my Maid, Sally Gunton, for sitting up with me when ill, 2. Yards of black Silk, being a hatband sent me by John Mann on the Death of his Mother. . . .

APRIL 6, GOOD-FRIDAY. . . . My Parishioners were much disappointed in not having Divine Service this Morning at Church as usual on G. Friday. Mr. Cotman promised me that he would attend this Day and declared the same last Sunday at Church. Mr. Custance with most of the Family with a great many of my Parishioners were at Church, and much displeased. It vexed me a great deal, as I told him of having Divine Service in the Morning of Good-Friday as usual on this Day. It hurt me very much to hear of it in my Weak State. . . . Dinner to day, Salt Fish, Eggs, & Fritters &c. Between one thing and another was made very uneasy.

APRIL 12, THURSDAY. . . . Mr. Ham. Custance called on us this Morning. Bottled off my last Mead this Morning, it filled twenty six Quart-Bottles—not so clear as I could wish. We were rather too late this Year in bottling it off. Dinner to day, Neck of Pork rosted, &c. By the publick Papers every thing appears on them most alarming not only respecting Great Briton but every other State in Europe, and beyond it—Oh Tempora oh Mores. I hope my Strength is increasing as I feel better to day.

APRIL 26, THURSDAY. . . . Js. Pegg called on me again this Morning with more Papers respecting an Invasion, the Names of all People in the Parish between 15. and 63. Years of Age &c. &c. . . .

APRIL 27, FRIDAY. . . . A Meeting of the Parish this Afternoon at the Heart, respecting a sudden Invasion from the French &c. what was necessary and proper to be done on a sudden attack. Mr. Custance attended as did most of the Parish—I could not.

JULY 1, SUNDAY. . . . There was no Service at Weston-Church to day, Mr. Cotman being gone to a Living of his in Kent which he has scarce seen yet. Dinner to day, hind Qr. of Lamb, not good tho' so lately recd.

JULY 15, SUNDAY. . . . Briton went to see his Friends at Reepham, came home drunk. Mr. Cotman neglected doing duty at Weston-Church this Aft. Many People displeased at it & it made me quite uneasy. . . .

AUG. 7, TUESDAY. . . . My poor Cow is a good deal better to day, Put her in my Garden. The old Gander very weak and lame and very poor indeed, had him into the Garden and gave him plenty of Barley. . . .

SEPR. 4, TUESDAY. . . . There was some small Rain this Afternoon, but did not last long. Never was known scarce ever so fine a Harvest Season. Lord! make us truly thankful & grateful for the same.

SEP. 15, SATURDAY. . . . The Rebellion in Ireland much abated. The French that have landed there have been defeated and the rest surrendered. The rebel Irish have most of them surrendered, and great discoveries made respecting the Rebellion there. It has been plotting & planning Schemes with the French for the last five Years, the Irish having so long been under French Principles.

Weston Longeville Church

View of Norwich, *Thomas Lound (1802-61)*

NOV. 8, THURSDAY. ... Very poorly and very weak this Morning as I was taken in a kind of fainting Fit, getting into bed, last Night. I had just time to open my Bed-Room Door before I fell down, wch. Miss Woodforde hearing, came to my assistance and our Betty also came soon after. I fell down and being so extremely weak could not get off my Breeches or get on my Legs. Dinner to day, rost Beef &c. Mr. Custance made us a Morning Visit, he had been to Mr. Townshend, alias, Lrd. Baynings.

NOV. 11, SUNDAY. ... Getting up this Morning I was taken very ill, with a giddiness in my Head, could not get down Stairs without Assistance (after some little time I got better)—owing to great Weakness & relaxation. Mr. Cotman being gone into Kent to a Living that he has got there, Weston Church was not served this Morn' as it ought to have been. Mr Cotman should have got a Substitute. It is not using me well by neglecting it. ...

NOVBR. 29, THURSDAY. ... Great Rejoicings at Norwich to day on Lord Nelsons late great & noble Victory over the French near Alexandria in Egypt. An Ox rosted whole in the Market-Place &c. This being a day of general Thanksgiving Mr. Cotman read Prayers this Morning at Weston-Church, proper on the Occasion. Dinner to day, Leg of Mutton rosted &c. I gave my Servants this Evening after Supper some strong-Beer and some Punch to drink Admiral

Lord Nelson's Health on his late grand Victory★ and also all the other Officers with him and all the brave Sailors with them, and also all those brave Admirals, Officers and Sailors that have gained such great & noble Victories of late over the French &c. &c. Miss Woodforde recd. a Letter this Morning from Richardson & Goodluck in London, informing her of her having a Prize in the Irish Lottery which was entirely done unknown to me. It was a 16th. Share in the Irish Lottery of a nine Pound Prize. She paid for the Share elevn Shillings & sixpence and she will receive for her Share only 11. Shillings and 3. pence, by which Prize, she will be out of Pocket 3^{d}. if not more when it is received. No rejoicings at all at Weston. I should have been very glad to have contributed towards some, if Mr. Custance had come forward.

Norwich market place in the early nineteenth century

DEC. 16, SUNDAY. . . . Nancy had two Letters this Morning . . . both very melancholy ones indeed, One was from Cole from Mrs. Grove at Cole, the other from Nancys Brother William. The former giving us the dismal Account of the Death of my dear Sister Pounsett on Tuesday last in the Afternoon of a putrid Fever at her House at Ansford. Nancys Brother did not mention her Death only that she was very dangerously ill. The melancholy News of the Death of poor dear Sister Pounsett made me very miserable indeed. It is our great Loss—but to her I hope great Gain. . . .

★ It was natural that Norfolk men should rejoice specially over the Battle of the Nile. Nelson had been born in 1758 at Burnham Thorpe of which his father was still Rector, and had been educated at Norwich Grammar School and at North Walsham.

DECBR. 22, SATURDAY. . . . Nancy had a Letter this Evening from her Brother William at Gallhampton confirming the bad News of my dear Sister Pounsetts Death and the unfeeling behaviour of her Son in Law, Grove respecting the burial of my poor Sister, none of her Relations invited to attend her to her last home. No Pall-Bearers & also even a Pall partly refused. From such unfeeling & base Hearts which Grove hath shewn to so deserving a Woman may we never more hear of such. What a miserable Prospect has my Niece his Wife before her! She would have him, and every device from her Friends respecting a proper Marriage-Settlement was thrown away upon her, So that Grove had everything not only all Jane's but her Mothers also—which now comes to him, every thing of my late poor Sister Pounsetts.

DECBR. 28, FRIDAY. . . . Frost last Night & this Morning & all the Day intense—it froze in every part of the House even in the Kitchen. Milk & Cream tho' kept in the Kitchen all froze. Meat like blocks of Wood. It froze in the Kitchen even by the fire in a very few Minutes. So severe Weather I think I never felt before. Even the Meat in our Pantry all froze & also our Bread. I think the Cold was never more severe in my Life. Giblett Soup & Piggs Fry for Dinner to day &c. This Evening, if anything, Frost more severe.

1799

JANRY. 19, SATURDAY. . . . Recd. a Letter this Evening from my Nephew Willm. Woodforde of Gallhampton in Somersett brought from Norwich by Mr. Custance's Servant. The Contents were mostly concerning the Cole Family, of the ill treatment of Grove to my late dear Sister Pounsett, but that she had made a Will and had given all she could give to her Sister White and her Family. It grieved me to hear so very indifferent a Character of Grove who married my Niece Jane Pounsett, and more so as he is a Clergyman—very unbecoming one. I was extremely sorry to hear he was such a Man.

FEBRY. 2, SATURDAY. . . . Still very severe Weather, much Snow & hard Frost. The Turnips have lost all their Tops and now look like so many large Bowls or foot-Balls. . . .

FEBRY. 3, SUNDAY. . . . The Weather more severe than ever with continued Snow all last Night and continued snowing all this whole Day with a good deal of Wind which have drifted the Snow in some Places so very deep as to make almost every road impassable—in many roads 15 feet deep. No Service at Weston Church to day. Such Weather with so much Snow I never knew before—not able to go to Jericho. Dreadful Weather for the poor People and likewise for all kinds of Cattle &c. &c. It is dangerous almost for any person to be out. Dinner to day a boiled Rabbit and Onion Sauce and a very fine Goose rosted &c.

FEBRY. 8, FRIDAY. . . . The very severe cold Weather that have so long prevailed, is to day if any thing, more piercing. I have felt it more to day, than any yet. Dinner to day, rost Beef &c. We want many things from Norwich, but am afraid to send any Servant in such bad Weather. Within these last few days have been afraid to go out of Doors by myself. Fear seems to have got great Power over me of late Days. Very fearful of being out of doors by myself having of late been very much afraid of having an Epileptic or falling fit—My Head inclining I have thought of late that way. It makes me very low indeed on that account. Mr. Custances Waggons returned home last Night in very good time, but had a most terrible Journey of it, but got home safe. They were four Hours in getting to the Turnpike Road at Honingham—The Road so deep. I am very glad that they got back all safe.

Norwich Fish Market, *David Hodgson (1798–1864)*

FEBRY. 26, TUESDAY. . . . Sent Ben, this Morning, to Norwich, on purpose to pay off two Bills for me, having been wrote to by the People, here mentioned. Messrs. Smith, Woolen-Drapers, and Forster, Taylor. I told Ben to take a stamp Receipt of each of them in full of all Demands having done with them. Dinner to day, a boiled Fowl & Pork & Beef-Steaks. Ben returned about 4. o'clock this Afternoon with proper Receipts on paying the said Bills. It pleased me much on the said Bills being paid but the remembrance of their being sent me by them, will not be by me so soon forgot having dealt with them for at least 23 Years. Smith the Mercer is a Presbyterian and I suppose, Forster, the Taylor, is of the same Persuasion. I have now done with them for ever for their late shabby, ungentleman-like behaviour. Fish at Norwich very scarce and very dear.

MARCH 22, G. FRIDAY. . . . Mr. Cotman called on me this Morning before he went to Weston Church to read Prayers being Good-Friday. He also wished to leave the Curacy of Weston at the expiration of the present Quarter. I cannot say that I was displeased at it, as he has been rather too inattentive to duty. Dinner to day, Salt Fish, Eggs & Fritters. I was rather a little giddy in my Head to day a little before dinner—but only a few minutes.

MARCH 31, SUNDAY. . . . Nancy had a Letter from her Brother William this Morning brought Yesterday from Norwich by Mr. Custance Servant—a most melancholy one indeed to us, as it announced to us the Death of our dear Friend my dear Brother John Woodforde, who died very suddenly at Mrs. Patty Clarkes

The River Wensum from Carrow Bridge, *Thomas Lound (1802–61)*

at Castle-Cary on Saturday last, having come from Bath. He came from Bath with Ralph Woodforde on the Sunday before, Ralph coming from Allhampton on the Death of his Mother—Ralph being executor. I sincerely pity poor Mrs. Woodforde my poor Brothers Wife for so dreadful a shock & not being with him at the time.

APRIL 2, TUESDAY. . . . Bitter cold again to day, hard Frost, but less Wind. There being but few sound Turnips, the poor Stock such as Bullocks, Cows, Sheep &c. are shockingly distressed, few Farmers have scarce anything to give them. Scarce ever known such distressed times for Stock of all kinds, nothing growing, no vegetation, every thing almost dead in the gardens, Beans & Peas &c. almost all gone dead. It is grievous to behold how every Vegetable is hurt— Not even a Daisy or any kind of flower seen. What dismal, dreary Aspect have we at present.

APRIL 19, FRIDAY. . . . To a poor old Sailor gave this Morning 0. 0. 6. I delivered this Morning my Income Tax-Paper to Js. Pegg in which I have charged myself 20£ per Ann.★ Dinner to day, a boiled Fowl & a Tongue &c. Very wet all the day long, but not very cold. Thank God! am not quite so nervous or fearfull as I was some time back but Spirits poorly.

APRIL 22, MONDAY. . . . Nancy busy to day in answering her Brother Willm. Woodfordes Letter. Rather low-spirited to day, all Family Affairs in the Country contrary to my desire or wish and those People which ought to be Friends by blood turn out the greatest Enemies on Earth.

MAY 6, MONDAY. . . . Saw the first Swallow.

MAY 26, SUNDAY. . . . Young Mr. Dade (who is to succeed Mr. Cotman in the Curacy of Weston) called on me also this Afternoon, and informed me that he would enter upon the Curacy of Weston by my desire on Sunday next. . . . I was pretty well to day, not so very nervous. Young Baker of Cawston was to have succeeded Cotman in my Church as Curate, but was very lately preferred to a Readers Place at Bury. I cannot say that I am very sorry for it, as of late I heard that Dr. Baker and whole Family are very violent Democrats indeed.

JUNE 8, SATURDAY. . . . I was finely to day, thank God, than what I have been for some days past. Appetite much better. Dinner to day, a boiled Codling & hashed B. Heart &c. A most heavenly Day, all Vegetation in the quickest growth and in the most flourishing State. Our News Papers did not come to day at all.

JUNE 19, WEDNESDAY. . . . Very cold indeed again to day, so cold that Mrs. Custance came walking in her Spenser† with a Bosom-Friend.‡ Neville Custance is a very chuff Boy indeed as I ever saw, seem displeased & cross with every

★Pitt's preliminary income-tax attempt having failed to produce the expected results, he repealed the Triple Assessment, and in January of this year introduced a direct tax on income from all sources.
†A close-fitting jacket or bodice named after Earl Spencer (1758–1834).
‡An article of clothing to protect the bosom from cold.

Cowherd and Milkmaid, *George Morland (1763–1804)*

thing—would not eat a bit of Cake when brought to him. Says little or nothing to any body and when he does speak, it is in a bluff and very rough & bluff way. He is not at all like his Brother or Sister in Temper.

JULY 16, TUESDAY. ... Rather more nervous and timorous to day. A Pigs Chop with Beans and Peas for Dinner. Fine Day for our Hay, almost all cocked.

AUG. 30, FRIDAY. ... Busy in carrying Oats to day, being a dry Day. A very late Harvest this Year indeed, we dont begin cutting Wheat till Monday next, if then. Last Year we cut Wheat on Monday Aug. 6th.

SEP. 25, WEDNESDAY. ... Just before Dinner, Nancy's Brother William from Somerset came riding into our Yard, and he dined, supped & slept here. His coming upon us to sudden affected us at first, but after dinner we were better. William slept in his usual Room. We had for Dinner to day boiled Eels &c.

OCTBR. 6, SUNDAY. ... Andrew Spraggs brought a Box for me this Morning to my House, which he brought Yesterday from Norwich, in which was a fine large Somerset Cheese, a present from my Nephew now with me, from a Relation of his Wife's at Mew near Stowton by name James Jules, a great Dealer in Cheese and employed for Government in that way and is getting a good fortune by it. It was a very kind Present from my Nephew. The Cheese was about a Qr. of a Hundred Wht. with the Kings Arms on the side of it. ...

DECBR. 10, TUESDAY. . . . This being my Tithe Audit-Day, the following People paid me their respective Compositions for Tithe &c. for the last Year to Michaelmas last. . . . They dined & stayed at my House, till abt. 11 at Night & went away then highly pleased. I did not see any of them the lest disguised. . . . It was the pleasantest & most agreeable Tithe-Audit, I ever experienced. Every thing harmonious & agreeable.

1800

JANUARY 24, FRIDAY. . . . Very busy all the Morning in looking over Family Accounts & Goods relating to Somersett that my Nephew Willm. Woodforde might take a Copy of the same with him into Somersett. After which I made him a Present of a Bank of England Note of 5. 0. 0. Also two Guineas, to be laid out in Town for things in remembrance of me to his Wife and Children—2. 2. 0. . . .

FEBRY. 25, TUESDAY. . . . The Price of Wheat being so very dear at present occasions very great grumbling amongst the Poor at this time, and makes them talk loudly. Three Pounds per Coomb★ for Wheat on Saturday last was said to be asked at Norwich Market. . . .

MARCH 10, MONDAY. . . . The same cold Weather still prevails, tho' fair. I made a bet with Nancy this Evening of 1. Shilling that it rained before to Morrow Night.

MARCH 11, TUESDAY. . . . It rained softly a good part of the Day, so that I got my bet with my Niece, but not recd. it. . . .

MARCH 24, MONDAY. . . . Nancy dined & spent the Afternoon and great part of the Evening at Weston-House, with Mr. & Mrs. Custance & their two Daughters, with their Sons Hambleton and William Custance, Lady Bacon with her Daughters Anne, and Maria Bacon, Miss Mary Anne Bacon from Devonshire, and Edmund Bacon eldest Son of Sr. Edmund & Lady Bacon. Nancy did not return till after 9. o'clock this Evening as the young folks at Weston House had something of a Masquerade-Ball this Evening. Dramatis Personae, Miss Custance in the Character of an Old Woman, Emily Custance a flower Girl, Devonshire Miss Bacon a Fortune-Teller alias Gipsy, Miss Bacon in the Character of a Fool, Miss Maria Bacon, a Ghost—None of the young Gentlemen acted at all or were dressed. . . .

MAY 9, FRIDAY. . . . Finely again this Morning before & at breakfast but being made uneasy soon after, was made quite ill again and very nervous &c. Poor Mr. John Buck was buried in Weston Church about Noon by Mr. Maynard. That added to my uneasiness also. My Maid Sally was invited to the Funeral as was also, my Man Ben Leggatt, both went. Ben was a near Relation to poor John Buck. Mr. Maynard called on me before the Funeral. . . . I told Mr. Maynard that he was to take 1. 1. 0. of the Undertaker, it being the usual Fee for burying a

★ This means the enormous price of £6 a quarter.

Person in the Church not living in the Parish, and that could be well afforded.

MAY 12, MONDAY. . . . Very cold indeed, to day—Wind ENE. Gave Nancy to day before Dinner a ten Pound Note of Kerrisons of Norwich, for the last Year due in January 1800 to her but did not give before, for Reasons of pertness. . . .

JUNE 2, MONDAY. . . . Our Maid (Betty Dade) taken very ill in the Night in her old Complaint, Hysteric-Wind Cholic. Very ill all the whole Day long—a little matter better in the Evening. We gave her Port-Wine and Water, Rum & Water, Lavender Drops &c. . . .

JUNE 22, SUNDAY. . . . Betty continues but poorly & weak still. Nancy thinks that it is owing to a Love Affair with my farming Man & Servant, Ben. Leggatt who hath for a long time taken notice of her. They have a long time been talked of. Whether he now slights her or not, I cannot say. I hope he hath not been too intimate with her. . . .

JUNE 27, FRIDAY. . . . I was finely to day thank God for it! and this Day I entered my sixtieth Year being born (old Stile) the sixteenth of June in the Year, 1740. Dinner to day, Shoulder of Mutton rosted &c. Accept my thanks O! Almighty God! for thy great Goodness to me in enabling me (after my Late great Illness) to return my grateful thanks for the same.

Weston Longeville Church

AUGUST 27, WEDNESDAY. . . . Our tame Hawk that we had so long in the Walled Garden fled away Yesterday and hath not been heard of since. The Lapwing also we had so long, have not been heard of some Days. Harvest quite at a Stand at present. . . .

OCTOBER 10, FRIDAY. . . . This being old Michaelmas Day, I paid my Servant Boy, Henry Daines, three Quarters of a Years Wages due this Day at two Guineas per Annum. 1. 11. 6. and dismissed him from my Service not behaving

in a manner that I expected from him, as he could not be trusted to do any thing if not overlooked, and also a very saucy, foul-mouthed Lad. . . .

DECBR. 11, THURSDAY. . . . A Man called here this Evening about 5. o'clock had Trowsers on and had he said been a Sailor. He walked as if he was lame, he asked Charity. He appeared rather a suspicious Character & that he had other

Wooded Landscape with Cattle, *Miles Edmund Cotman (1810-58)*

things in view than mere asking Charity, this time of the Day. I rather suspect of his being after Poultry. As he might however be in want, gave him 0. 1. . . .

DECBR. 22, MONDAY. . . . Yesterday being Sunday & St. Thomas's Day the Poor deferred going after their Christmas Gifts till this Morning, I had at my House fifty five, gave only to 53, the other two not living in the Parish. Gave in the Whole this Morn' at 6ᵈ each in Number 53. 1. 6. 6. Dinner to day, boiled Beef & a rost Chicken. I was but poorly to day after dinner, giddy &c. Sitting too long to day at one time I think. The Poor to day behaved extremely well indeed tho' times were extremely hard for them—They all appeared very patient & submissive. . . .

1801

JANUARY 31, SATURDAY. . . . Ben returned home from Norwich about 5. o'clock this Evening, safe & well (thanks to God for it) and brought me Cash for my Wheat from Mr. Bloome at 3. 15. 0. pr Coomb. 30. 0. 0. an enormous Price I must confess indeed and sincerely wish that it might be cheaper e'er long for the benefit of the Poor who are distressed on that Account—tho' much alleviated by the liberal Allowance to them of every Parish. Pray God! send us better Times and all People better. . . .

FEBRUARY 5, THURSDAY. . . . Very fine Weather indeed for the Season. Bees quite brisk. Crocus's & Snow Drops out in full blossom. Gooseberry Trees coming into Leaf very fast indeed.

MARCH 10, TUESDAY. . . . Gave my Niece this Morning 10. 0. 0. Mr. Aldridge called here this Morning with Cottons of different Patterns &c. &c. I paid him for divers things as under 3. 10. 11. Viz, 8. Yards of Purple and White Cotton for a Morning Gown for myself at ˢ2/3ᵈ 0. 18. 0. To 6. Yrds and ¾ Callico-Lining at ˢ1/4ᵈ. 0. 9. 0. To 2. Coloured Handkerchiefs for my two Washerwomen, Downing & Richmond 4. 8. To 2. Waistcoat Pieces for my two Men, Benj: Leggatt & Bretingham Scurl, of Woolen but of pretty Pattern, red, green & brown in stripes about one Yard in length, each pd. 0. 14. 0. To a Waistcoat-Piece for my boy Robt. Case also, about a Yard also of Woollen 0. 4. 0. So that I paid Aldridge in toto 3. 10. 11. He had also besides, both Victuals & Drink. So that upon the whole, he did not make a bad-Calling here this Morning and his obliging behaviour merited it also. Paid also to Alldridge (omitted before) for 2. Cotton Gowns for my two Maids of Pink & White 17. Yards at ˢ2/dᵈ. 2. 2. 6. . . .

APRIL 16, THURSDAY. . . . Mrs. Custance with her two Daughters made us a Morning Visit & stayed upwards of an Hour. Brought us great News, that Lord Nelson had taken several Men of War from the Danes, had demolished Copenhagen, a great Part of it at least. The Danes defied him. They have of late behaved very shabby towards us. The Emperor of Russia also is said to be dead supposed to have been put to death. He had long behaved bad towards England. . . .

JUNE 26, FRIDAY. . . . It being a fine Day, I had all my Hay carried, only five Cart Load from four acres, very well made indeed & without a drop of Rain. It makes but little Show but smells like a Violet.

JULY 14, TUESDAY. . . . Sent Briton this Morn' to Mr. Ansons of Ling after a Puppey promised me by him, and a very nice little bitch he sent me back of a reddish Colour, all over—quite of the Fairy Size, therefore we named her Mab. Mrs. Custance with Lady Bacon made us a Morning Visit, they came walking and were much frightened by a Cow coming across the Field. They appeared much agitated, they had each a Glass of Port Wine & other refreshment. They came about 2. o'clock and stayed till 3. as they stayed till we could send to Weston House after the Coach. Briton went to order it directly. It came in about an Hour after it was ordered. They were pretty well composed when they went. . . .

AUGUST 10, MONDAY. . . . Begun cutting Peas this Morn' in the Field. A Parish Meeting held this Evening at the Heart to take into consideration the Papers lately recd. concerning what is to be done in case of an Invasion of the French on this Country. Dinner to day, Beans and Bacon &c. I was very nervous and weak to day, much agitated not knowing what to do at the present Crisis & wanting Health & Strength am scarce able to do even the most trivial action.

SEPBR. 27, SUNDAY. . . . Mr. Dade read Prayers & Preached this Morning at Weston-Church. Mr. Dade read the new Thanks giving Prayer to Almighty God! for his late blessing to us in a fine & plentiful Harvest. Mr. and Mrs. Custance at Church to day. Miss Woodforde also at Church. Dinner to day, Loin of Veal rosted & a Pudding. Ben abused Betty this evening on his hearing that she had accepted his Cousin Thos. Leggatt of Ringland for a Paramour.

OCTBR. 21, WEDNESDAY. . . . Great Rejoicings to be to day on Account of Peace.★ A bullock to be rosted in the Market-Place &c. It raining all the Morning rather against them. About 6. in the Afternoon it cleared up and many went from Weston. Ben went about that time and had my Mare, Jenny, to go thither. Dinner to day, Ham & 2. Fowls boiled &c. Whilst we were at Dinner to day, there was a large flash of Lightning and one loud Clap of Thunder. The Lightning shone on Nancy's Plate. It rained hard for about an Hour afterwards. N.B. No Bullock rosted at Norwich as talked of.

DECBR. 7, MONDAY. . . . I was very indifferent & very unwell indeed to day so blown up with gouty Wind & strange feelings. Dinner to day, boiled Beef &c. Towards the evening I got something better. Cow, Beauty had a Cow-Calf.

DECBR. 25, FRIDAY. . . . Mr. Dade read Prayers, Preached and administered the H. Sacrament this Morn' at Weston Church, being Christmas-Day. None from Weston-House at Church to day. Old Thos Atterton, Robt Downing, Roger Sherwood, Eliz. Ward Widow and the Clerk Willm Large, dined at Weston-Parsonage to day, being Christmas Day and had each in Money ^s1/0^d— 5. 0. Poor old Mary Heavers, Widow, very old & infirm I sent her Dinner to her and likewise—0. 1. 0. Dinner to day, Surloin of Beef rosted & plumb Puddings boiled for both Parlour & Kitchen. We had also in Parlour some Mince-Pies.

Cattle Watering, *John Sell Cotman (1782–1842)*

★ The preliminaries of peace were signed in London on Thursday, Oct. 1st, 1801, were confirmed by Bonaparte on Oct. 5th, and finally incorporated in the definitive Peace of Amiens on March 27th, 1802. No one could foresee that the peace would last for only a year and a half.

1802

JANRY. 1, FRIDAY. . . . The New Year came in with Frost & Snow and with it very cold Weather indeed, which pinched me much—being an invalid. . . . Our Servants being invited to Weston-House to Dinner to day, Briton & Sally went, but returned in good time about 10. o'clock at Night Much fatigued & tired, it being very bad & cold walking—The Snow in places quite high and No Moon. I hope they will not be ill after it.

FEBRY. 20, SATURDAY. . . . Mr. Thorne (alias Dr.) called about Noon and stayed about an Hour with us. He says Nancy's Complaint is an internal one. The Dr. drank a small Tumbler of Brandy & Cold Water he having a bad Cold. The Dr. says that it will take a little time to set her right by a due course of Medicine. . . . Very low, faint and very unwell all the Morn'. I dont know that I ever felt myself so depressed and so spiritless as this very day. Nancy out of Temper all the Whole day, very saucy.

APRIL 7, WEDNESDAY. . . . I was rather faint & weak to day. Dinner to day, a Pike rosted &c. Sent my poor Neighbour Will: Richmond to day a Bottle (and the last I had) of very old strong Beer 10 y^{rs} old, he being dropsically inclined.

APRIL 13, TUESDAY. . . . To James Pegg this Morn' by Betty, pd. 3. 6. 8. being two Months Income Tax—at twenty Pounds Pr Annum—Valued at 200£ p^r Annum N.B.—The above Tax to be repealed this Month—is now pretty generally believed if not already done—it being universally disliked. ⋆ Very cold to day with Hail, Snow and Rain at times. . . .

MAY 30, SUNDAY. . . . Mr. Dade read Prayers & Preached this Afternoon at Weston Church—Mrs. Custance there. There was Bread given to the Poor at Church this Afternoon by Briton from Money which he had received for that Purpose from some Person who desired that it may not be known from whom it came in value abt. 1. 5. 0. . . .

JUNE 1, TUESDAY. . . . This Day being appointed for a general Thanksgiving for Peace, Mr. Dade read Prayers and Preached this Morning at Weston-Church. . . . I was rather poorly this Morning, so very cold & giddy & weak. . . . Mem. great Doings in many Places to day. At Weston nothing at all—Mr. Custance against it.

JUNE 2, WEDNESDAY. . . . Rather odd feelings about me immediately after breakfast this Morning, just as was going to shave, attended with the Cramp in my right hand, thank God! it did not last long, but alarmed me. Mrs. Custance by herself called on us this Morning and made us a long Visit. Miss Woodforde shewed her a new Bonnett (by name Pick-Nick) which she had sent her from London . . . Mrs. Custance said it was very handsome and had seen nothing like it at Norwich as yet, tho' only at Norwich last Week to see the new Fashions. . . .

⋆ Pitt's Income Tax was repealed in this year. The repeal was short-lived. War
broke out again in May, 1803, and the tax was reimposed in a modified form
by Addington.

JUNE 18, FRIDAY. . . . This Morn a Person by name Richard Page, dressed as a Clergyman, walked up boldly to our Front Door through the Garden and knocked. I went and let him in, and walked into my Study and there informed me before Nancy, that he was a reduced Clergyman from Oxfordshire, was born at Bath in Somersetshire, had read Prayers &c. at the Abbey Church there for 12. Years. That a Dr. Lawrence of Doctors Commons was his great Friend &c. He seemed well acquainted with Oxford and with many of my old Contemporaries there, was formerly of Baliol College or at St. Edmund Hall, a short Man and thin, talked rather fast and made a plausible Story. Shewed me his Letters of Orders, signed by the late Dr. Lowthe when Bishop of Oxford &c. He stayed about half an Hour with us, drank a Glass of Table Beer and then walked away. I gave him before he went, half a Guinea 0. 10. 6. . . .

AUGUST 29, SUNDAY. . . . I felt finely this Morning thank God! & stronger. Very hot indeed to day, especially at Noon. Dr. Thorne was with us to day between 12 and 1 o'clock. He stayed some little time with us. My Throat is daily getting better he says. . . .

SEPBR. 8, WEDNESDAY. . . . Very weak & indifferent again to day & all day. So depressed in Spirits to day made me miserable. I was assisted down Stairs & up to day. Dinner to day, Leg of Mutton rosted &c. The lest Uneasiness affects me very much.

SEPBR. 12, SUNDAY. . . . Very weak still, if not weaker, had a hard Matter to get down Stairs this Morn' tho' help'd. So tired after I got down, that I panted for breath. . . .

SEPBR. 17, FRIDAY. . . . Thank God! that I rather think, I am somewhat better than I felt myself Yesterday, and I hope stronger. Mr. Stoughton of Sparham called on us this Morn' since his return from Cromer, having been there some time for his Health, it being close to the Sea. To a travelling Woman by Name (Falling), a married Woman, who sold divers things, for a Pound of different kinds of Thread for the use of the Family—paid 0. 7. 0. Dinner to day, Shoulder Mutton rosted &c. Mr. Salisbury brought us a brace of Partridges this Evening—very weak towards bed-time. Briton still sleeps in my Room upon the Sofa, and a Candle burning all Night in the Chamber.

OCTBR. 2, SATURDAY. . . . I was rather better this Morning when I got up I think, than I was Yesterday Morning. Mr. Custance sent us a brace of Partridges. Dry Weather still continues to prevail. Dr. Thorne called here about 4. o'clock this Aft. Dinner to day, boiled Calfs Head, Pork & Greens and a Pigeon-Pye hot. My Legs & Thighs still continue much swelled, if any thing rather more and higher. Spirits much depressed to day upon that Account.

OCTOBER 17, SUNDAY. . . . Very weak this Morning, scarce able to put on my Cloaths and with great difficulty, get down Stairs with help. Mr. Dade read Prayers & Preached this Morning at Weston Church—Nancy at Church. Mr. & Mrs. Custance & Lady Bacon at Church. Dinner to day, Rost Beef &c.

The rest of the page is blank. The Diary has come to an end. On New Year's Day, 1803, Parson Woodforde died.

Coastal Scene near Cromer, *James Stark (1794–1859)*

A NOTE ON THIS EDITION

The diaries of the Reverend James Woodforde cover almost every day of his life from 1759 to 1802. The original manuscript is contained within sixty-eight closely written booklets. In 1924 the Oxford University Press published a first volume of selections, edited by John Beresford. This was followed by four further volumes of extracts, the last of which appeared in 1931. A one-volume edition, roughly a third of the original edition in length, was then prepared by Beresford for publication in 1935. This selection was subsequently re-issued in The World's Classics and Oxford Paperbacks. The text contained in this volume has been further edited and reduced in length by James Michie with the intention of making Woodforde much more accessible to today's general reader.

For the sake of consistency within the main body of this book, the eighteenth-century spelling of Parson Woodforde's parish has been retained in the introductory matter and captions: 'Weston Longeville'.

A NOTE ON THE ILLUSTRATIONS OF WATERCOLOURS OF THE NORWICH SCHOOL

During the latter part of Parson Woodforde's life, Norwich became an increasingly important centre of artistic activity. The painters who eventually became to be known as the 'Norwich School' were often connected by family and teaching relationships, which resulted in a homogeneity of approach to their favourite subject matter: the streets and buildings of Norwich and the countryside of Norfolk. This association of aims and activity was embodied more formally when the Norwich Society of Artists was founded in 1803, the year of Woodforde's death, and its first annual exhibition held in 1805. The paintings of the Norwich School very much reflect the life and landscape of Norfolk as Parson Woodforde would have seen them, both in his frequent trips to Norwich and in his daily life as a Norfolk country parson.

Artists whose work is reproduced in this volume:

Henry Bright (1810–73)
John Joseph Cotman (1814–78)
John Sell Cotman (1782–1842)
Miles Edmund Cotman (1810–58)
John Crome (1768–1821)
David Hodgson (1798–1864)
Thomas Lound (1802–61)
John Middleton (1827-56)
Henry Ninham (1793–1874)
Alfred Stannard (1806–89)
Eloise Harriet Stannard (1829–1915)
Emily Stannard (1803–85)
James Stark (1794–1859)
John Thirtle (1777–1839)
George Vincent (1796–1831)

Painters not in Norwich School

George Morland (1763–1804)
Michael Angelo Rooker (1746–1801)
Edward Seago (1910–74)

Acknowledgements

The artist, publishers and copyright owners gratefully acknowledge the following for their kind assistance:
Dr Paul Howell
Mrs Richard Meynell
The Rector, All Saints, Weston Longville
Mr Roger Otton
Mr Michael Sayer
Miss Norma Watts
Mr Oliver Woodforde
Dr A Woodforde

Picture Credits

Courtesy of The Rector and Churchwarden, All Saints, Weston Longville: 8
Abbot Hall Art Gallery, Kendal, Cumbria: 89
BBC Hulton Picture Library: 19, 20, 38, 43, 49, 74, 79, 107, 126–127, 128, 152–153, 158, 161, 182, 204
Haworth Art Gallery, Accrington/Bridgeman Art Library: 219
John Luard: 167
The Mansell Collection: 18, 41, 103, 159, 179, 180
Mary Evans Picture Library: 45, 152
Norfolk County Library: 177
Norfolk Museums Service (Great Yarmouth Museums): 52
Norfolk Museums Service (Norwich Castle Museum): 53, 57, 64, 65, 72, 80, 85, 97, 100, 101, 104, 108–109, 113, 116, 120, 121, 132, 133, 137, 141, 143, 144, 145, 149, 160, 164, 168, 171, 172, 173, 176, 185, 193, 196, 199, 201, 203, 206, 207, 212–213, 216
Oxford University Press: 135, 186
The Royal Opera House Archives: 183
The Tate Gallery: 209
The Victoria and Albert Museum: 189